Start Where You Are,
But Don't Stay There

Start Where You Are, But Don't Stay There

Understanding Diversity, Opportunity Gaps, and Teaching in Today's Classrooms

H. Richard Milner IV

HARVARD EDUCATION PRESS
CAMBRIDGE, MASSACHUSETTS

Fifth Printing, 2016

Library of Congress Control Number 2010931407

Paperback ISBN 978-1-934742-76-1
Library Edition ISBN 978-1-934742-77-8

Published by Harvard Education Press,
an imprint of the Harvard Education Publishing Group

Harvard Education Press
8 Story Street
Cambridge, MA 02138

Cover Design: Sarah Henderson

The typefaces used in this book are Minion and Helvetical Neue.

This book is dedicated to my daughters:
Anna Grace Milner and Elise Faith Milner
(Born July 30, 2010)
You are my heartbeats . . .

Contents

Foreword

Some twenty years ago, when I began researching successful teachers of African American students, I could never have imagined that it would create a kind of epistemological split among those whose work is aimed at issues of equity and diversity. I just wanted to search for some existence proofs that demonstrated that the very students who some claim cannot—or will not—learn could indeed learn and perform at high academic levels. My work with the eight teachers known as "The Dreamkeepers" was highly praised by some and deeply criticized by others. The supporters seemed to use my work as a way to advance a "no excuses" agenda. The detractors seemed to think that I was ignoring the material reality of institutional and structural racism and other inequalities. The truth is somewhere short of both perspectives. I did not think that teachers alone could ensure student success, and I did not think that structural factors were irrelevant. But, I did think that teachers can, and do, make a difference and that the work of the teachers I studied supported that assertion.

In *Start Where You Are, But Don't Stay There*, Rich Milner continues the scholarly tradition of examining effective practice among teachers who work with those students whose profiles rarely spell success. However, he extends this work to include secondary teachers—a group that has been under studied in this research genre. But it is not merely Milner's choice of subject that makes this book an important addition to the literature; he also introduces us to a new concept—"opportunity gap"—that helps us move the discourse from the exhausted "achievement gap" lament to a more robust and nuanced discussion of why school failure persists for some groups of students.

American education has gone through several waves of reform. We have witnessed restructuring, reconstitution, high-stakes testing, accountability, and standards-setting. President George H. W. Bush promoted the National Education Goals that were an outgrowth of Reagan era concerns about the deterioration of U.S. public schools. The National Education Goals advocated some ambitious targets for American education that included universal school readiness; universal high school graduation; and competency in reading, mathematics, science, and computer technology. During the Clinton administration, the first President Bush's agenda was renamed "Goals 2000" to signal the urgent need to meet these ambitious goals by the year 2000. In addition to the goals outlined by President Bush, President Clinton also included what was called an "opportunity-to-learn standard." This "kinder, gentler" approach to national standards acknowledged that without proper academic supports, it would be impossible for the nation's most needy students to meet those goals.

The opportunity-to-learn standard addressed the fact that some students attended poorly resourced schools with teachers who were either unqualified or underqualified. It was impossible to be an excellent physics or chemistry student in a school that did not have a well-equipped, or even functioning, physics or chemistry lab—or a qualified physics or chemistry teacher. In the mid 1990s, personal computers were not ubiquitous, and if you attended a school without a computer lab you were unlikely to develop computing skills. The opportunity-to-learn standard was crucial to coping with the persistent inequity that characterized the nation's urban—and rural—schools. Unfortunately, the very first standard to be jettisoned in the clamor for accountability was the opportunity-to-learn standard. Somewhere between political pressure and economic priorities, federal, state, and local governments decided they could not afford to meet the opportunity-to-learn standard.

In this volume, Milner's unique concept of *opportunity gaps* moves us away from the exhausted talk of achievement gaps. This work points out that even with dedicated teachers, an insistence on high standards, and constant pressure to produce high test scores, students can still fall short because they are missing some important opportunities. Sociologist Annette Lareau's work *Unequal Childhoods: Class, Race, and Family Life* draws distinctions between middle class children's lives of "concerted cultivation" and poor and working class children's "accomplishment of natural growth."[1] Clearly there are opportunity gaps between the kinds of lives these two groups of students experience.

Fortunately, Milner does more than simply identify opportunity gaps. Rather, his book offers fresh evidence and insights about what is possible—and what is happening—in schools and classrooms where teachers successfully negotiate diverse settings, and where they see working in such settings as opportunities for both their students and themselves. Imagine that—the classroom as a space for opportunity for teachers and for students!

I should add that this volume is not a neatly tied up recipe for teaching diverse students. Like Gregory Michie does in *See You When We Get There*, Milner shares both triumphs and challenges.[2] He shows us real teachers doing the hard work of simultaneously being teachers and learners. This is the real stuff of teaching, and it should remind us all to start where we are—but not stay there.

Gloria Ladson-Billings
University of Wisconsin-Madison

Acknowledgments

I have always been cautious about listing names of people who have been helpful to me in my personal and professional life. Indeed, because so many people have believed in me, supported me, opened doors for me, and served as role models for me, I run the risk of leaving someone off the list. However, it is important for me to name some of the most influential people in my professional work and personal life to demonstrate to readers that I understand that no one achieves excellence in this profession (or life in general) without the assistance of others.

Family First!

My family is very important to me. I thank my extraordinarily supportive wife, Shelley Banks Milner, for her unwavering commitment to me and our family. Thank you for allowing me the time to complete this project. Also, I cannot thank you enough for all you have done to enrich my life and to empower me to reach my full capacity in all aspects of my life. You are a magnificent person, and I love you beyond words. And to my daughters, Anna and Elise, you bring me joy beyond words! Thank you for being the gifts. I am also grateful to my parents, Henry III and Barbara Milner, for teaching me what it means to live life in a meaningful way. What I appreciate most is how you taught me to be a good person who cares about others and who operates with integrity in my journey. Thank you for teaching me to see the good in people and in situations! I am also thankful to my sister, Tanya, a gifted elementary school teacher of two decades. You are a mentor whom I love and honor. Your work in the trenches with students makes a difference. I would also like to thank my sister-in-law Kimberly Banks Martin for supporting our family and taking care of her little sister (my wife, Shelley) growing up. I am also thankful for the wisdom and love of my grandparents, Henry and Jessie Milner. You both inspire me and bring a huge smile to my face whenever I see you.

Of course, all my nieces and nephews inspire me, and I encourage you to dream unthinkable dreams and then do what is necessary to reach them. My aunts and uncles have been in my life to guide, correct, and support me: Annie (and the late Clifford) Cook, Betty (and Roosevelt) Blackman, Lou (and Edward) Morris, Lottie (and Dickie) Pyron, Lena (and Mike) Starks, Annie (and Jesse) Milner, Barbara (and Michael) Wyatt, Darlene Milner, Tammy (and Jonny) Milner, Linda (and Walter) Milner, Lynn (and Cornelius) Milner, Sherrie Wilson, and Joyce (and James) Izzard.

I almost listed all the cousins who have been influential in my journey but decided not to because the acknowledgment section of this book would far exceed the page limit. The absence of the names of my cousins, however, does not minimize my gratitude toward them. Every positive word you have spoken about me in my absence and every good and supportive thought and action on my behalf is very much appreciated. Thank you, cousins, for being there and for holding our family together.

And special recognition to my "other mothers" and "other fathers": Willie C. and Margaret Banks (my mother- and father-in-law who have filled in the gap so many times for us and whom I value as other parents), Christine and Tom Hill, Geraldine Ford, Portia and Willie Ogletree, Vernordor Taylor, Gladys Allen, Laura Lowe, Marilyn Middlebrooks, Essie (and Lee) McRae, Geneva (and David) Woods, Carolyn (and Ernest) Holston, and Cheryl (and Eddie) Gilbert.

MEMORIES!

I am also inspired and empowered by the memories of my grandparents—Annie M. Williams, Henry Williams, Eunice Milner, and Emitt and Corine Williams—to do good work on behalf of those who have been marginalized and simply mistreated. I miss you much but am grateful for the wisdom you shared. I also honor my cousin, Angela Cook, for her life and many contributions. Other family members and friends who have transitioned but whose legacy and deeds remain close to my heart are Annie M. Stanley, Annie Domineck, Annie L. Sutton, Iris Byrd, and Jeanelle Berry.

Standing on the Shoulders of Giants!

I would also like to thank colleagues whom I respect for their outstanding work in the field of education. In a sense, I stand on your shoulders as I do my work. To my professional mentor, big brother, and true friend, Dr. Tyrone Howard, thank you for leading the way. And to my major professors from The Ohio State University: Dr. Gail McCutcheon and Dr. Anita Woolfolk Hoy, I am grateful for the knowledge and skills you "brought out of me." To Dr. Cynthia Dillard, Dr. Robert Ransom, Dr. Kofi Lomotey, Dr. Jackie Irvine, Dr. Christine Sleeter, Dr. Bill Tate, Dr. Gloria Ladson-Billings, and Dr. Peter Demerath: thank you for all you have done and continue to do to help me do my best work and for being excellent role models on the journey.

Dr. Linda Tillman is a model mentor from whom I have learned so much. I thank you for helping me understand so many of the implicit rules of the academy and for being a true friend. Dr. Mark Gooden is a trustworthy brother who has been on the journey with me since graduate school. I value your brotherhood and respect you immensely.

Support from mentors from South Carolina State University is also appreciated, particularly from the following: Dr. Sarah Favors, Allen Fleming, Howette Davis, Dr. Ronald Speight, and Dr. William Pruitt.

In addition, I am thankful to the many teachers and students I have worked with over the years, particularly those showcased in this book.

Friends!

I realize that some friendships come and go, but I would like to acknowledge some friends who will be lifetime brothers and sisters to me. Indeed, friendship is something you do (a verb), and I am thankful to have friends who truly understand the nature of friendship and who have helped me understand what friendship is through their actions. In particular, Dr. John Singer is a true friend who has challenged me intellectually and influenced my thinking about pertinent issues in education. I value your friendship and am thankful to have you on my side. Dr. Perry Daniel has been a friend since little league football. It is refreshingly rare to have a friend who is not seasonal and who will be there through thick and thin. Keep up the excellent work you do for your students in urban middle and high schools, Dr. Daniel. Brian Crump is another childhood friend who is not a seasonal friend but one who has been there and will be there forever. I am proud of the man you have become and value you as a true friend and brother! Another childhood friend who has "kept it real" and remains valuable in my life is Shalanda Few.

Matthew and Dr. Audra Davis, Dante and Roselyn Lawson, Chris and Christa Leslie, Patrick and Roselyn Hicks, Vincent Windrow, Thomas Barr, Jr., Chad Bright, Michael Thompson, Jamal Brown, Valinda Burks, Mike Prude, Jason and Daneen Farrington, Dr. Jason Irizarry, Tawio Barksdale, Dr. Pickens Patterson, Dr. Terry Husband, Dr. Jamel Donnor, Dr. Marvin Lynn, Dr. Sarah Buchanan, Ira Murray, Charles Pryor, Dr. Carl James, William Moseley, Dr. Eric Toshalis, Dr. Sheneka Williams, Micah Sheppard, Raymond and Tselanie Mitchel, Dainon Sidney, Morris Goggins, A. Clifford Jones, Edward McKinney, Ricky Gordon, Dr. Chance Lewis, Terry Stone, Terry Jones, Bobby and Talisa Smith, Dr. Leon Caldwell, Leon and Rebecca Stevenson, Carla and Doris Copeland, Chanda Brooks, Tyangee

Ette, Corey Posey, Toby Jenkins, Dr. Alric Simmonds, Angela Fairwell, Natalie Ford, Sharonda Glover, Dr. Darrell Cleveland, Yolonda Robinson, David Swett, Erik Wilson, Keith Jordan, Kesa Brown, Tammi Boyd Brown, Stephanie Sinkfield, Dr. Na'im Madyun, Dr. Quaylan Allen, Dr. Richard Reddick, Reco Dallas, Robert King, Mike Sertic, Maria Ogletree, Allen and Monet Young, and Michael P. Jackson. You all have supported me, my girls, my wife, and my family in general. Every encouraging word or positive word to or about us—phone call, e-mail, visit, card, gift, prayer, or positive thought—is appreciated. I understand that your commitment to me is authentic, and I am grateful to have your support. If space would allow, I would write about how each of you has inspired me. For now, though, *thank you*! Please know that I do not take you for granted.

Vanderbilt and Harvard Education Press Support!

I am so thankful to many of my Vanderbilt colleagues (both faculty and staff) for supporting me. While I appreciate the support of colleagues and mentors from afar, I have a splendid group of colleagues with whom I have the honor of working at Vanderbilt University daily. In particular, my Department of Teaching and Learning colleagues have been, in the words of Tina Turner: simply the best! I value each of you and appreciate your support of me, even when I do not hear or see you. I have chosen not to list names of Vanderbilt colleagues here, but please know that I appreciate those who have been there for me.

Several former colleagues from Vanderbilt University remain, as do those who I am confident have cheered from afar or made a lasting influence on me and my work. I would like to acknowledge Dr. Margaret Smithey, Dr. Brian Williams, Dr. Patrick Thompson, Dr. Ana Christina Iddings, Dr. Chuck Kinzer, Dr. Alfredo Artiles, and Dr. Carolyn Evertson.

I have worked with some outstanding undergraduate and graduate students over the years. As their major professor, I would like to acknowledge Judson Laughter, F. Blake Tenore, Britnie Kane, and Elizabeth Self, for learning with me over the years. I have learned so much from you and value you as scholars, friends, and people! I encourage you to carry forward the important work that you/we do wherever you may go.

Finally, I must thank and acknowledge the unquestionable professionalism and outstanding support of the Harvard Education Press team. In particular, Douglas Clayton, Jeffrey Perkins, Marcy Barnes, and the copyeditor, Sarah Weaver, were nothing short of a dream team throughout this journey. My work is better because of you. Thank you!

Introduction

Start where you are, but don't stay there.

—African saying

THERE ARE MOMENTS in our lives that help define and shape them, times and experiences that we never forget. I recall such a moment during my first semester of doctoral studies, when then associate dean Charles Hancock began his comments to a group of us, all first-semester doctoral students, with the African saying above: *Start where you are, but don't stay there*. I was astonished—simply stunned. I cannot tell readers what else occurred or was said during that meeting. All I can recall was that moment when he uttered those words. I knew then that Dean Hancock had shared some wisdom with us that would forever change how I thought about my personal and professional life. He had encouraged us to embrace a lifelong cognitive, social, and emotional journey that would allow us to do our best work, realizing that we were never really finished learning and contributing to education and society. At that moment, I immediately started to transfer and apply what he had shared to a plethora of experiences I was working through. He had spoken directly to me on that day, in that moment.

As I have thought about the many roles I have assumed and continue to assume in education, such as student, former high school teacher, teacher, teacher educator, social scientist, and researcher, I have pondered how to improve and move forward in these various aspects of my professional life. Moreover, as a father of two daughters, watching them grow and develop, I find something powerful about the idea of embracing a journey that by definition is incomplete. In a similar way, I am hopeful that readers of this book—teachers, preservice teachers, administrators, graduate students, teacher educators, and researchers—will critique, embrace, and learn from the ideas presented here, with the ultimate goal of improving their work and progressing in their own journey. Each of us, from those early in our careers to those more seasoned, has room to grow and to improve. Thus, I invite readers to think about the lessons and the moments captured in this book as sites from which to learn and to grow. My goal in this book is not to beat up on teachers. As a former public school teacher, I believe that teachers are sometimes blamed for situations and issues far beyond their control. Instead, I encourage readers to address and work to improve the areas of their work that are in their control and that have a bearing on students' opportunities to learn.

I care deeply about what happens to students, all students, in schools. I have been perplexed, frustrated, and baffled for many years, though, about why some students—students of color (particularly African American students and Latino/a students), those whose first language is not English, and/or those living in poverty—too often struggle to succeed in schools. I have found it difficult to understand how to prepare all teachers with the essential knowledge, skills, attitudes, and practices they need to embark upon their teaching journeys and, hopefully, to teach all students well. Among the many questions I have pondered over the last twelve years are: How do we design learning environments that build on the many talents and strengths that all P–12 students bring into the classroom? Why do some teachers and students succeed while others do not? How do (and should) we prepare teachers to teach all students well in a variety of subject matter areas and educational institutions? Ironically, the questions that I have avoided throughout my time as a social scientist, teacher, researcher, and teacher educator are ones that many teachers, researchers, policy makers, superintendents, public officials, and other educators have now placed front and center: those dealing with an "achievement gap."

TOO MUCH TESTING, NOT ENOUGH TEACHING

While the achievement gap discourse in education usually focuses on students' scores on standardized tests, it also concerns student graduation rates, patterns in gifted and advanced placement and talent programs, as well as other measurable outcomes that allow comparisons between White students and other racial groups of students. Standardization, in many ways, is antithetical to diversity because it suggests that all students live and operate in homogeneous environments with equality of opportunity afforded to them. In this way, standardization is the opposite of diversity. While on the one hand it is necessary to hold educators accountable for providing optimal learning opportunities for students, on the other hand, our instructional practices need to be tailored for students in a relevant and responsive way to address the range of differences that students bring into the classroom.

There is not much debate in U.S. society and in education that people are diverse and that their situations and experiences vary significantly. In an era of high-stakes standardized testing, I (and many others) have often wondered if we are focusing on *too much testing and not enough teaching*. In other words, I want to suggest that we focus our attention more on meaningfully constructed instruction that meets the needs of diverse learners rather than focusing so much attention on standardized examinations.

A scan of the books, chapters, and articles that I have written over the years reveals a clear avoidance of a direct emphasis on an achievement gap. My decision to sidestep the many achievement gap conversations has been both deliberate and subconscious. I have struggled with what it means to have an achievement gap and why such gaps have persisted, with only minor improvements, over the years. My analyses of empirical research and policy reports will not allow me to accept, for instance, the "eugenics" explanation for an "achievement gap"—that there is a "biological basis for the superiority of Whites."[1] Put simply, White people are not biologically, genetically, or innately superior to other groups in terms of intelligence. If educators agree with this reality—that no group of people is intellectually superior to another—then they should be willing to delve into the complex social maze of rationales for what are perceived as achievement gaps. Even at a time in U.S. and world history when formal sanctions of slavery and Jim Crow have long since ended, there are still deeply ingrained social realities that disallow certain populations of students to reach their full capacity to learn. The question is: why?

In this book, I suggest that we need to refocus attention away from an achievement gap and toward an opportunity gap. I invite readers to engage in a *paradigm and mind-set shift*—to alter their thinking, ideologies, belief systems, and overall worldviews in terms of how we socially construct achievement and success. Consider four important questions regarding this necessary mind shift: (1) To what extent is achievement synonymous with learning? (2) What does it mean to learn and achieve in one school community in comparison to another? (3) Who decides what it means to achieve and why? (4) How do (and should) we address the kind of learning that never shows up on achievement measures—including high-stakes tests?

Critical theorist Michael Apple stresses that those of us in education must continue to question what knowledge is, how it is constructed and validated, and who decides the worth, value, and meanings of knowledge and knowledge construction.[2] I believe similar questions should be posed about achievement. As with knowledge, certain areas of achievement are privileged over others, and there is a socially constructed hierarchy of which achievements and knowledge matter more in comparison to others. In this sense, there are societal high and low cultural ways of looking at achievement and knowledge. For instance, in literacy, knowledge about and achievement related to traditional canonical readings from authors such as William Shakespeare and Charles Dickens are considered high culture, while African American literature written by authors such as Zora

Neale Hurston and James Baldwin may be classified as low culture (from a White-dominated societal perspective).

I am asking readers of this book to rethink their conceptions of why many culturally diverse students do not fare well in a range of schools across U.S. society, from urban to suburban to rural settings, and why we focus on the measures of success and achievement that we do. It is important to understand that I am not suggesting that educators should not be concerned about achievement gaps and test scores. I realize that educators operate in systems that require them to focus on these matters, and I believe we should be preparing students for success on these examinations because their success in this society can depend on such achievement. However, concurrently, I am arguing that in order to assist teachers in addressing matters of achievement with students, we need to focus more on the processes (teaching and learning) and not so much on the final outcome (test score). In short, in this book, I demonstrate the importance of the interrelated nature of processes associated with diversity, opportunity, and teaching in a range of different classrooms.

CONVERGENCE OF DIVERSITY, OPPORTUNITY, AND TEACHING

This book demonstrates the interrelated nature of diversity, opportunity, and teaching. It is difficult for teachers to teach their particular content area if they do not understand the diversity-opportunity nexus. As students at our nation's schools become increasingly diverse, it is becoming more difficult for teachers to teach them and for teacher education programs, whether traditional or nontraditional, to prepare them to teach.[3] These diversity aspects include but are not limited to race, ethnicity, gender, sexual orientation, language, religion, ability, and socioeconomic background. These general, more traditional (yet still essential) categories are complicated by individual circumstances, such as whether students are supported and encouraged to complete homework, whether parents have the ability and skill to help students complete their homework, or whether parents have the resources to hire a tutor to assist their children with homework if they are not able to.

This book addresses at least two critical aspects of the diversity-opportunity nexus in the classroom: (1) focusing on diversity and opportunity to better understand social relationships between teachers and students and (2) focusing on diversity and opportunity to incorporate and infuse those dimensions into the curriculum and overall learning opportunities made available to students. The first emphasis—on teachers' developing the knowledge, skills, and abilities that will enable them to get along with students from culturally diverse backgrounds—seems logical. Educators do generally grasp that they need to understand themselves and how their experiences shape who they are in relation to others. Similarly, educators seem to understand that they should design a learning environment that promotes respect and care between students. However, educators often struggle with how to develop social contexts where they are able to relate to their students. Moreover, they can struggle to design and construct classroom settings where all their students feel empowered to speak and to participate in the learning opportunities available. Teachers may wonder how to help students from different cultural backgrounds to feel that they possess valuable knowledge and skills that can contribute to the classroom culture.

A second focus—how teachers can incorporate aspects of diversity and opportunity into the curriculum—is also essential because research demonstrates that all students, both culturally diverse and White students, become disengaged, disinterested, and disconnected from lessons and learning opportunities when they do not see themselves reflected in the curriculum and related opportunities to learn. Researchers and theoreticians agree that a race-centered,[4] culture and diversity-focused,[5] and multicultural[6] curriculum are essential for student academic and social success.

All students need and deserve to encounter and experience a curriculum that highlights and reflects the life experiences and contributions of people of color, women, and other marginalized groups—not just those of the White mainstream. In addition, they need to be empowered to critique the curriculum and to provide counterpositions to what they are reading and engaging. The very *nature* of this content and *how* it is actually incorporated into learning opportunities are critical for students. Multicultural educator Geneva Gay asserts that students often feel "insulted, embarrassed, ashamed, and angered when reading and hearing negative portrayals of their ethnic groups or not hearing anything at all."[7] Thus, it is not enough to incorporate the historic, political, and social experiences, events, and challenges of various ethnic groups into the curriculum. Educators must recognize that the essence of that curricular content (what is actually included, how, and why) is very important as students come to understand themselves and others in a pluralistic and ever-changing society, because students need to see themselves and their cultural group from positions of strength and tenacity. These two matters, presented only briefly here, are discussed at length in later chapters.

I have intentionally separated race from diversity in some of the discussions throughout this book, although I realize that race is a concrete dimension of diversity. I have done this because too many educators gloss over race as an important area of consideration in broader diversity discourses, for a variety of reasons: (1) They are uncomfortable talking about it, (2) they find it irrelevant to do so, (3) race is sometimes considered a taboo subject due to its horrific history for some in U.S. society, and (4) race is misunderstood by so many, both within and outside of education. A much more nuanced and elaborate discussion of these and related issues will be explored in chapter 1 and other parts of the text.

ACHIEVEMENT AND OPPORTUNITY NEXUS

I have often wondered why so many people focus on the outcome (test score) rather than on the processes that lead to the outcomes—that is, teaching and learning. Rather than focus on an achievement gap to explain students' educational outcomes, I suggest we think about what I call an *opportunity gap*. As an explanation of disparate outcomes, opportunity is multifaceted, complicated, process-oriented, and much more nuanced than achievement. Further, some sociologists would argue that it is ineffectual to spend extensive amounts of time comparing one group with another.[8] I agree, and focusing on an achievement gap inherently forces us to compare culturally diverse students with White students without always understanding reasons that undergird disparities and differences that exist.

I will not spend pages comparing the opportunity gaps between White students and culturally diverse students. Rather, I invite readers to think about opportunity in a broader sense, as all students and teachers deserve to be engaged in opportunities that can improve their own lives and those of others as they work to make meaningful contributions to their families, their communities, and to society. For instance, students from different racial and ethnic backgrounds bring assets into the classroom that should be maximized. Students in predominantly White settings should have chances to engage in race- and diversity-related learning opportunities as well. However, this kind of learning, where students are actively involved with understanding issues of diversity in P–12 schools, may never show up on a standardized test, although developing such skill, knowledge, and awareness is important.

I am a product of opportunity. People in society, in institutions, and in education have given me many chances to demonstrate my capacity. Ultimately, it was up to me to embrace and to maximize those opportunities, but others first had to give me a chance to succeed. Too many students in P–12 institutions have not been provided an opportunity to develop into successful students because our educational system has not been structurally designed to do so. Opportunity is at the core of success and failure in *society* as well as in *schools*.[9] I believe a focus on an achievement gap places too much blame and emphasis on students themselves as individuals and not enough attention on why gaps and disparities are commonplace in schools across the country. Opportunity, on the other hand, forces us to think about how systems, processes, and institutions are overtly and covertly designed to maintain the status quo and sustain depressingly complicated disparities in education.

Educational researcher and teacher educator Gloria Ladson-Billings has concluded that in U.S. society there is not so much an achievement gap as an "education debt" that the educational system owes to the many students it has poorly served.[10] Moreover, educational researcher and teacher educator Jacqueline Irvine suggests that a perceived achievement gap is the result of other gaps that seduce people into believing that an achievement gap actually exists.[11] Rather than focus on a perceived achievement gap, Irvine asserts that we should shift our attention to closing the other gaps that exist in education; these include "the teacher quality gap; the teacher training gap; the challenging curriculum gap; the school funding gap; the digital divide gap; the wealth and income gap; the employment opportunity gap; the affordable housing gap; the health care gap; the nutrition gap; the school integration gap; and the quality childcare gap."[12] I believe that when we address opportunity gaps, achievement results and the validity of our data can improve. With a focus on achievement gaps, culturally diverse students—including African American students, Latino/a students, English language learners, and students living in poverty—are positioned as somehow deficient in the minds, practices, and designs of educators. From an ecological perspective, many teachers design the learning milieu believing that their culturally diverse students are underachievers, poorly prepared and lagging behind their White classmates. Such a position can lead teachers into mind-sets and practices that do not recognize the strengths and expertise (even genius) among entire groups of students.

A dominant, oppressive, and repressive view is that the performances, experiences, and outcomes of White students are "the norm" by which others are compared, measured, assessed, and evaluated.[13] For instance, culturally diverse students are too often placed in remedial courses to "catch up" or "live up" to a norm—as modeled by their White classmates. Research and astute observation suggest that people of color may experience a different type of "normal" life and that excellence can and does emerge in multiple and varied forms: people of color from all walks of life are successful. Yet this paradigmatic way of seeing the world—of viewing an achievement gap as something that's "wrong" with students—sometimes prevents teachers and others from recognizing and accepting that excellence emerges in different ways in various communities. Static and exclusively Eurocentric views of normality are problematic.[14] In essence, it is difficult for many to embrace what multicultural educator and teacher educator Cynthia Dillard explains: people of color are not simply White people with colored or pigmented skin.[15] Their normality is shaped by (among other qualities) their racial, ethnic, gender, and cultural heritage. So, who decides what is normal and acceptable? How can we broaden our mind-sets and our conceptions of difference so that our work in education benefits all the culturally diverse learners in a classroom?

HOW TERMS AND CONSTRUCTS ARE USED

Throughout this book, I use *culturally diverse students* to represent students of color, those whose first language is not English, and those who live in poverty or are from lower socioeconomic backgrounds. I understand that every person represents racial, cultural, gender, and ethnic diversity, even though White people are usually classified as the norm and others are considered diverse. I understand that there is a great deal of diversity among people within every racial, cultural, gender, and ethnic background. However, for the purpose of this discussion, I am defining racially, culturally, and ethnically diverse people as those groups that are not White or European American. I do not use the term *minority* because the word carries a historically negative connotation and because White people and others in the mainstream of society are sometimes in the "minority" in particular places at particular times.

Also, when I use the term *we* throughout this book, I am referring to those in education and society, from parents to teachers to policy makers, who are interested in the educational experiences of all students. In some cases, I use *preservice teachers* to refer to those who are in traditional or nontraditional teacher education programs and may not yet be employed in school systems. When I use the term *inservice teachers*, I am referring to those who are already teaching in schools. I use the terms *teacher* and *educator* interchangeably, as I do *African American* and *Black*. Also, I consistently use *P–12* to refer to prekindergarten through grade twelve.

AUDIENCE FOR THIS BOOK

While the book has a clear teacher focus, there are important lessons and ideas that are also relevant for other educators, such as principals, guidance counselors, teachers' assistants, and athletic and academic coaches. While the narratives given in chapters 2 through 4 are from middle and high school teachers, the six White teachers showcased in chapter 5 demonstrate teacher learning challenges and successes encountered in grades P–12. Practicing teachers in urban, rural, and suburban schools as well as students in teacher education programs should read this book, as should teacher educators and researchers interested in students' opportunities to learn.

ORGANIZATION OF THE BOOK

In chapter 1, I share what I call a diversity and opportunity gaps conceptual framework to ground and shape the narratives that follow. This framework includes five interrelated areas or tenets: (1) rejection of color blindness; (2) ability and skill to work through and transcend cultural conflicts; (3) ability to understand how meritocracy operates; (4) ability to recognize and shift low expectations and deficit mind-sets; and (5) rejection of context-neutral mind-sets and practices.

In chapters 2, 3, and 4, I showcase narratives from real teachers in U.S. public middle and high schools who capture the nexus of diversity, opportunity, and teaching in their practices. The teachers highlighted are not perfect, and the social contexts in which they work present very challenging realities. They live and function in complex and difficult circumstances. However, they persist despite the difficulties as they work tirelessly to address students' opportunities to learn, opportunity gaps, and diversity. Mr. Hall is a White science teacher who successfully navigates an urban middle school, Bridge Middle School, to meet the diversity and opportunity needs of his students. Mr. Jackson, an African American mathematics and science teacher, and Ms. Shaw, an African American social studies teacher, also teach at Bridge Middle School. Dr. Johnson is an African American language arts teacher who expands her notions of the opportunity-diversity connection by infusing her curriculum and instructional approaches with cultural and gender content in a mostly White, wealthy suburban high school, Stevenson High School.

In chapter 5, I discuss the learning and some related practices of six White female preservice teachers learning to teach for diversity and opportunity in elementary through high school. I believe their experiences represent the kinds of challenges and successes that those learning to teach may face. I conclude the book with a chapter on the importance of building relationships, a recurrent theme throughout the chapters. I provide recommendations and suggestions for both teachers and school leaders to build and sustain meaningful relationships for the benefit of diversity and opportunity. In the epilogue I explain my research process so readers can learn in more depth about the journey that led me to share these narratives and also about the people and social contexts of the schools presented.

In summary, in this book I focus on three important areas that I believe are crucial for empowering students and teachers to succeed: diversity, opportunity gaps, and teaching. I challenge readers to shift their focus from an achievement gap to those areas related to processes of teaching and learning as well as opportunity gaps.

Finally, although broad and structural changes can make a powerful impact on students' opportunities, individual teachers can also play a role in their classrooms every day! Indeed, teachers *can* make a difference even when they are operating in institutions and systems that do not support their passions and commitments to meeting the complex needs of all students. It is in this vein that I hope educators read this book. Systemic and broad-level change is ideal. Individual-level changes in mind-set and practices among teachers is a place to begin the journey in order to construct those moments that serve students as experiences they shall never forget. Thus, I invite you, the reader, to start where you are—but don't stay there!

1

A Diversity and Opportunity Gaps Explanatory Framework

OPPORTUNITY GAPS, especially those linked to diversity, exist at all levels in education and in the lives of both educators and students. The case studies in the following chapters have important implications for how educators can address diversity and opportunity gaps in a range of school contexts across U.S. society—urban, suburban, and rural; public and private; independent and parochial. In this chapter, I introduce a conceptual framework that creates a context for and serves as an analytic tool to explain these case studies. The issues raised throughout this book are grounded in, related to, and shaped by many of the concepts presented in this chapter. These concepts emerge from theory, research, and practice established in the literature. While this explanatory framework will be used to analyze the thinking and practices of the teachers and students showcased in this book, it is also meant to challenge educators to broaden their belief systems, shift their mind-sets, and transform their practices in order to better address opportunity gaps that persist in P–12 educational contexts.

The framework covers five interconnected areas that I believe are critical in helping educators bridge and shed light on opportunity gaps: (1)

rejection of color blindness; (2) ability and skill to understand, work through, and transcend cultural conflicts; (3) ability to understand how meritocracy operates; (4) ability to recognize and shift low expectations and deficit mind-sets; and (5) rejection of context-neutral mind-sets and practices.

1. *Color blindness:* Educators are challenged to rethink persistent notions that they should avoid recognizing race and how race operates on individual and systemic levels in education. They are challenged to understand and acknowledge how our race-central experiences can influence our ideologies, attitudes, and belief systems, and consequently our practices. Rejecting color blindness allows educators to understand fundamentally that *race matters* for all involved in education, even White people, and to recognize the multiple ways in which race intersects with educational practices—particularly the teaching and learning exchange. Educators are particularly challenged to move beyond individualized ideas about race and racism to an understanding of how systemic barriers continue to marginalize certain groups of students. In addressing opportunity gaps, educators consider individual realities as well as systemic and structural realities related to race and are challenged to think through how race shapes what happens both in society and in the classroom.

2. *Cultural conflicts:* Educators are challenged to become mindful of the conflicts that can emerge in classrooms as a result of the culturally grounded and shaped experiences of both teachers and students. Cultural conflicts can cause inconsistencies and incongruence between teachers and students, which can make teaching and learning difficult. Opportunity gaps can persist because educators' cultural ways of knowing, which are often grounded in Eurocentric cultural notions and ideologies, take precedence over those of their students. To address opportunity in a constructive way, educators are challenged to understand the important role culture plays in curriculum

development, instruction, and broader decision making, such as when teachers correct student (mis)behavior.

3. *Myth of meritocracy:* When educators approach their work through meritocratic lenses and mind-sets, they believe that student performance is primarily and summarily a function of hard work, ability, skill, intelligence, and persistence. Educators believe that student success is a consequence and result of merit—that is, students (and people in general) deserve their success and failure in school and society because they have earned them. Educators are sometimes consciously or subconsciously aware of how situations far beyond students' control and merit can bear on their access to opportunities. To address opportunity, educators are challenged to become mindful of, or at least willing to acknowledge, the many factors beyond merit that shape students' academic and social success.

4. *Low expectations and deficit mind-sets:* Educators sometimes have low expectations of particular students, which can become a self-fulfilling prophecy, setting those students up to perform only to minimal expectations. With this mind-set, educators also tend to focus on what students do not bring to the classroom; that is, they may focus on student deficits rather than their many assets. When addressing opportunity, educators are challenged to be mindful that students will generally meet the expectations that are set for them—including high ones. Educators are challenged to understand that students bring assets into the learning environment that should be valued and capitalized on in the design of learning opportunities.

5. *Context-neutral mind-sets:* Educators sometimes approach their work with students without understanding and attending to the nuances and idiosyncrasies inherent to their particular teaching environment. This approach fails to consider the social contexts of teaching and learning, such as the state, the city, the local community surrounding the school, or the sociology of the school itself. For instance, a teacher may learn to teach a subject such as math, language arts, history, or

science but fail to understand how to teach that subject well in a particular location, the social context. To address opportunity, educators are challenged to become aware of the contextual complexity that influences their ability to design learning opportunities and teach their subject matter. By recognizing the ways in which the social context can influence how the world works and how education works, educators are better able to empower their students to learn, think, and challenge existing forces that place them at a disadvantage in a particular community or social context.

The following sections expand on these five concepts. I begin with color blindness because I have come to understand that educators seem to struggle most to understand the role and relevance of race in teaching and learning.

COLOR BLINDNESS

The research literature suggests that student learning opportunities can be hindered when teachers fail to consider their own and their students' racial backgrounds and think carefully about how race can and does emerge in classroom learning opportunities. The research also suggests that teachers who adopt and embrace color-blind beliefs, worldviews, ideologies, mindsets, and consequently practices can neglect important features of students that should be included in how teachers come to understand their students and construct learning opportunities in the classroom for them.[1] When teachers ignore the racial component of students' identity, they are in effect treating their students as incomplete beings, and student performance can suffer as a result. For instance, if teachers are not conscious of students' racial background, non-White students may not "see themselves" in the curriculum because the curriculum may be constructed using a "business as usual" approach where the curriculum is developed mainly to meet the needs of White students. Moreover, when a color-blind worldview is adopted, instructional practices may be Eurocentric in nature and not take into consideration non-White students' lived experiences. There is also a sociological dimension to color blindness, beyond curriculum and instruction, which can prevent teachers from empathizing with racially and ethnically diverse students. Consider, for instance, a Latino student who has been racially profiled and followed around a corner convenience store in which he stops before going to school. Also consider an African American student who is called a nigger by a group of older students from a car window as she walks to school. These two experiences can influence how these students interact with their classmates, their teacher, and the curriculum. Still, many teachers refuse to acknowledge the prevalence and salience of race in their work as teachers because, in their minds, race is inconsequential, and they often believe that we live in a postracial society.

Feminist theorist Audre Lorde maintains that individuals who adopt color-blind ideologies and approaches to their work believe they can "conquer it [racism and discrimination] by ignoring it."[2] I have heard educators, including non White teachers, proclaim in many different contexts that they "do not see color," they "just see students." Multicultural education researcher James Banks explains that "a statement such as 'I don't see color' reveals a privileged position that refuses to legitimize racial identifications that are very important to people of color and that are often used to justify inaction and perpetuation of the status quo."[3]

Furthermore, teachers who adopt color-blind mind-sets and practices can lack the racial knowledge, sensitivity, and empathy necessary to successfully teach racially diverse students, especially those who are often relegated to the margins of teaching and learning. Because teachers can fail to attend to the multilayered identities of students and may even intentionally avoid race as a central identity marker in their decisions regarding curriculum and instructional designs, students are sometimes expected to just assimilate and adjust to expectations that do not consider the role and relevance of their race. Teachers with a color-blind mind-set may not recognize how their own race and racial experiences shape what they teach, how they teach it, and how they assess what has been taught. For example, when teachers do not include curriculum content related to

Native Americans, that omission itself teaches students something about the importance (or lack thereof) of Native Americans.[4] Omitting Native American content from the curriculum not only denies Native American students the right to recognize their cultural contributions to the fabric of the curriculum, it also denies students from other racial and ethnic backgrounds the opportunity to deepen their knowledge of that group. The result is that students very often learn from a curriculum dominated by White contributions and White norms to the exclusion of contributions from other racial and ethnic groups. Moreover, students are learning something based on what is *not* included in the curriculum. What is absent in the curriculum is actually present in student learning opportunities. At the heart of what is and is not emphasized in the curriculum is teachers' racial identity—who teachers are, how they represent themselves to others, and how they come to see themselves as people who benefit from or are discriminated against due to matters associated with race in society. Consider the demographic data in tables 1.1 and 1.2.

The research literature is clear that a racial demographic divide between teachers and students in P–12 classrooms, as illustrated in the tables, can

TABLE 1.1

Racial demographics of teachers in U.S. public elementary and secondary schools, 2007–2008

Race	Elementary public school (%)	Secondary public school (%)
White	82.7	83.5
Black	7.1	6.9
Hispanic	7.5	6.8
Asian	1.2	1.3
Pacific Islander	0.2	0.2
American Indian/Alaska Native	0.4	0.5
More than one race	0.9	0.9

Source: National Center for Education Statistics, *Digest of Education Statistics, 2008*, http://nces.ed.gov/programs/digest/.

TABLE 1.2

Racial demographics of students in all U.S. public P–12, 2003–2008

Race	2003 (%)	2004 (%)	2005 (%)	2008 (%)
White	60.5	59.9	59.4	57.8
Black	14.9	14.9	14.8	16.0
Hispanic	17.7	18.2	18.7	20.4
Asian	3.6	3.7	3.7	4.4
Pacific Islander	0.2	0.2	0.2	n/a
American Indian/Alaska Native	0.9	0.9	0.9	1.4
More than one race	2.2	2.3	2.3	n/a

Source: National Center for Education Statistics, *Digest of Education Statistics, 2003–2005,* http://nces.ed .gov/programs/digest/; NCES, *The Condition of Education,* http://nces.ed.gov/programs/coe/. National Center for Education Statistics.

be a disadvantage for teachers and students alike.[5] Data illustrating a demographic divide can include gender, race, ethnicity, and socioeconomic background, for instance. For the purposes of this discussion, tables 1.1 and 1.2 provide racial demographic percentages of teachers and students in public schools, where teachers tend to be White and students are increasingly non-White. White teachers and students of color have had different racial experiences both inside and outside the classroom, a gap that may create roadblocks to learning opportunities and consequently roadblocks to students' academic and social success in the classroom.[6]

The idea is that when teachers have the same racial background as their students, there are more opportunities for teachers and students to connect, and there are fewer situations for misunderstandings to occur in the learning environment. However, as Gay asserts, even if students and teachers are of the same race, it "may be potentially beneficial, but it is not a guarantee of pedagogical effectiveness."[7] Educators from any racial background can be successful with any group of students when the educators have (or are willing to garner) the knowledge, attitudes, dispositions, and skills necessary to understand and be responsive to their students' social, instructional, and curriculum needs.[8] In other words, it is what teachers know and are willing to learn that matter more than their racial background. However, it is clear that teachers of color, because of their racialized experiences in the world, often have a deeper understanding of students of color, and are accordingly able to create learning opportunities that students can relate to and connect with.[9] Consequently, given the racial demography of students, increasing the percentage of teachers of color is an important aim for public schools across the United States. Teachers of color often possess life experiences that allow them an insider's perspective in understanding and interpreting what students of color are grappling with and working through.[10] The reasons for paying attention to racial demography are copious. The research literature suggests, for example, that teachers of color

- Can relate to their students of color and empathize with them during race-related experiences, such as feeling discriminated against or experiencing acts of racism by others in the school
- Consciously decide to incorporate materials in the curriculum that showcase and speak from the point of view of their students of color
- Develop examples in the curriculum and make instructional decisions that are explicitly related to students of color
- Address disciplinary conflicts in the classroom to avoid sending students to the office, and provide "tough love" when necessary
- Serve as role models for all students, including students of color
- Recognize "diamonds in the rough" and build on the knowledge and skills that students of color bring to the classroom because they recognize a wider spectrum of the brilliance and talents that students possess[11]

Where color blindness is concerned, I have discovered at least three common dangerously disadvantageous conceptions among teachers:

Mind-set 1: If I acknowledge the racial or ethnic background of my students or myself, I may be considered racist.

Mind-set 2: If I admit that people experience the world differently and that race is an important part of people's experiences, I may be seen as "politically incorrect." I may offend others in the teacher education classroom or my P–12 faculty meeting if I express my beliefs and reservations about race.

Mind-set 3: I should treat all my students the same regardless of who they are, what their home situations are, or what their experiences happen to be. Race does not matter and racism has ended; thus racial considerations have no place or relevance in the design of classroom learning opportunities.

These misguided assertions can manifest in seriously destructive ways in the P–12 classroom. Sociologist Amanda Lewis found in her study of a mostly White school, for instance, that many educators and adults refused to discuss or acknowledge the ever-present social and institutional race-related matters in their social context.[12] When Sylvie, a student of color, brought up her experiences of racism in the school, educators in the community ignored her concerns and rationalized that the student was "playing the race card" (whatever this means!). Lewis explained that the adults essentially adopted a color-blind approach and mind-set to their work and lives. The adults in Lewis's study believed that issues of race were not important in their learning environment because most of the students, educators, and parents were White. Consequently, as her study made clear, some educators believe that when there is not a critical mass of people of color, race is insignificant. Such educators may fail to understand that race affects all people in society and in education, even White people.

The 2008 election of Barack Obama to the presidency led too many people in the United States and abroad to believe that his election transcended centuries of racism, oppression, marginalization, and discrimination. White Americans as well as those from other racial and ethnic groups, including some Black Americans, proclaimed what seemed to be a modern cliché: that it was "a new day" in U.S. society. Some believed that we as a country had arrived at a postracial, postoppressive, postdis-crimination era because White voters had helped elect an African Ameri-can president. Indeed, many did support him—but many others did not. Regardless, this position does not recognize the pervasiveness of race, racism, and other more general forms of discrimination and prejudice. While individual educators may not be racist, broader policies and prac-tices (constructed by a collective of individuals) are often rife with racism. Accordingly, educators who do not view themselves as racist individuals can have trouble recognizing how racism works and how it can manifest in broader systems and institutionalized structures to prevent certain groups of students from succeeding in the classroom and beyond. In particular, educators who voted for President Obama may especially find it difficult to believe that we are still living in a racist U.S. society.

In short, it is critical that educators recognize their own and their stu-dents' racial backgrounds in order to treat their students as complete hu-man beings rather than fragments of their full identity.

How do teachers contribute to individual and structural forms of rac-ism that can influence student opportunities? Clearly, color-blind ideolo-gies, orientations, and practices make it difficult for educators to recognize disparities and dilemmas in education, such as

- An overrepresentation of students of color in special education
- An underrepresentation of students of color in gifted education
- An overreferral of African American students to the office for disci-plinary actions and consequences
- An overwhelming number of African American students who are ex-pelled or suspended
- An underrepresentation of students of color in schoolwide clubs, or-ganizations, and other prestigious arenas, such as the school's home-coming court and student government
- An underrepresentation of faculty and staff of color in school posi-tions, including professional staff, teaching, and leadership positions

These disparities and dilemmas are complexly important and seem to persist despite decades of clear evidence of their existence. For instance, as gifted education researcher Donna Ford maintains, little progress has been made in the demographics of gifted education over the past twenty years.[13] Black and Hispanic students tend to be grossly underrepresented in gifted education programs and overrepresented in special education across U.S. society. Educators who take a color-blind approach are apt to be unaware of or unconcerned about disproportionate representation and enrollment in different courses and on various academic tracks. In addition, the lack of microlevel race-conscious policies and procedures can be dangerous for students if schools do not centralize matters of race as a proxy for who is representing the school in organizations and in what ways. For instance, if students of color continually do not hold offices such as school president or are not represented in the student government association, school officials and educators should be concerned and take steps to address that reality. Similarly, they should take corrective action when students of color participate primarily in athletics and rarely in accelerated academic programs. Some believe that the students themselves cause their underrepresentation, not the school's race-neutral, color-blind policies and procedures. Thus it is critical that educators remember race and racism in their work with students on both individual and systemic levels. By adopting color-blind ideologies, practices, and mind-sets that ignore the importance of race, educators can contribute to and actually exacerbate the persistence of opportunity gaps.

CULTURAL CONFLICTS

Like color blindness, cultural conflicts in classroom practice are widespread.[14] Researchers have found that the conflicts, incongruence, and inconsistencies that educators and students encounter in the classroom can limit students' learning opportunities.[15] When teachers operate primarily from their own cultural ways of knowing, the learning milieu can be foreign to students whose cultural experiences are different and inconsistent with teachers' experiences. Such cultural conflicts can have negative consequences because there are few points of reference and convergence between teachers and students. A student, for instance, may be immersed in hip-hop culture, and his teacher may have no interest or awareness of it. This can result in a cultural conflict and, consequently, a missed opportunity for teacher and student to develop a meaningful relationship. Moreover, teachers may miss the opportunity to incorporate aspects of hip-hop into their instructional practices in order to explain an idea or to help students solve a complex math problem. The idea is that "some groups of students—because their cultural characteristics are more consistent with the culture, norms, and expectations of the school than are those of other groups of students—have greater opportunities for academic success than do students whose cultures are less consistent with the school culture."[16]

Educational researcher and educator Lisa Delpit advanced the idea of a "culture of power" that exists in classrooms and that can have lasting influence on the types of learning that can take place in a classroom.[17] Cultural conflicts sometimes result in a resistant, oppositional, or confrontational environment in which educators are fighting to control students and to exert their power, and students do not want to feel controlled. Students can similarly work to be heard and to have some power in the classroom. Consequently, educators and students can *work against* each other, which can leave students feeling that their preferences are insignificant, disrespected, irrelevant, or subordinate to educators and to classroom/school life. As a result, students may refuse to engage in the classroom culture and refuse to learn.

Cultural conflicts and power struggles carry important associations. Delpit outlines five aspects of power, culture, and conflicts:

(a) issues of power are enacted in classrooms; (b) there are codes or rules for participating in power; that is, there is a "culture of power;" (c) the rules of the culture of power are a reflection of the rules of the culture of those who have power; (d) if you are not already a participant in the culture of power, being told explicitly the rules of that culture makes acquiring power easier; and (e) those with power are frequently least aware of—or least willing to acknowledge—its existence. Those with less power are often most aware of its existence.[18]

In this sense, educators create a culture of power in the classrooms because they do in fact have power over their students; this culture can be gravely inconsistent with students' cultural experiences and how they construct meaning and relevance. Several common mind-sets and assertions can reinforce conflicts of power and culture between teachers and students:

Mind-set 1: I must teach students based on how I teach my own biological children, not based on their culture and experiences in the world (which may or may not be consistent with my own).

Mind-set 2: I'm not going to tolerate students joking around during class. If they misbehave, I'm sending them to the office—period!

Mind-set 3: "Those" students need to adapt and assimilate into the culture of "my" classroom and accept the consequences if they do not.

What constitutes acceptable behavior and appropriate discipline for students at home can be significantly different from the discipline and rules of behavior experienced in the classroom.[19] At the core of these cultural conflicts is what it means to be "normal." Normal classroom behavior can be informed by different cultural frames, such as race, socioeconomics, language, or even geography. For example, students may be accustomed to joking around with family members when a conflict arises in order to deescalate or to avoid a confrontation. They may have found that using humor helps family members ease away from or work through confrontation and conflict. Teachers, on the other hand, may consider it inappropriate when students invoke humor to defuse a conflict, which can then escalate cultural conflict between a teacher and a student.

Delpit reports that students deserve to overtly be told the "rules" and the consequences of breaking them.[20] For students to have a chance at success in the classroom, and thus in society, they must understand that they live in a system that can be oppressive and repressive. Those in power decide what is normal behavior and conduct. If joking around to resolve a disagreement in the classroom is not acceptable, then students need to be taught this and not be punished for using a coping or resolution ideology and approach that they have found effective at home. Students too often are punished for not behaving in a particular way, even when that way has not been well explained and taught to them. The onus, therefore, is on educators, those in power, to help students learn to behave in ways that the dominant culture finds acceptable. Otherwise, conflicts can emerge, and students almost always lose what I have come to call cultural battles in the classroom—mainly because students do not necessarily think, act, and live as their teachers do or as their teachers' biological children do. In short, it is irresponsible and simply unfair to expect students to behave in a way that has not been well explained to them. Teachers should not assume that students understand the culture of power; teachers must teach it!

Even while students are told explicitly about the culture of power and are learning to survive and thrive within it, they should be empowered to challenge and question oppressive structures, rather than conform to systems that make them feel, according to urban educational researcher Pedro Noguera, like "prisoners."[21] In essence, Noguera's research suggests that some students in urban schools, particularly those living in cultures of poverty, are treated more like they are prisoners than students learning to navigate and negotiate educational structures. Teachers in these schools are obsessed with straight lines, hand raising, and control of students. Such educational institutions are inundated with instructional practices that teacher educator Martin Haberman calls the "pedagogy of poverty"—teaching practices that reinforce and prepare students to take orders and to eventually assume roles in the larger society either as prisoners or as those trained to take orders.[22] The educators in Noguera's study identified students they believed would eventually end up in jail. Such a mind-set, where educators predict who will eventually go to prison, is grounded in a culture of conflict that surely has a bearing on opportunity. If teachers believe their students will fail and become incarcerated, they likely will treat them in ways that essentially guarantee such an outcome. Again, students usually meet the expectations teachers establish—whether high or low. In fact, structural and sustained practices can covertly be designed to prepare students for "jail-bound" paths. In this sense, schools can structurally produce and perpetuate inequity, poverty, and cultures of apathy while pretending to be designed to do the opposite.[23]

Although students should be empowered to counter oppressive practices that place them in situations of prisonlike insubordination, they must also be able to operate within these cultural systems in order to change them. Knowing what the culture of power actually is, how it works, and how power can be achieved are important tools for students to develop. Not only should students be taught explicitly about the culture of power, but their parents should also be informed about what expectations teachers have for their children. Again, educators cannot maintain tacit beliefs about expectations, assuming that parents know what is expected of them or of their children. Being explicit is critical in building partnerships and solid relationships between teachers and students—and their parents. Thus, simply assuming that students will be taught the culture of power outside the classroom can be considered irresponsible because students' parents may operate from a different worldview regarding expectations in their homes. Moreover, parents of these students may not fully understand (or embrace) how to negotiate and live in the dominant culture or may not possess those dominant cultural views and values about how to function in society.

Cultural conflicts are apparent in patterns of school discipline and office referrals, especially those that occur in the classroom. The findings in the research literature are straightforward in that most disciplinary student referrals originate in the classroom and are disproportionately for students of color and those from lower socioeconomic backgrounds. Researchers Russell Skiba et al. analyzed disciplinary documents for 11,001 students in nineteen middle schools in a large midwestern urban public school district during the 1994–1995 academic year. They reported a "differential pattern of treatment, originating at the classroom level, wherein African American students are referred to the office for infractions that are more subjective in interpretation."[24]

For instance, if a Latino/a student talks back or mouths off to an educator, the behavior may be interpreted as disrespectful, based on the educator's cultural frame of reference. However, the student may be behaving in this way (mouthing off) because of peer pressure—not wanting friends to see him or her as weak—rather than out of disrespect; malice may not be at the core of the student's actions. Skiba et al. point out that students of color received harsher punishments for misbehavior than their White peers.[25] Thus, cultural conflicts are serious areas of consideration in addressing opportunity gaps, and educators must be mindful of them.

MYTH OF MERITOCRACY

The third category in the framework, the myth of meritocracy, is another critical consideration when addressing diversity and opportunity gaps. While many educators, White educators in particular, have a difficult time confronting matters of race, they readily identify disparities in students' socioeconomic status and education as causes of opportunity gaps. Educators appear to be more confident and comfortable with the idea that socioeconomic factors, particularly resources that determine wealth and poverty, influence educational inequities, outcomes, and opportunities. However, they sometimes misunderstand the historic and structural forms of resources that give people their positions in society. Their conceptions of what class is and how it affects their students, their students' parents, and their own families are sometimes sorely inaccurate, underdeveloped, and therefore inadequate, especially in terms of how socioeconomics can shape the kinds of learning opportunities that are afforded students in schools.

Educators sometimes embrace the notion that their own, their parents', and their students' success and status have been earned. Conversely, they may believe that failure is earned as well—that it results solely from the wrong choices, such as an individual's choice not to work hard or put forth effort. Unearned opportunities, however, are often passed down from one generation to the next; yet, many educators believe that their own success is merited because they have worked hard, followed the law, had the ability and skill, and made the right decisions. They have little or no conception of how privilege and opportunity manifest (see McIntosh's article "White Privilege" for an excellent discussion of the nature of privilege).[26] For instance, White teachers may fail to see that they are privileged based on their race and the opportunities Whiteness has afforded them. Moreover, wealthy teachers of any racial background can fail to recognize their economic privilege and to understand how they have acquired that privilege. People rarely become wealthy overnight. Wealth and related resources are built and established over time and through generations of families. Teachers in general can fail to understand that they have gained their status through a wide range of unearned advantages. In contrast, students who grow up in poverty or from a lower socioeconomic status generally do not start their educational or life experiences in a fair or equitable position.

In wealthier families, inherited wealth may afford opportunities that are not directly "earned." Consider the following examples of what generational and family wealth and resources afford people:

- Trust funds established and passed down through generations
- Property (as in homes and land) that is passed down from one generation to the next
- A college education financed without student loans
- Private and independent school tuition and education
- Private tutoring in academic subjects
- Exposure to different cultures and languages
- Financial support and assistance with graduate studies
- Kaplan and tutorial programs to prepare students for the SAT, ACT, and GRE
- Vacations and getaways, both domestic and international
- Zoned school systems with superior educational resources and curriculum materials as well as strong educators and administrators

At the center of the meritocracy argument for student success is opportunity. That is, U.S. society is predicated on the philosophical ideals expressed in the Declaration of Independence, that all people are created equal and have the same opportunities for success. In reality, however, educational practices and opportunities are anything but equal or equitable. The enormous variation in students' social, economic, political, and educational opportunities is in stark contrast to the "American dream," which has meritocracy as its core. Still, many educators believe that if people just work hard enough they will be rewarded and achieve their full potential, regardless of historic or contemporary economic structures. Educators can fail to recognize the systemic barriers and institutional structures that prevent opportunity and thereby hinder success. Several assertions regarding meritocracy are common:

Mind-set 1: All people are born with the same opportunities. If students just follow the formula for success—work hard, put forth effort, and follow the law—then they will be successful.

Mind-set 2: If students do not succeed, it is because they are not working hard enough, not because of other factors that may be outside their control.

Mind-set 3: Some students just do not have the aptitude, ability, or skills for success; the "system" has nothing to do with academic achievement.

However, if the meritocracy argument were accurate, as sociologist James Henslin writes,

[A]ll positions would be awarded on the basis of merit. If so, ability should predict who goes to college. Instead, family income is the best predictor— the more a family earns, the more likely their children are to go to college . . . while some people do get ahead through ability and hard work, others simply inherit wealth and the opportunities that go with it . . . in short, factors far beyond merit give people their positions in society.[27]

Thus, the meritocracy argument appears to be a myth because it maintains that any person living in U.S. society can achieve the "American dream," as long as he or she has the ability, works hard, follows the law, and makes good decisions. However, opportunity gaps can "undermine one of our most powerful and core beliefs that we as Americans cling to: that no matter what circumstances children are born into, all have the opportunity to become educated and, if they work hard, to pursue their dreams."[28] By way of rationalizing a meritocratic philosophy and position, successful, isolated cases are offered of individuals (mainly successful athletes and celebrities) who have pulled themselves up by their bootstraps and transcended poverty, such as Oprah Winfrey, Tom Cruise, and Bill Gates.

This philosophy can reject institutionalized and systemic issues and barriers that permeate policies and practices, such as racism, sexism, classism, and discrimination both in the classroom and in society. Teacher education researcher Marilyn Cochran-Smith explains that "U.S. society writ large is not a meritocracy but is embedded in social, political, economic, and educational systems that are deeply and fundamentally racist."[29] Indeed, the meritocracy argument does not appropriately take into consideration the resources, advantages, and privileges that wealthier students often inherit—materially, physically (in terms of health and health care they receive), socially, and culturally—capital that has been and continues to be passed down from one generation to the next.[30]

A pervasive theme of a meritocratic mind-set centers around a we/they binary that some adopt as they position themselves and their "earned" success in opposition or in relation to others. Apple maintains that

> the binary opposition of we–they becomes important . . . For dominant groups, "we" are law-abiding, hardworking, decent, and virtuous. "They"—usually poor people and immigrants—are very different. They are lazy, immoral, and permissive. These binary oppositions act to exclude indigenous people, women, the poor, and others from the community of worthy individuals.[31]

Thus, these dichotomous mind-sets can allow people to rationalize and view their successes as having been "earned" by being law-abiding, hard-working, and virtuous. However, Ladson-Billings asserts that it is unfair and inconceivable to expect all students to finish their education in the same place when they do not begin their education in the same place. In other words, how can we expect all students to cross the same finish line when they do not have the same starting point and equitable support systems throughout the race? Further, how can we expect equal outcomes on achievement measures when structural inequities place some groups of students in poorly run schools with fewer resources and underquali-fied teachers? Bafflingly, we wonder why populations of students who have been poorly served in education cannot necessarily transcend our poorly run educational system.

Figures 1.1 and 1.2, based on the 2000 U.S. Census data[32], capture the correlation between people's earnings and their level of education. These graphs summarize annual salaries as well as lifetime earnings. It is clear that people's ability to pursue higher education has serious implications for the amount of money they will earn in their lifetime. These graphs pro-vide an important picture of the educational and economic landscape that has direct implications, I believe, on the kinds of experiences and oppor-tunities people have in society. Logically, education is a strong predictor of economic success. Understanding these deep-rooted societal realities is crucial for teachers as they work to level the playing field inside schools.

However, as ethnographer Jay MacLeod explains, sometimes "schools actually reinforce social inequality while pretending to do the opposite" because educators refuse to see meritocracy for what it really is, and they blame students for realities far beyond students' control.[33] Moreover, when educators do not understand (or when they understand but do not acknowledge) how educational opportunity and economic realities are linked, they are unlikely to make decisions that help students under-stand inequity and learn how they can transform their lives to circumvent poverty and low-paying jobs and careers. Moreover, students need to be empowered to improve and mobilize their own communities to get out

FIGURE 1.1

What people earn annually

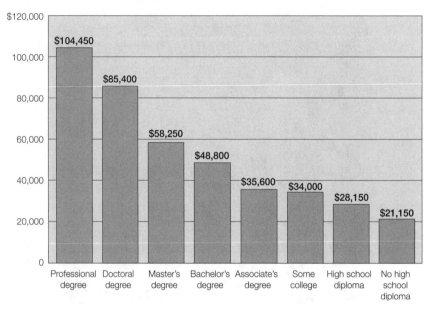

Adapted from U.S. Census Bureau Current Population Reports, Special Studies, *The Big Payoff: Educational Attainment and Synthetic Estimates of Work-Life Earnings* (P23-210), http://www.census.gov/prod/2002pubs/p23-210.pdf.

of poverty. For example, elementary students cannot control how much money their parents earn, the school zone in which they live, or the availability of private tutoring. It can be distressing for educators to move beyond a strictly merit-based mind-set and approach in the classroom, however, because as curriculum theorist Beverly Gordon asserts, it is difficult for educators to critique and work to change the world when the world works (and has worked) for them.[33] Myths of meritocracy make it difficult for educators to understand the complexities of opportunity, hard work, and ability, and students are the benefactors of mind-sets and practices that have sometimes overlooked factors far beyond merit that have placed them in their educational positions.

FIGURE 1.2
What people earn over their careers

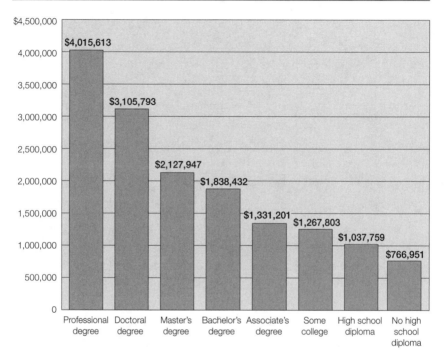

Adapted from U.S. Census Bureau Current Population Reports, Special Studies, *The Big Payoff: Educational Attainment and Synthetic Estimates of Work-Life Earnings* (P23-210), http://www .census.gov/prod/2002pubs/p23-210.pdf.

LOW EXPECTATIONS AND DEFICIT MIND-SETS

So far I have explained three tenets of the diversity and opportunity gaps framework: color blindness, cultural conflicts, and merit-based ideologies. A fourth explanatory lens for analyzing these gaps concern the low expectations and deficit mind-sets that teachers sometimes have of students. Where cultural deficit theories are concerned, Ford writes,

> These theories carry a "blame the victim" orientation, and supporters look upon Blacks and other minority groups as not only culturally but also in-

tellectually inferior. According to deficit theories or perspectives, "different" is equated with deficient, inferior, and substandard.[35]

Low expectations and deficit mind-sets make it difficult for educators to develop learning opportunities that challenge students. For instance, teachers may believe that some students cannot master a rigorous curriculum, and consequently may avoid designing important learning opportunities for those students. They may see the knowledge and skills that culturally diverse students possess as liabilities rather than assets. And when educators do recognize student assets, they sometimes struggle to understand how they can scaffold those assets or strengths with learning opportunities. At times, student assets are not appropriately used as anchors to make instructional connections in the classroom, and educators continue teaching in ways that avoid or overlook the brilliance and talents that students possess.

Educators' beliefs that can lead to low expectations may materialize out of (1) conversations they have had among themselves about students in the teachers' lounge or hallway, (2) their interpretations of student results on standardized tests, or (3) parents' views about particular groups of students. Regardless of the source, teachers can transfer such mind-sets, expectations, and beliefs into their instructional designs and practices. Several common beliefs are related to low expectations and deficit mind-sets:

Mind-set 1: I need to distance students from the "horrors" of their home conditions. Students lack so much, and their home environments make it difficult for me to teach them.

Mind-set 2: I am being sensitive to culturally diverse students when I feel sorry for them. If I expect too much, then I am setting the students up for failure.

Mind-set 3: Students need educators who make up for what students lack rather than teachers who build on what students have because some students "bring so little."

Mind-set 4: "Those" poor students cannot meet high expectations because they do not have the resources to do so.

Such mind-sets and expectations make it difficult for educators to build on the strengths that students bring into the learning environment. It has become clear to some researchers that

> the under-representation of diverse students in gifted education is primarily a function of educators holding a deficit perspective about diverse students. Deficit thinking exists when educators hold negative, stereotypic and counterproductive views about culturally diverse students and lower their expectations of these students accordingly.[36]

Because of a deficit mind-set, educators sometimes believe they are actually doing students a favor by not developing challenging learning opportunities. These lowered expectations emerge in how and what they teach, and unchallenging content is often irrelevant to their students. For example, educators do not give students opportunities to engage in critical thinking, or they fail to design a learning environment where students can be creative, exert voice, or offer views that differ from those presented by a teacher or textbook.[37]

The deficit mind-set contributes to an unending cycle: educators do not teach with rigor and high expectations; students do not learn; students' test scores suffer; and then all involved wonder why. I have learned that the blame for failure is too often placed on students, without any serious interrogation of the role that teachers and school structures play. In short, deficit mind-sets and low expectations can have negative outcomes for both educators and students.

Additionally, stereotypes can play a huge role in teachers' expectations of students. Social psychologist Claude Steele's research points to the psychological burdens that marginalized people have endured as a result of stereotypes about them in U.S. society.[38] His research shows that people's performance and achievement, such as women in mathematics, can be hindered due to what he calls "stereotype threat," where members of the stereotyped group worry that they will reinforce or confirm a stereotype through their performance in a particular domain. The stereotype becomes an additional burden that people believe they must counter. Educators' expectations coupled with students' understanding of their "deficiencies" have direct consequences for students' psychological, social, and emotional well-being. Stereotyped students know what is being said about them through the media, for instance, and their performance can be influenced by these views because they may be working overtime to counter or disrupt the stereotypes. Students understand when teachers buy in to pervasive, negative stereotypes about certain groups, and they realize when low expectations and deficit mind-sets shape what happens in the classroom.

CONTEXT-NEUTRAL MIND-SETS

The fifth and final concept in this framework, a context-neutral mind-set, is also essential in thinking about opportunity gaps and diversity. Social contexts have a huge bearing on human development and opportunity structures, for both educators and students. Communities can be classified as suburban, rural, or urban. Suburban communities often offer educational resources that many urban and rural contexts cannot. The social context of schools and communities therefore reinforces opportunity and the status quo. Context-neutral mind-sets do not allow educators to recognize the realities embedded in a particular place, such as a school in a particular community—what multicultural education researcher Francisco Rios calls the cultural context.[39]

The social context should be taken into account when attempting to understand opportunity and diversity and the impact they have on educators' and students' performance and outcomes. Consider, for instance, the following contextually grounded realities that inevitably influence the nature of opportunity for both teachers and students. I have adapted many of these examples from Paul Barton's policy analysis, *Parsing the Achievement Gap: Baseline for Tracking Progress:*[40]

- Urban and high-poverty schools have a disproportionate number of new teachers; students whose teachers have five years of experience or more make three to four months more progress in reading during a school year.
- Teachers in urban and high-poverty schools are absent more often than teachers in other locations; as a result, students in urban schools are taught by substitute teachers, many of whom are not trained in subject-matter domains of teaching.
- There is often a lack of commitment and persistence among educators in urban and high-poverty schools. Teachers graduate from college/ teacher education programs and work in urban and high-poverty schools until another position becomes available in a "more desirable" location.
- A disproportionate number of educators teach outside their field of expertise in urban and high-poverty schools.
- Money and resources are unequal in different social contexts: high-need districts where resources are low too often receive the same assistance as districts with much greater resources.[41] Some districts distribute "equally funded programs into schools regardless of how many students need them. For example, a district might allocate $100,000 to each school with English-language learners, even though one school might have 200 students with limited English proficiency and another—often a more affluent school—might have only 20 [students]."[42]

Thus, it is no secret that urban and high-poverty schools face persistent challenges that put student learning opportunities in jeopardy. Educators' understanding of how factors presented above influence students' opportunities is important as this awareness allows us to examine how a social context shapes opportunity rather than focusing primarily on the students themselves, on achievement gaps, or on an outcome, such as test scores. I believe that focusing on what happens when these contextual factors exist allows us to address opportunity and to get at some of the more logical reasons why too many culturally diverse students are underserved in schools across the country. For instance, focusing on absenteeism among educators in urban and high-poverty schools can help us make sense of student achievement when we consider that students have received instruction from a substitute teacher who may or may not have the educational credentials (especially the knowledge of the subject being taught) to teach. In a similar vein, it is not enough for educators to have deep subject-matter knowledge if they lack strong context-centered knowledge. Sadly, many education researchers treat these two important dimensions of knowledge (subject matter and social context) separately, in terms of both research and practice.

An added problem arises when educators believe that issues of race and diversity are insignificant in mostly White learning contexts. Researchers and theoreticians agree that race, diversity, and multicultural education are a necessity for the intellectual, academic, and social success of students of color.[43] Understandably, because the number of culturally, racially, and linguistically diverse students in the United States is increasing at a high rate, and because educators are still largely White, middle class, and female, emphasizing race and diversity has consistently focused on White educators teaching in predominantly African American or other settings with large populations of students of color—namely, highly diverse urban settings. However, Banks explains that diversity studies and multicultural education are "to help *all* students, *including White mainstream students* [emphasis added], to develop the knowledge, skills, and attitudes they will need to survive and function effectively in a future U.S. society in which one out of every three people will be a person of color."[44] Consider Banks's demographic profile (both historical and projected): in the year 2000, 28 percent of U.S. society consisted of people of color; in 2025, it is projected that 38 percent of the population will be of color and by 2050, 50 percent will be of color. Moreover, Banks notes that one of six students in U.S. public schools speaks a language other than English.[45] Understanding these broader social realities can provide a window for educators to more deeply understand the world in which they (will) teach.

Issues of race, diversity, and multicultural education, then, are important not only for students of color, linguistically diverse learners, and students who have a special learning need, but also for students in the mainstream of learning; White students and students who grow up with some degree of wealth in a range of social contexts should also focus on these matters. However, in suburban and mostly wealthy schools "in which the population is basically white and middle-class, multicultural education is often viewed as unnecessary."[46] The idea that racial discrimination and cultural misunderstandings do not exist in predominantly White settings is a fallacy. Moreover, students who attend mostly White settings do not live in a vacuum; they will experience matters of race and diversity in the world they inhabit and inherit, and they must be prepared to function effectively in that world in order to understand their own position and opportunities, as well as those of others.

I have learned that many future teachers enter teacher education with context-neutral mind-sets like these:

Mind-set 1: Kids are just kids. If I learn my subject matter well, I can get all my students interested in the subject; the type or location of the school and who is enrolled in the school do not matter.

Mind-set 2: It is not necessary for me to rally the local community to help empower, energize, and motivate students inside the school and classroom.

Mindset 3: There are few differences between the various schools in the United States. It is not necessary for me to develop skills to understand the historic and contemporary realities of the school communities where I teach.

It is important for educators to deeply understand both the broader and the more localized social contexts that shape their teaching. Relevant, effective, and responsive teaching requires that educators know more than their subject matter; they must understand the differences, complexities, and nuances inherent in what it means to teach in urban, suburban, and rural environments. Such an understanding of the context in which they teach can move teachers beyond stereotypes to a mind-set that allows them to learn continuously about their communities and the people in them. While I am in support of educators learning about the social context in which they teach, I am also stressing that teachers refuse to accept commonly held ideas that place particular communities in a negative light. Educators need to learn about the social context so that they are able to grasp how communities are classified and what they might encounter; concurrently, educators need to be deliberate in their efforts to locate the "good" in social contexts that others have written off as hopeless.

In essence, educators need to understand that they are working in service *with* the community. As Brazilian critical theorist Paulo Freire explains, those of us in education are working with communities to empower the community to improve their own situations.[47] Educators are not the only, or even the main, arbiters of knowledge in a community.[48] Moreover, as curriculum theorist Gail McCutcheon reminds us, we must take control of our beliefs and positions before they control us. Indeed, community knowledge is an essential aspect of understanding opportunity, and educators must be vigilant in their efforts to learn about the social context of their work.

Table 1.3 summarizes the five core concepts that address the interrelated essence of opportunity and diversity that is discussed throughout this book. The table includes an explanation of each concept, several mind-sets or assertions educators may hold that substantiate the concepts, and possible instructional and related consequences connected to opportunity drawn from the concepts.

The following chapters showcase teachers in particular social contexts and how they address issues of opportunity and diversity in their practices.

TABLE 1.3

An explanatory framework on opportunity

Construct	Explanations	Educators' mind-sets	(Instructional) consequences
Color blindness (conceptions of race matter)	Educators avoid and reject their own and their students' racialized experiences in their decision making. Educators see race as a taboo topic that is irrelevant and inconsequential to the success of their students. White educators do not recognize the multiple layers of privilege associated with their race and how race can manifest in teaching, learning, and curricular experiences.	M1: If I acknowledge the racial or ethnic background of my students or myself, then I may be considered racist. M2: If I admit that people experience the world differently and that race is an important dimension of people's experiences, I may be seen as "politically incorrect." I may offend others in the teacher education classroom if I express my beliefs and reservations about race. M3: I should treat all my students the same regardless of who they are, what their home situations are, or what their raced experiences happen to be.	Educators teach their students in a myopic manner; they do not consider how racially diverse students experience the world inside the classroom, inside the school, and in society. Curriculum and instructional decisions are grounded in a "White norm" that students of color have to just "deal with." Race is seen as a marginal, not central, issue in developing lessons and enacting those lessons (teaching).
Cultural conflicts (conceptions of culture matter)	Inconsistency emerges in the teaching and learning context based on (among other factors) race, gender, age, geography, and socioeconomic disconnections between educators and students. Conflicts may be historically or currently shaped. Educators see their culture as superior to that of their students.	M1: I must teach students based on how I teach my own children, not based on their cultural ways of knowing. M2: I'm not going to tolerate students joking around with me during class. If they misbehave, I'm sending them to the office—period! M3: "Those" students need to adapt and assimilate into the culture of my classroom and accept the consequences if they do not.	Educators refer students of color to the office when they "misbehave." Educators refer culturally diverse students to special education when they are not grasping instructional material rather than attempting to adjust their instructional practices to better meet the learning styles of those students. A disproportionate number of African American students are suspended and expelled.

(continued)

TABLE 1.3 *(continued)*

An explanatory framework on opportunity

Construct	Explanations	Educators' mind-sets	(Instructional) consequences
Myth of meritocracy (conceptions of socioeconomic status matter)	Educators accept the idea that people are rewarded based (solely or mostly) on their ability, performance, effort, and talents. Systemic and institutional structures and barriers are not considered. Individual achievement is seen as an independent variable.	M1: All people are born with the same opportunities; if they just follow the formula for success—work hard, put forth effort, and follow the law—then they will be successful. M2: If students do not succeed, it is because they are not working hard enough, not because of other factors that may be outside of their control. M3: Some students just do not have the aptitude, ability, or skill for success; the "system" has nothing to do with academic achievement.	Educators do not give students multiple chances for success because they believe the students are not working hard enough. Educators do not delve deeply into the reasons behind students' lack of engagement or the reasons why students do not complete their homework. The reality that performance may be a consequence of students' financial problems is not considered as a source of "problems" in the classroom.
Deficit mind-sets and low expectations (belief systems matter)	Educators approach their work focusing on what students do not have rather than on the assets students bring into the learning environments. Educators have a narrow view of what it means to be "normal" or "successful"; these views are based on their own cultural references, which may be inconsistent with others.	M1: I need to distance the students of color from the "horrors" of their present cultural conditions. The students are lacking so much. M2: I am being sensitive to culturally diverse students when I feel sorry for them. If I expect too much, then I am setting them up for failure. M3: Students need educators who try to make up for what they lack rather than build on what students have because some students "bring so little."	Educators spend their time remediating students instead of building on the knowledge students actually bring into the classroom. Educators refuse to allow students to develop their own thinking skills. Students are expected to regurgitate a right answer that the educator has provided.

(continued)

TABLE 1.3 *(continued)*

An explanatory framework on opportunity

Construct	Explanations	Educators' mind-sets	(Instructional) consequences
Deficit mind-sets and low expectations (belief systems matter) *(continued)*	Educators do not believe that culturally diverse students are capable of a rigorous academic curriculum, so they provide unchallenging learning opportunities in the classroom.	M4: It is my job to concentrate mostly on students' test scores and to "close the achievement gap." M5: "Those" poor students cannot meet high expectations because they do not have the resources to do so.	Very little discussion and creative learning opportunities are available. Students are given busywork in hopes that they will not talk; the classroom is viewed as the educators' space, and students are expected to conform and to be quiet. Educators water down the curriculum and have only minimal curricular expectations. Educators focus on basic skills only and push students to get a "right" answer in all academic subject matters. Students are not allowed to think outside the box, to develop critical and analytic thinking skills, or to question power structures in order to improve unfair, inequitable realities.
Context-neutral mind-sets (social contexts matter)	Educators approach their work without a keen sense of how contextual, ecological, and environmental realities shape opportunities to learn. Educators concentrate on learning subject matter (such as math, science, social studies, and language arts) and consider it unimportant to understand the complexities inherent in teaching that subject matter in different contexts, such as urban, suburban, or rural spaces.	M1: Kids are just kids. If I learn my subject matter well, I can get all my students interested in the subject; the type of school does not matter. M2: There are few differences between the various school contexts. It is not necessary for me to develop the skills to understand the historical and current realities of the school communities where I teach. M3: It is not necessary for me to rally the local community to empower, energize, and motivate students inside the school/classroom.	Educators do not build on or draw from the knowledge or established resources of the local community. Rather than constructing knowledge with the community, educators act as if they are omniscient and miss or possibly consciously avoid opportunities to build substantive partnerships in the social context.

2

White Male Teacher, Diverse Urban School

Relationships and Race Matter— Even in the Science Classroom

The students were resistant [to me] because they did not know me when I first started teaching here. There was all this pushback because the kids were like: "I don't care who you are, I don't know you."

—MR. HALL, urban middle school science teacher

MR. HALL, A WHITE SCIENCE EDUCATOR, had been teaching for three years at Bridge Middle School when he made the comment above. He explained that when he first entered the teaching profession, his students were sometimes unwilling to engage in class and were resistant because they did not "know" him. In this chapter, I demonstrate the transformative nature of Mr. Hall's work in the science classroom by focusing on the role and relevance of race and relationship building in addressing opportunity. Some students in Mr. Hall's classes struggled to make a connection with him, which had an influence on the kinds of learning opportunities that Mr. Hall was able to make available in the classroom. However, rather than accepting that tensions would emerge and that opportunity gaps were inevitable in his classroom, Mr. Hall learned from his students and adjusted his practices accordingly. In reality, Mr. Hall started where he was but refused to stay there. He was willing to look at himself and his own life experiences and to examine his classroom practices in order to address broader issues related to opportunity. Had Mr. Hall not been tenaciously vigilant in addressing problems and tensions as he experienced them, opportunity gaps could have taken several serious forms.

To maximize opportunity and avoid serious opportunity gaps in his classroom, Mr. Hall realized early in his career that he would need to (1) learn from his students and adjust his practices based on what they taught him; (2) develop a deeper understanding of the impact of race in the science classroom; (3) create opportunities to develop relationships with his students that transcended cultural differences; and (4) understand how uncomfortable situations could become opportunities to learn for both his students and himself.

The growth in this educator's conceptions, mind-sets, and practices was driven by the students themselves—the very students who insisted that Mr. Hall did not "know" them when he arrived at Bridge Middle School. Like many educators early in their careers, Mr. Hall had not thought about how or why race, culture, or diversity was important in his teaching practices, especially in a science classroom. He explained that he went to work to "teach science," and that he had to work to understand that teaching science would require much more than knowledge of his subject. Mr. Hall learned that he would have to address race, even though it was not something he necessarily wanted or expected to do as a science teacher. He had to think about race because the students needed him to.

In my work preparing teachers, I have learned that preservice educators are sometimes skeptical or uncertain about the relevance of race and other dimensions of diversity in their P–12 classrooms. For years, I have been met with persistent and assertive resistance from preservice educators who struggled to understand how race or diversity would matter to their teaching. In their defense, I should note that the educators with whom I worked had not experienced firsthand what it meant to teach in a diverse classroom. They seemed to recognize that they would experience diversity among their students but were unclear about how diversity, and race in particular, might influence their actual teaching practices.

The case study in this chapter describes how a White male middle school science educator, Mr. Hall, developed into what one of his colleagues called a "shining star" and what a group of students called a "with-it" teacher. His story shows how a White male educator was able to learn from his students, build relationships with them, and transform his teaching in the process. In essence, it demonstrates how the students themselves helped their teacher become responsive to what they believed they needed. Mr. Hall was able to transform his practice by learning from and with his students about how to deal with the challenges and roadblocks that they faced together in their journey to teach and learn. The case addresses some critical questions: What experiences shaped Mr. Hall's mind-set, beliefs, and consequently his practice in the highly diverse context of his urban classroom? Why and how did these conceptions change over time? What might other educators learn from this case about teaching in similar contexts?

INTRODUCING MR. HALL

When I met Mr. Hall, he was in his early twenties. He usually dressed in blue jeans or khakis and a polo shirt. Describing his own identity and background, he proclaimed that he was a part of a "rural Southern" culture. Approachable yet firm, Mr. Hall projected a "tough love" demeanor that was also what some students called "cool" and "with-it." I observed that, over the years, his manner seemed to intensify as he developed into a more attentive, conscientious, and conscious educator; as he built knowledge about the idiosyncratic needs of his students, he transformed his practices with zeal and attentiveness. He was "cool and with-it" enough that students enjoyed hanging around him between classes or before and after school. While Mr. Hall rarely raised his voice, when he did, it was not in a condescending, demeaning, or arrogant manner. His interactions with students reminded me of a parent or older sibling who clearly was not willing to accept nonsense but who also realized that every situation was not going to be perfect, and that he would sometimes have to let some things go and negotiate with his students in order to succeed. In this sense, Mr. Hall reminded me of a father or older-brother figure with his students (a point I will expand upon later). Mr. Hall seemed to realize that he needed to choose his battles wisely and that his real challenge would be to create and manage learning opportunities, not to dominate his students. He did not try to control his students based on some predetermined rules that were often out of date and irrelevant in the real classroom.

Throughout the two years I observed at Bridge Middle School, I never saw Mr. Hall take much of a break. During his planning time, he was in his classroom talking with students or preparing for the next class: cleaning lab materials, grading papers, or writing on the board. During an assembly I attended, Mr. Hall sat with his students and was constantly making sure they were being respectful to their classmates, whereas some other teachers used the occasion to take a bit of a break. In 2008, Mr. Hall was chosen by his colleagues as Teacher of the Year—a major feat for someone in the profession for only a few years. However, I was not surprised by this honor because Mr. Hall not only knew his subject matter well but was also smart enough—and perhaps more important, open enough—to realize that knowing his students well was equally important. His instruction, curriculum development and enactment, assessment, classroom management, and vision for his students and related learning opportunities were dynamic, responsive, iterative, relevant, and always evolving.

KNOWING SCIENCE, KNOWING STUDENTS

Teachers cannot teach science until they understand and acknowledge who they are teaching science to. Subject-matter knowledge is essential but not sufficient for success in the classroom.

I recently had a conversation with a preservice math teacher who declared, "I respect people who want to deal with all that diversity stuff, but that's not for me. I just want to teach math and help my students develop a love for math." This future teacher explained that what mattered most in urban and highly diverse schools was that students develop mathematical thinking and be able to understand math beyond getting a right answer. He went on to tell me that he was "beyond" and "so past" the diversity aspect of his work. In his view, it was a waste of time for him to engage in diversity-related matters because he believed that his knowledge of math and his ability to teach it would supersede such issues. I reminded him that he would indeed be developing *people* into those who love math and that he would be working with *people* as they developed mathematical thinking beyond getting a right or wrong answer. I explained to him that without *understanding* and *acknowledging* whom he would be teaching, he would probably find it difficult to succeed in transforming students into the avid mathematicians he aspired to create. I reminded him that students are grappling with the demands of living, learning, and thriving in the classroom and also in their broader social worlds and realities. Furthermore, students are human beings with diverse preferences, interests, belief systems, worldviews, experiences, successes, failures, needs, and desires, all of which are shaped by a range of influences, including their race, socioeconomic status, culture, language, religion, sexual orientation, gender, geography, and ability.

Like this math teacher who declared that he was "so over" the diversity aspect of his work, science teachers may wonder *how and why race should be considered in the teaching of science.* It is well known that the biological roots of race can be traced through scientific methods. However, science educators may not see the relevance of understanding the manifestation of race beyond such investigation and analysis, let alone among their students. In other words, attempting to wrestle with matters of race as a social phenomenon, construction, and reality in a classroom can take on much more complex nuances that need to be considered. For a science educator, thinking seriously about diversity may seem irrelevant or even inappropriate for the science curriculum. As a teacher educator, I have learned that science teachers often cannot or will not understand how or why learning about race or diversity in a teacher education program or professional development workshop has any real bearing on their work in the classroom. When he first started teaching, Mr. Hall was among this group. He noted, "I came here to do one thing, and that was to teach science."

However, Mr. Hall soon began to understand that he could not teach science until he understood and acknowledged *to whom* he was teaching science as well as the social context in which he was teaching it. Stated differently, teaching science in one context can be qualitatively different from teaching it in another, which means that educators have to be equipped to deal with matters beyond the science curriculum and instructional designs beyond those focused exclusively on science content. Finally, educators need to be aware that some of their students may have been exposed to scientific ideas for years, others not at all. It became evident to Mr. Hall that he had to be equipped to deal with all kinds of diversity among his students in order to construct opportunities for them to learn.

Although Mr. Hall initially embraced a color-blind and diversity-blind philosophy, his experiences teaching and interacting with his students propelled him to a space where he understood how much race and diversity mattered in his work as a science educator. Outside the school, race seemed insignificant to him. As a White male, he did not have to consider race because his life experiences did not necessarily require or warrant it. Indeed, a person who has never experienced racism and does not find race germane to how people function in society may find it difficult to understand why students would invoke race in situations where it seems arbitrary. For me, as an African American male, race is a salient reality in my everyday experiences; thus I am empathetic when race emerges in situations for others. Although race was not a critical element in his life outside of Bridge Middle School, Mr. Hall's thoughts evolved as his students insisted that he expand his notions of race, racism, and diversity. When he began teaching, several students called him a racist. He explained: "Just coming from a rural country [town] and coming into the urban areas, the first couple years here, if I got onto some of the 'harder' African American kids, you know, who are really into rap . . . because I don't listen to rap . . . they'd say, 'You are racist.' They'd walk out the door saying, 'You're racist, you're racist.'"

Mr. Hall believed that these students saw his attempts at correcting their misbehavior—that is, his "getting onto them," as racist. Some African American students viewed him in terms of race, and he struggled with this because he did not consider himself a racist, just someone who had not thought much about race until he was compelled to do so by his students. Mr. Hall wanted the students to realize that he did not have anything against them, especially in terms of race. He merely expected the African American students, like all his students, to engage and take advantage of the many opportunities afforded them in class. Mr. Hall rationalized the students' concerns: "I think some [students] have it in their minds that because I am up here, I get on to you, that I am attacking you personally. That is one of the hardest things to get across to children—that I am not attacking you; I am attacking your behavior."

So, while Mr. Hall explained that he held no malice or racist motives and that he was only correcting students' behavior, not "attacking" them personally, some students still perceived him as a racist. It may be easy for some readers to dismiss the students' claims, insisting that the students were just playing a race card (again, whatever this means!), being immature, or simply had it all wrong. Others may believe that the students were in fact upset with Mr. Hall and were using race to exacerbate the tension between themselves and their teacher. However, it is critical to remember that the students were expressing their view of reality, which Mr. Hall rightly refused to dismiss. Indeed, the students' perceptions were their realities, which should not be ignored. One of Mr. Hall's most powerful attributes was his ability to gauge what was happening with his students and to respond to those realities. He wondered why the students would default to race in situations when they had conflicts about his "getting onto them," and he wondered how he could reinvent himself and develop a reputation as a caring, committed, and competent educator for all his students through his practices with them.

As inaccurate as he may have considered the comments, accepting his students' perceptions allowed him to develop into an educator I would describe as caring deeply for his students—all his students. It was important for him to be willing and able to improve his practices based on what he learned from his students; listening to them gave him that opportunity. Had he failed to consider their reality, he could have missed important opportunities to forge deeper connections with his students. The question is, how was Mr. Hall able to work through this difficult experience and ultimately use it as an opportunity for him to learn?

In essence, Mr. Hall realized that his students were right in saying they needed to get to know each other. He realized that he needed to build solid relationships with his students in order for them to grant him entry into their worlds, and to see that he challenged them not because he was racist but because he wanted them to reach their potential; he cared whether they did what was necessary for them to succeed. Mr. Hall realized that while there were differences between him and his students, there were also commonalities that could become catalysts for building connections in the classroom. In searching for those common threads with his students, Mr. Hall remembered his poverty.

REMEMBERING POVERTY

Educators must recognize cultural points of connection that allow them to bridge differences; shared experiences enable students to see their teachers as real people who have known and worked through difficult circumstances, such as poverty.

Mr. Hall learned that it was essential for his students to learn more about him and to understand some of what they had in common. Demonstrating and sharing commonality would allow the students to see that when he was "getting onto them" it was because he expected excellence from them—not because he was a racist or did not care about them. He needed to get his students to understand that they were on the same team. To build such trusting relationships, he and his students had to learn to share aspects of their lives. To do this, he needed some *points of reference* and *points of convergence* that would enable them to open up to each other.

When he began his career at Bridge, some students had questioned Mr. Hall's loyalty to them, in part because he was not into rap music/hip-hop, but primarily because they felt they did not know him. He later realized that while race was an important identity marker, his students needed to see him as a real person who could connect with their experiences on other levels. He explained: "I grew up in rural west Tennessee, and I've told a couple of kids—I said, I grew up poor and we didn't have anything, you know? I told them I didn't know what real money looked like until I was about fifteen and had my own job because . . . my family bought food with food stamps . . . I thought all money was purple, green, and brown. I didn't know what real money looked like."

Mr. Hall started to see that the difficult economic conditions he faced growing up were a bridge to his students. Having a sense of his history upended their assumption that all educators have "had it easy" and have not had to struggle to reach their current positions. Once his students realized that he had had difficult times similar to their own, they became more receptive in the classroom. Mr. Hall had learned that students had to *allow* teachers to teach them. It now seemed impossible for the teaching of science to occur until students were ready and willing to learn it from their teacher. In short, Mr. Hall could teach once the students were in a posture to learn.[1] Sharing his own story about poverty allowed his students to see the links between his growing up "in the woods" and their growing up in a "tough neighborhood." Mr. Hall came to understand that some of his personal experiences could be incorporated more consciously into his teaching practices as a way to facilitate interactions with his students.

Mr. Hall recognized that sharing his childhood poverty experience with some students could provide an important learning perspective for them: "I haven't brought that [childhood socioeconomic status] out to everybody, but every once in a while you'll get a couple of attitudes, and you know, you just kind of sense that [the students think], 'You don't know where I'm coming from . . . You don't know what it's like to live here' . . . You know? I told them it's like living in the woods is similar to living in a tough neighborhood. The house I grew up in for about three years didn't have indoor plumbing. It was an outhouse. We went outside to go to the bathroom. And a lot of them find that kind of amazing . . . because even they have never not had a toilet [sic]." Revealing his early poverty seemed to precipitate students' "opening up"; by sharing some of his life experiences that linked to their own, they, in turn, began to grant him entry into their experiences.

Mr. Hall believed it was those *situations of struggle* that often helped him connect with the students in his classes. He stated: "The struggle of being a human being is that every day is not going to be sunshine and roses—that's what I told them . . . I said every day is not sunshine and roses; some days it clouds up; some days it rains; but hey, there's always tomorrow. So don't worry about it." Because some of his students struggled with finances and grappled with other tough situations outside the classroom, Mr. Hall believed they would "give him attitude." They saw him in his present successful position as a teacher and didn't realize that he too had struggled with basic resources and a low socioeconomic status in the past. Despite their outward bravado, some of the students were hurting on the inside. Their pain appeared to increase their need to feel confident that their teachers understood what it was like to "be here" and to "be them." Eventually, as Mr. Hall's connections with his students deepened and improved, the claims that he was a racist subsided, but the accusations remained sharply entrenched in his mind.

In sum, Mr. Hall attempted to inspire his students with features of his story: he grew up living in deep-rooted poverty and yet was able to persevere. His students were afforded an opportunity to glance into a window on his past and to think about his developmental journey to his present professional situation. At the core of Mr. Hall's vision and decision making for his students were *possibility, optimism, hope,* and a *commitment*—not just to help students work through difficult science-related content, but also to help them deal with situations outside of school. He refused to allow students to feel sorry for themselves. He developed high expectations for his students—even though he realized his middle school had fewer resources than neighboring schools. One of his goals was to prepare his students with a toolset to work through difficult situations outside of school as well as give their best effort in the classroom. He wanted his students to anticipate life beyond their present situations and to realize that if he could transcend poverty, they could, too. He realized that he could not teach the students if they felt too distant from him, so he used his experiences as *opportunity anchors*—sites to build and scaffold relationships with his students that would be critical for teaching and learning to occur.

Mr. Hall refused to be defeated by the challenges of his work and instead used the difficult situations (such as being called a racist) as an opportunity to learn, to sharpen his pedagogical skills, and to grow. Admirably, Mr. Hall never complained about the limited resources at Bridge Middle School. While he worked to increase the resources available for his students, he realized from the beginning that he would need to do more with fewer material resources and that he should not expend his energy on matters (such as scarce resources) beyond his control.

DOING MORE WITH FEWER RESOURCES

Student and teacher potential cannot be limited by a lack of material resources. Resources matter, but teachers cannot allow inadequate resources to deter them from challenging students to reach their potential or from exposing them to the types of knowledge and experiences necessary for success.

Mr. Hall did, in fact, do more with fewer resources, such as laboratory equipment—but he also did something about the problem. When Mr. Hall was uncharacteristically absent from school, I learned that he was participating in professional development workshops offered by local universities in order to earn laboratory equipment for his school. His participation forced him to miss school, which placed him in a quandary—he wanted to be with his students, but he also realized what having more sophisticated laboratory equipment could mean for them and for the school. So, distressed by the lack of resources in his lab, he did something about it. His actions are consistent with Freire's assertion that those who are marginalized and treated unjustly cannot wait for others to rescue them or act on their behalf.[2] Rather, those on the fringes of dominant economic structures must be empowered to do what is necessary to improve their own situations. Mr. Hall worked to bridge the resource opportunity gap by earning lab equipment for his students. It is important to note that I am not excusing the inequitable funding of urban and highly diverse school contexts. At a minimum, all students in public schools deserve equitable funding, resources, and materials, which can make a huge difference in terms of their learning opportunities. But Mr. Hall understood that some inequities were structurally unavoidable, and he was unwavering in his commitment to address the resource shortage in the school.

Although he was disappointed by the lack of resources, Mr. Hall was not willing to merely complain about it and play the role of victim; he did something about it. In practice, Mr. Hall believed that if he and his colleagues were to succeed, they would have to "never give up . . . You got a lot of people here who are bound and determined to succeed no matter what obstacles are put in front of them . . . even though we are at one of the oldest buildings in the [school] system. We've got [fewer] materials than anybody else, and it's just like—so what—who cares? You know the kids can do it; so *we're going to find a way to do it. I think that's it, you know? They never give up, never surrender—we're going to make it work no matter what*" [emphasis added].

Clearly, Mr. Hall did not feel defeated by the lack of resources or by the outdated building. Perhaps most important, he did not want his students to feel defeated or to adopt a victim mentality. However, he realized they were not blind to the inequities, and that they needed to understand and critique what they may have perceived as inequitable facilities and resources. A critique of the resources appeared to be a first step to addressing a much more complex array of issues. He did not make excuses for the fact that he was teaching in one of the "oldest buildings in the system." He just taught in spite of this reality. He was able to build confidence in himself and confidence in his students because he placed opportunity at the core of his mind-set and practices. For instance, when they engaged in laboratory experiments, students participated without any real consideration of the quality or age of the equipment they were using. In my observations, Mr. Hall's confidence was portrayed by his tireless energy, displayed from the beginning of a class period to the end. He taught with the equipment that he had, was enthusiastic about the content he covered, and never complained publicly about the quality of the equipment or materials the students had to use. He was teaching and the students were involved in learning activities from bell to bell. The students had few chances to think about the lack of resources or the building's shortcomings because there was work to be done.

Another issue related to resources was the size of Mr. Hall's classes—he was teaching more students than most science teachers and with fewer resources. His classes were even disproportionately larger than others at Bridge Middle School. He told me, "These are actually the smallest classes that I've had in my three years that I've taught. My largest class was last year, and it was at one time thirty-nine, but then it went up and down as the year went . . . People transferred out and transferred in . . . usually I average about thirty-one or thirty-two [students] per class. I do have one class this year, sixth period, and it is sixteen students. I am used to big classes; it's all I've ever known." Mr. Hall estimated that he had taught as many as one hundred fifty students throughout the day in previous years. My inquiries revealed an average science classroom at neighboring suburban schools had twenty to twenty-five students.

When I asked Mr. Hall what he considered his greatest success, he stated, "My greatest success would be with my high school class [eighth graders preparing for high school] . . . The first year that I got here [I learned that] the high school science class . . . had three people who passed the high school exam the year before . . . My first year only five people passed. Last year, I had thirty-one students who passed the exam." He knew that many science teachers in other schools had a higher percentage of students who passed the exam, mainly because they had more resources to work with. However, even with fewer resources, Mr. Hall was able to significantly increase the passing rate among his students. Think about it: six times as many students passed the high school science examination after just one year of teaching. The students' engagement and performance increased as Mr. Hall continued to bring innovative materials into the school. Clearly, learning was taking place in Mr. Hall's classroom, despite the inequities.

EQUITY IN PRACTICE

Educators need to understand that equity *does not necessarily mean sameness.* Equality *tends to connote sameness, while* equity *implies parity. To achieve equity, educators provide resources, take actions, and make decisions based on particular needs in a particular context. This means that it may be necessary to distribute more resources in a school based on the needs of that space.*

Mr. Hall appeared to understand equity, and he worked to achieve it in his practices. He seemed aware that he would need to develop different learning opportunities and curricula for his students and establish individual connections with them, based on their specific needs. Mr. Hall worked to build solid and sustainable relationships with all of his students, both individually and as a class, paying close attention to where they were cognitively, socially, emotionally, psychologically, intellectually, academically, and behaviorally. His interpretation would require him to respond to students in different ways. He explained: "I think that you have to develop a relationship with *each student* [emphasis added]. Every kid that you have has a different story, and if you show interest in what they've gone through, they're going to show interest in what you're trying to convey to them. Then they will show interest in what you're doing."

Mr. Hall was known for giving students multiple opportunities for success. He did not want to place a student's destiny in the hands of another, such as an administrator who had the power to suspend or even expel a student from school for "misbehavior."[3] Clearly, the kind of learning necessary for success is not taking place when students are outside the classroom, so Mr. Hall did not dismiss students without making a serious attempt to learn why they were misbehaving. From my observations, it appeared that some students misbehaved or joked with their classmates to offset pain—laughing was better than hurting or crying. They wanted to appear strong and jovial when they were in fact experiencing inner turmoil.

In general, it seemed that students cared more about how they would be perceived by their friends than by their teacher. Being disrespectful to teachers when they joked or played around seemed not to matter as long as they felt they were receiving praise for being the class clown or making everyone laugh. During one class session, one student continued to be disruptive, joking around as Mr. Hall was lecturing. I asked the student after class why he had chosen to be disruptive, and the student made it plain for me: "It was all good for me. Mr. Hall is cool; I have no problem with him. He's all right. He can't take what we say personally. We are just trying to get through the day and have some fun, that's all. Sometimes we have a lot on our minds and we are just letting off steam, that's all." Understanding that students were dealing with a range of difficult realities (some he was aware of; others he was not), Mr. Hall gave disruptive students multiple opportunities to straighten up; he also gave them multiple opportunities to succeed on their assignments and was not quick to allow a student to fail. During my entire study at Bridge, I never witnessed Mr. Hall dismiss a student from the classroom for disruptive behavior (although this does not mean he never did). From my observations, though, and based on my conversations with him, he refused to give up on students and continued to work with them even when they were difficult to work with.

This approach—giving multiple opportunities to some students and responding to each student's particular needs—could lead some to question how Mr. Hall was able to avoid problems associated with equity. In other words, how could he treat all students fairly if he treated them differently? I asked him how he responded to adults or other students who questioned the equity of his practices. He explained: "Well, I'd ask: who hasn't gotten a second chance in life? I mean, everybody messes up, and not everybody messes up at the same time [and in the same way] . . . It's a different situation for everybody. I mean, I know there are times in my job that I said the wrong thing, did the wrong thing, and . . . alarms didn't go off and the swat team didn't come in . . . People, my peers—people above me pulled me aside and said: 'Hey, you know, we don't do it this way.' You know, I wasn't terminated on the spot . . . You know I'm not going to [give them failing] grades or hurt their self-esteem right there on the spot just because they did it wrong that time . . . Everybody's different, you know . . . We are not robots . . . we can't all just crank out the same stuff every time. It's going to take one kid five times to get it . . . and it's going to take one kid one time."

Importantly, Mr. Hall connected how he dealt with and interpreted the needs of his students to his own experiences. For example, he himself had received multiple opportunities to succeed, even at Bridge Middle School, and he transferred these life lessons into his teaching practices. The idea that teachers can empathize more fully with students when they have had parallel experiences is a constant theme of the teachers portrayed in this book. However, what should teachers do if they do not have those parallel experiences from which to draw? Thinking about Mr. Hall's narrative and how he made decisions for students based on his own experiences reinforces the idea that teaching is identity work. That is (as will be demonstrated throughout this book), it can be difficult for teachers to separate themselves and their own life experiences when making decisions that affect students.

Mr. Hall's approach of providing multiple opportunities for success seemed to empower his students to participate in classroom activities and discourse without worrying so much about the consequences of their off-target or "incorrect" responses. Based on what I observed in his classes, it appeared that he had designed the learning environment around an opportunity structure that valued the different cognitive and social spaces that students were in at a particular time. The students seemed unafraid of participating in the classroom learning opportunities because they understood that while Mr. Hall expected their best work and expected them to excel academically, he recognized that excellence would show up in different forms, at different times, and at different developmental stages for his students.

He seemed determined not to "tear the students down" when they were (mis)interpreting scientific content and context. For instance, based on my observations, students regularly participated in class discussions, and Mr. Hall consistently pushed them to think deeper about the content by not accepting answers that were off-target; but at the same time he never belittled or dismissed student comments. One student, for instance, was consistently off base for several weeks, but as Mr. Hall put it, he "never gave up." Some teachers might have grown weary and frustrated by the student's consistently incorrect responses, but Mr. Hall appeared excited that the student continued to put forth effort and develop scientific thinking. In fact, Mr. Hall continued to invite the student into discourse even though his participation seemed to complicate the discussions for everyone else. He refused to silence the student, and the student continued to give his all.

When some students had the "wrong" answer, Mr. Hall and other students would pose additional questions to guide them to more appropriate responses. Overall, students did not appear intimidated by the scientific knowledge available in the classroom or threatened by the expectations and discourse in the classroom because the classroom context supported participation and engagement. Mr. Hall had created a classroom context where many of the students (including some society might not expect) appeared confident, capable, and enthused about what was happening. The students wanted to learn, and they seemed to realize that even if it took them a few times to "get it," Mr. Hall was not going to give up on them. In Mr. Hall's words: "I think as long as they get it—that's the ultimate goal. It doesn't matter how fast you get it; it's that you do get it."

In sum, Mr. Hall cared deeply about ensuring that each of his students was able to master the information and skills being taught. This meant that he regularly allowed his students multiple opportunities to turn in work and that he would explain a concept or procedure repeatedly until they got it: "Maybe that's bad—[that] I give so many second chances, that I care about them too much—but I think it works for me. And I wouldn't know how else to do it. And I couldn't be one of those who say, 'Uh oh, Timmy, you didn't get your homework done; well, that's your fifth zero.' You know I couldn't be like that."

However, he would not accept nonsense or allow his students to "run over" him. He had high expectations of his students but also would do everything in his power to help them succeed as long as each student was putting forth the effort necessary for both academic and social success—a clear demonstration of his care for them. He gave multiple opportunities for success, but he would not accept mediocrity; he pushed his students to produce and expected their best work. An important feature of Mr. Hall's work was his ability to understand equity and to design learning opportunities that were responsive to students' individual academic and social needs.

To be responsive to his students, however, Mr. Hall had to work through cultural conflicts.

WORKING THROUGH CULTURAL CONFLICT

Unavoidably, there will be times when conflicts between teachers and students will emerge in a range of different social contexts. The real questions are, how do teachers work through those conflicts, whom do they blame for them, how and what do they learn from them, and how do they move beyond them in order to refocus attention on opportunity?

Inevitably, there were times when Mr. Hall had conflicts with students who did not want to engage in class, refused to complete their assignments, and were disruptive. He told me about one such conflict: "[There was one student]—he was a foot and a half taller than me, a big old guy.

He wanted to chitchat and talk about sports and basketball and stuff, and he didn't like me coming up to him telling him 'get on task, get on task' every five minutes. And one day he stood up to me and just went off. And I went off [too]—you know, it's like two brothers fighting. He let me know what he was thinking. And I let him know what I was thinking, and we went our separate ways . . . It took us about a week, but one morning he just walked up to me, and said, 'We're cool now.' It was almost like, 'I didn't know what happened.' I was cool from the minute he walked out the door. That's just me: I am going to tell you how I feel, what I didn't like, and I am done [with it]." In short, Mr. Hall expressed his feelings, allowed the student to do the same, and the two moved forward.

Mr. Hall realized that his students, regardless of their grade level, were still adolescents dealing with all kinds of developmental matters that he might or might not be aware of. As a teacher and as an adult, he understood also that he could not allow misunderstandings to hinder his relationships with his students. He explained how important it was for him to not hold grudges, that when students walked back into the classroom after a previous misunderstanding with him, he did everything in his power to move forward and not hold the conflict against the student: "If I get upset at you or if you screw up . . . tomorrow is going to be new. I'm not even going to mention it. Unless you do the same thing . . . Every day is a new slate." He also was not one to gather with colleagues to discuss his students' faults. It simply was "not my style," he said, and he wiped the slate clean each day.

Mr. Hall explained that he had to constantly reset the parameters in the classroom so that students realized he expected them to do their best work at all times; he was willing to accept *only their very best*. Mr. Hall had to establish his motives and his vision with the students by making explicit why he was "getting onto them." Making rules and expectations explicit is consistent with Delpit's suggestions about how power works and should work in the classroom.[4] Although one could argue that students should have a voice in making decisions and setting expectations in the classroom, it is also essential for teachers to make their goals clear so that students do not have to guess what is expected of them. Mr. Hall had developed some powerful relationships with his students partly because they understood what was expected of them and what would be accepted in the classroom. At times, he encountered students who would not put forth effort and who were not interested in learning. However, Mr. Hall's mind-set for dealing with the conflicts seemed to be what mattered most in resolving them.

Another important reason for Mr. Hall's success was the way he "sowed seeds" with his students to build lasting relationships with them.

SOWING SEEDS

Building relationships means that teachers develop knowledge and understanding about students, to enhance both present learning and future opportunities. Teachers need to establish powerful relationships with students as a way to "plant seeds" that will enable the teaching and learning relationship to grow over time.

I have learned, based on my research over the last twelve years, that at the heart of successful teaching—and perhaps especially in urban contexts—is teachers' ability to develop solid and sustaining relationships with students. Such relationships are essential for both educator and student success. When opportunities to develop meaningful relationships arise, educators must be prepared to seize them. Mr. Hall recognized the importance of relationships as a foundation for the kinds of learning opportunities that he hoped to design in the classroom. After students called him a racist and insisted that he needed to "get to know" them, he realized that he needed to develop the skills to build relationships with his students so that they could recognize him as someone who was fighting for them, who wanted to provide opportunities to enhance their lives both in and out of school. Developing this ability required him to reflect deeply about who he was, who his students were, how his and his students' multiple and varied identities emerged and converged, and how he wanted to grow as a teacher. He discovered that personal and professional reflection was critical before the teaching of science could occur.

Mr. Hall described the evolution of his relationship with one student: "I had a kid named Mike, and last year, he was one of the biggest troublemakers that I had. I couldn't get him to do homework. I couldn't get him to study for a test or anything. And this year he made the basketball team and made the football team. And every week I was asking him, 'Hey, how you doing [with basketball]? Did you score a basket? What did you do in the game?'"

The now easy relationship between Mr. Hall and Mike took some serious work—lots of seed sowing—before Mike's engagement, participation, and ultimately learning in the science classroom increased. Mr. Hall would query Mike about his games in the classroom and also in the corridors when he saw him. He took an interest in Mike outside of school (in athletics) in order to build a strong relationship with him inside the classroom. He was constantly asking Mike about what was happening in his games, which gave Mike a sense that Mr. Hall was interested in his life experiences beyond academic success and beyond what was expected of him in the science classroom.

Out-of-school experiences and extracurricular activities mean much more to some students than their classroom experiences. With Mike, Mr. Hall needed to engage in the "extra" curriculum to get Mike to engage more fully in the science curriculum. *The idea that Mike was experiencing any curriculum—albeit extra—is important.* He was learning something from the athletic curriculum, and Mr. Hall engaged that more meaningful curriculum in Mike's world with him. Beyond simply asking questions about Mike's performance in basketball (and football) games, Mr. Hall realized that he also needed to more assertively sow seeds to ultimately get Mike to "grab onto" learning opportunities in the classroom: "I've gone down to a couple basketball practices and played one on one against him, and he missed two assignments the whole year in homework. And his grade, average-wise, last year is up about fifteen points. He's gone from being a C student in my class to being an A student. He's just one example of how you show interest in a kid and how [his or her] output goes up in your class." In short, Mike refused to learn from Mr. Hall until he believed that Mr. Hall was concerned about him as a person, not just a student in the science classroom. Mr. Hall clearly credits Mike's increased participation, engagement, and improved science grade to the building of a solid relationship with the student.

Ultimately, Mr. Hall came to understand that some of his students, like Mike, would refuse to perform, engage, and provide "outputs" for educators they did not believe had an interest in them. Basically, some of his students refused to learn from him and to engage in his classroom until they felt that he cared about them. Moreover, they did not seem to realize or care about the consequences of their (in)actions when they refused to complete learning tasks and assignments or were disruptive. (This was perhaps a function of where the adolescents were developmentally.) Interestingly, it seemed that the students believed they were "hurting" the educator they did not like when they were disengaged, underprepared, or disruptive. I had a conversation with a female student who had been sent to the office by another teacher. I asked what happened and why she had been sent to the office to be reprimanded. Her response was quick and direct: "[The teacher] doesn't like me, and I don't like her." For this student, what precipitated her dismissal from class was a consequence of being "liked." I learned that some other students were battling teachers because they did not feel the teachers had their best interests at heart or simply did not like them.

I have spoken to countless educators, both preservice and inservice, who give up on students like Mike. These educators place most or even all of the blame on their students, and rarely examine their own practices as sites that could be transformed to strengthen their relationships with students. Might some classroom practices stifle the participation of students like Mike? Or should all the blame lie with the students? An educator facing a student like Mike could easily put all the blame on Mike, his parents, or other external factors. However, Mr. Hall took some responsibility and initiative, decided to learn about the areas of Mike's life that piqued his interest, and then used that deepened understanding to build a relationship with him.

In other words, Mr. Hall realized that in some cases he would have to go *beyond* the walls of the classroom before he could connect with a student *in* the classroom. Based on my observations and my conversations with students, it is clear that Mr. Hall was an educator students came to know and respect. Of course, this took time and required Mr. Hall's ability to recognize opportunities to build meaningful relationships when they presented themselves. In my conversations with students, they would tell me what they thought about the teachers at Bridge Middle School, both positive and negative. As for Mr. Hall, the students saw him as "cool," "with-it," and a "good teacher." At the same time, they perceived his class as "hard" but "fun." The students commented on how Mr. Hall watched the Discovery Channel, and many of them had developed an appreciation for the channel as well. In class, students would often reference a recent program, and Mr. Hall was right there with them. A television channel had become a *bridge* to learning in the classroom. Such bridging seemed essential to the development of strong relationships between Mr. Hall and his students.

In short, Mr. Hall wanted what was best for his students, and he would not allow them to get away with things that would be destructive or disadvantageous to them in the present or the future. As he put it, "One thing I try to let kids know this year is that I really do care about them, you know, whenever [and wherever] I see them. You know, I love you. I want to see you play basketball. I want graduation invitations. You know, that's not going to happen though, if you don't straighten up in class. And I've tried to be more expressive, but at the same time, stay on them." As Mr. Hall developed his teaching repertoire at Bridge Middle School, he found that sowing the seeds of strong relationships was vital to his success in the science classroom. He also learned that constructing narratives was an important way to forge deeper connections both with students socially and with the curriculum.

POWER OF STORY

The sharing of personal narratives allows students a window into a teacher's life. Personal and professional stories can be powerful tools for building connections with students and bringing the curriculum to life. Story can be a compelling scaffolding tool in the classroom.

It appeared that Mr. Hall's students developed a heightened interest in his class when he shared narratives that connected his own life with the course content. For instance, students seemed to become more attentive when Mr. Hall shared aspects of his home life. When he described a recent episode with one of his children or a debate with his wife about an issue, student interest seemed to escalate. Mr. Hall explained: "If you can relate what [the students] want to know and put some science in there with it . . . I mean everybody remembers what happened Tuesday whenever Ricky and Jane broke up. There was a big screaming match outside; they will remember that for six months and make connections to science."

Mr. Hall shared that he had begun to share personal stories that enhanced the learning opportunities for his students. The lesson here is that it is important for educators to bring not only students' cultural experiences into the classroom, but some of their own as well. As Mr. Hall related, "I've gone real personal. I mean, my second year that I was teaching here, me and my wife [sic] were expecting our second child. We were talking about reproduction. I brought the little video from where they show the little baby before birth; we talked about how whenever an embryo is developing . . . the cells are multiplying, and we showed how it [the baby] looked like a real person, but it was only two inches long. And just that connection—the kids really have never seen a picture [video] like that . . . It was just amazing to them that it could be two inches long and yet still have all the features and characteristics of a person. You can see the outline of the head. [The narrative] gives them *something to hold on to* [emphasis added], and it puts a picture in their mind that they're not going to forget."

According to Mr. Hall, the students needed something to hold on to during lessons, and sharing personal (appropriate) stories helped make the content real and relevant to their lives. The students seemed mature enough not to intrude and pose inappropriate personal questions. While it can be advantageous for teachers to share aspects of their own story with students, it is also important that teachers maintain a professional distance between themselves and students. Mr. Hall said that eventually students would ask, "How is the baby doing? How is your wife doing?" By granting students entry into his personal life through the power of narrative, he made a difference in their interests and engagement; it was one more way in which Mr. Hall just refused to allow his students to fail.

JUST CAN'T LET THEM FAIL

When educators truly understand the stakes for students if they fail, they simultaneously should understand that their mind-set must be that they will not allow them to fail.

Mr. Hall seemed to embrace the idea that he could not let his students fail because they were "like family." Moreover, he believed it was important that he demonstrate "good" behavior so his students would understand that he was not only telling them what kinds of behavior were necessary for success, such as treating oneself and others with respect, but practicing them himself. He stressed that educators often have to play various roles with their students: "For some kids you are going to be mama, daddy, brother, auntie, uncle, grandmother, and granddaddy. I mean, you're going to be the one person who they're going to tell everything to. Some of them, it's going to be almost like a big brother. They're going to do what you do. Now if you're modeling good behavior, they're going to act like you, almost like a younger sibling would."

Mr. Hall stressed that family members are not willing to let other members fail. They do "whatever it takes" for their family to succeed: "I like the family aspect because, I mean, if family's not important to you, then what [or who] is? I mean, family should be the thing that's most important to everybody. And I mean that for some people it's not, so hopefully in here [in Mr. Hall's classroom] they kind of get that aspect . . . I care about everybody; I love them all . . . just like I would my own . . . If I holler at you it's because I know you can do better. And if I get on to you, I know that you're slacking; you're not pulling your weight."

Mr. Hall added that family and community are established not only with students in the classroom; he also developed strong relationships with colleagues at the school: "Another thing [I] started doing last year is, we had a couple of new teachers who were on the first floor. And during my planning time I'd just walk in and check on them. So kids who I didn't even have, they were seeing me. And if they were acting crazy, I was taking them, and we were coming up here, and we were doing sixth-grade science in my room. And I think just to gain that reputation now, you know, you might not teach them that year but you're always watching them. And if you're around they'd better be acting right. So the school is the community." Thus, Mr. Hall believed that he needed to develop relationships (1) with the students in his classroom, (2) with other students in the school, even those he did not teach, and (3) with his colleagues, particularly new teachers, in order to build a school community. Communities are established and nurtured by the people in them, and Mr. Hall seemed committed to building the kind of school community in which students and teachers alike understand that they are on the same side.

Mr. Hall clearly believed that "if you quit caring about what you're doing, that's when you stop improving. You [can't] quit caring about the kids." Therefore he was constantly thinking of ways to connect with his students and others in the learning environment. He recognized the many opportunities that opened up when he did things "outside the box" at Bridge Middle School. Mr. Hall believed to some degree that there was a sense of urgency in his practices; when he was teaching he felt he was fighting for the lives of his students: "You've got to fight against everything else in their life for their attention for that one hour. And if you can win the battle, you've won the child for that one hour, and 99 percent of the time they are going to remember the important things you talked about." Mr. Hall's point here is consistent with Ladson-Billings's idea that educators in schools across the country are actually fighting for the lives of students when they are teaching.[5] It is not enough to simply teach their subject; educators must think about the enormous responsibility that working with students entails. Mr. Hall had a mission to teach his students because he realized the possible consequences the students might face if he did not teach them, and if they did not learn. An undereducated and underprepared student from an urban school (and possibly any school) could too easily fall into destructive and dangerous activities, possibly leading to drug abuse, prison, gang activity, or, unthinkably, death.

In the next section, I conclude this discussion with suggestions for explicit reflection regarding diversity and teacher identity. I also provide heuristics to guide educators as they build the knowledge and expertise to transform their practices in ways that can make a difference for their students.

RECOGNIZING RACE, RECOGNIZING CULTURE

In teacher education courses I have taught and in professional development sessions I have led for experienced educators, I have observed great resistance to acknowledging the importance of diversity (especially race) and its relationship to teaching. Thinking about race, culture, or diversity requires educators not only to consider others, such as their students or their students' parents, but also to reflect on themselves. Reflection on race, in particular, should begin with the self; that is, teachers should conduct their introspective examinations before they even start to think about their students. Such self-reflection on race can help them build a positive personal racial/ethnic identity and also think about how their racial identity can influence their work as teachers.

In order to build a positive racial identity as a teacher, I have discovered that educators, all educators, must engage in deep, explicit reflection about matters of race. When examining their own privilege and their experiences as educators, it can be easy for teachers to engage in general self-reflection and to avoid reflecting on race altogether. However, thinking about the role race plays can be a critical dimension of teachers' work, as Mr. Hall learned from his students. Mr. Hall's experience as a White male with African American students who called him racist suggests that White teachers need to be especially well prepared to confront matters of race in their classrooms. But it is also important for culturally diverse teachers to engage in race reflection. All teachers need to think seriously about themselves as people who operate in and through systems that are shaped significantly by race and racialized mind-sets. It may be difficult for some educators, especially science educators, to find the relevance of race in their work, to understand how to think about race, or to realize what they should focus on relative to race in their teaching. Table 2.1 provides a list of questions and a brief explanation of each to help educators undertake meaningful introspection regarding race.

The purpose of this table is to demonstrate the necessity for educators to understand the self as a forerunner to understanding their students (and why, for example, a student could perceive a teacher as a racist). It is important that educators from all ethnic backgrounds think beyond simplistic and/or static answers to the questions. The potency of the exercise of reflecting about race lies in provoking analysis of such critical questions, not in the answers per se, which will vary from person to person and from situation to situation. This important reflection relates back to the idea that teaching is a journey, and therefore educators should work to answer the questions more completely and accurately throughout their careers. The questions are critical because they ask educators to contemplate higher-level, deeply contextualized issues that go beyond closed-ended, simplistic queries, and that allow them to think about a range of matters related to opportunity and to opportunity gaps in their particular situations. The power of the table is in actively engaging in the questions, not necessarily in articulating finite answers.

TABLE 2.1

Questions to guide teachers' self-reflection about race

Critical questions	Reflective purpose and significance
How does my race influence my work as an educator with my students, especially my students of color?	This question challenges you to reflect on the race-based privileges and/or the lack thereof that you experience inside and outside of the classroom. Then consider how your race connects with or diverges from your students to either hinder or enable learning opportunities.
As an educator, what is the effect of race on my thinking, beliefs, actions, and decision making?	This question challenges you to reflect on your conceptual and cognitive positions and positioning that may have been hidden previously. Beliefs and ideas may become more visible through such conscious deliberation. Then, connect your racial beliefs with your practices and think about how your race shapes the kinds of examples you use to elucidate curriculum content with students.
How do I, as an educator, situate myself in the education of students, and how do I negotiate the power structure in my class to allow students to feel a sense of worth regardless of their racial background?	With these questions comes reflection about the relationships between race, power, and actions. You are challenged to think about whose voice matters in the classroom and to recognize that students can feel marginalized and insignificant when teachers do not recognize the important contributions and assets that they possess and bring into the classroom.
How do I situate and negotiate students' knowledge, experiences, expertise, and race with my own?	This question challenges you to decide whether you are willing to negotiate expertise and ways of knowing with your students. Start by considering the important relationships between knowledge, experience, expertise, and race. Then work to understand that you may need to learn from your students and others how to negotiate knowledge and expertise in the classroom and how some groups of students have been silenced because of their race.

As educators reflect on themselves and build knowledge about themselves, their own experiences, and worlds related to race, they should eventually engage in reflection about their students' race and racial experiences and also about the context in which they are teaching. That is, teachers should begin their introspective journey about race by focusing on themselves and then transition to broader reflections about themselves in relation to others as well as to the social context. Table 2.2 provides questions that support teachers' reflections about race relative to their students and also the teaching environment.

TABLE 2.2

Questions to guide teachers' reflection about students, race, and social context

Critical questions	Reflective purpose and significance
How will my students' race influence their work with me as the teacher? What conflicts might emerge due to racial differences and disconnections?	This question challenges you to reflect on the way students' race might influence their perceptions of you as the teacher. Consider how your ways of seeing the world might be quite different from those of your students (or your students' parents). Be mindful that conflicts can surface between you and your students, and you may be compelled to find points of convergence in building relationships with them and in planning and implementing the curriculum and related learning opportunities.
What matters are most important to my students and to me? What is the relevance of race to these important issues?	This question challenges you to think about becoming (re)searchers in your environment with race as a focus to determine how student priorities can overshadow those of teachers. Students experience a raced world inside and outside of the classroom and what they find significant may be quite different from what teachers find important.
To what degree are my role as educator and my experiences superior to the experiences and expertise of students, and is there knowledge to be learned from my students? How might race shape these roles?	This question encourages you to reflect on your evolving roles as an educator, the knowledge and expertise among students, and how race can shape these matters. Educators should be deliberate in rejecting, disrupting, and countering racial superiority in the classroom.
Am I willing to speak about race on behalf of those who might not be present in the conversation, both inside and outside of school, and am I willing to express what I find to be unjust regarding race and racism in difficult spaces?	These questions challenge you not to separate your personal and professional racial philosophies. If you believe that racial oppression is wrong, then you are challenged to speak out against it wherever you find evidence of it, even in spaces where hegemony emerges (through discourse and actions).

I hope educators find the questions in tables 2.1 and 2.2 useful as they work to transform their mind-sets and practices from color/diversity/ culture blindness to those that are race/diversity/culture conscious. Of course, the term *race* in the tables can be replaced with a range of different identity markers such as culture, gender, socioeconomic status, or religion. Still, I have included the term *race* because so many teachers find it difficult to confront it in their personal and professional lives and because

I believe that until we begin to really penetrate race and its role in teaching and learning, we will continue to see significant disparities in education. The questions presented here challenge all educators, regardless of their racial or ethnic background, to critically examine how race can matter for teachers and their students. Race reflection, for instance, is essential for teachers of color because they can be what I have come to call "kidnapped" into believing negative information even about themselves and their racial group.

SUMMARY

Overarching themes of this chapter are that race, culture, and relationship building matter, even in the science classroom. There were many positive facets of Mr. Hall's thinking, mind-set, and practices related to his work. He learned from his students and readjusted his practices based on what they taught him. He developed a deeper understanding of how race mattered, even in a science classroom, after being called racist by some African American students. He created opportunities to develop relationships with his students that transcended cultural conflicts and differences. Importantly, he did not necessarily view cultural conflicts with his students as impediments to teaching and learning. Rather, he perceived the conflicts as opportunities that he could learn from and work through. In short, he understood how uncomfortable situations, such as those dealing with race or other cultural conflicts, could become opportunities for him and for his students to learn and develop.

Mr. Hall understood that knowing science—that is, having deep subject matter knowledge—was absolutely necessary but also insufficient for success in his urban classroom. He needed to know his students in order to teach science. He needed to develop knowledge about whom he was teaching science to, and this effort had to be ongoing. Many of the students with whom he worked claimed that they would not learn from a teacher they did not like or who did not know them. So, much of the work for Mr. Hall involved getting to know his students and for his students to feel confident that Mr. Hall cared about them.

To connect with his students and build solid and sustaining relationships with them, Mr. Hall decided to share areas of his life that would help them recognize some of the commonalities that existed between them. For instance, he revealed to some of his students how he grew up in poverty, worked his way out of it, gained an education, and became a teacher. He connected his experiences growing up "in the woods" with growing up in a tough neighborhood. Mr. Hall not only shared stories about his youth that he believed connected with his students, he also told them about his own family. He found that sharing personal narratives was advantageous on at least two levels: (1) in developing relationships with his students and (2) in helping students make subject matter (here, science) connections in the classroom.

In essence, Mr. Hall worked through cultural conflicts, using them as opportunities to learn, and he developed relationships with his students by sowing seeds that he would nurture and develop over time. He understood that at times he needed to take an interest in students outside the classroom in order for them to perform and engage inside the classroom.

Finally, Mr. Hall understood what it meant to maintain high expectations despite limited resources. In his view, the students were capable of academic success and of meeting rigorously constructed learning opportunities. So, he did more with fewer resources. While I am not condoning, by any means, inequitable funding in urban or any schools, Mr. Hall did not allow the scarce resources to deter him from what he was confident that his students needed. He taught in spite of the resource shortage. Moreover, Mr. Hall attended professional development workshops to address the resource gap; his participation earned sophisticated laboratory materials for the school. He attempted to do something about the lack of resources rather than just complain about it.

Mr. Hall treated his students equitably and realized that he needed to be responsive to his students as individuals. He provided them with multiple opportunities for academic and social success. Even when students were "off-target" with their comments or thinking, he invited them to continue contributing to the discussion rather than silencing them. He was tough but did everything in his power to keep his students in the classroom, even when they were being disruptive. More than anything, Mr. Hall simply refused to let his students fail!

3

Black Female Teacher, Suburban White School

Addressing and Transcending Cultural Conflicts

You teach what you know; you teach what you've experienced; you teach who you are . . . My students know me. They know how I live, and there's no misunderstanding, no misinterpretations about that. I am a Black woman, and they need to understand that there are some differences between myself and them.

—DR. JOHNSON, suburban high school language arts teacher

IN THE QUOTE ABOVE, Dr. Johnson, an African American language arts teacher with twenty-six years' experience, eleven of them at Stevenson High School, explained how important matters of race and diversity are in predominantly White spaces. In our conversations, she also explained how teachers' various identities and experiences shape what they teach, how they teach, why they teach, the amount of time they spend on issues, and why they emphasize what they do. Dr. Johnson was deliberate in deciding to teach with race, culture, and diversity at the center of her curriculum.

In contrast, consider Mr. Hall's initial approach to teaching. In chapter 2, I shared the story of Mr. Hall's transformation, especially regarding the centrality of race and relationship building in his science classroom and his ability to bridge opportunity gaps. But when Mr. Hall first began his work in his school, he purposely avoided matters of race in his teaching. He also did not fully understand the relevance and importance of developing solid relationships with his students. Initially, he declared that he came to school to do one thing: "to teach science." He transformed his practices by listening to the voices and requests of his students. The students, especially African American students, expected Mr. Hall to think about race and "get to know" them, although such a focus was not his goal in the beginning. In essence, Mr. Hall learned that he had to know more than science in order to teach it in an urban social context. He needed to know whom he was teaching science to in order to be successful in his work.

Dr. Johnson did not begin her work at Stevenson High School deliberately avoiding issues of race and diversity. On the contrary, because of what she had observed and experienced both within and outside the school context, she had come to understand how important race and diversity were to her teaching practices. She found that although she was teaching in a predominantly White setting, issues related to race, culture, and gender were still salient to her work.

In this chapter, I focus on an African American teacher working in a context that might easily be overlooked in a discussion of race and diversity, in that her school has a small population of students of color, children living in poverty, or English language learners. There is scant evidence about the nature of multicultural education, particularly matters of race and diversity, in suburban, primarily White school environments. Opportunity gaps related to diversity exist in many such schools, but few people working in them seem aware of the interplay between race, diversity, and opportunity, leading to a lack of understanding of how diversity curriculum and instructional opportunities can and should manifest in mostly White spaces.

In this case study, I demonstrate that matters of race and diversity should be incorporated into a school's curriculum even if most of the students, faculty, and staff are White. Students live in a multicultural society, which requires them to be able to understand their own and others' privileges, or lack thereof, and the many ways in which people experience the world. Some believe that race and diversity are inconsequential and insignificant in White spaces, until they actually confront uneasy and unsettling situations, such as these:

- Someone in the community makes a racist, sexist, or homophobic comment.
- Parents become uncomfortable with interracial dating among students.
- Adults in a school start to question why all the members of one racial group sit together during free time, such as at lunch, at an assembly, or during sporting events.
- Parents insist that their students not be taught by a teacher of color.
- It becomes evident that culturally diverse students are showcased in sports, while White students are showcased in honors courses or with academic awards.
- The number of teachers of color is disproportionately low in comparison to White teachers.
- Students and parents become concerned that the school curriculum is Eurocentric and male dominated and excludes contributions from other ethnic groups and women.

Avoiding discussions of race and diversity can make it difficult for teachers to provide optimal learning opportunities for all their students. Moreover, teachers and administrators are sometimes not prepared to respond to parents when students select to date outside their race.

Students from all racial and ethnic backgrounds will interact with multicultural, multiracial, multilingual, and multiethnic people in the United States and in a global society for the remainder of their lives. It is essential that all students have the opportunity to develop knowledge, skills, awareness, attitudes, belief systems, and understandings of what it means to function productively in society in order to live healthy and productive lives. Research has found that "both children of color and White children develop a 'White bias' by the time they enter kindergarten."[1] These biases, assumptions, and worldviews need to be recognized as problems and disrupted in order to help students broaden and complement their mindsets related to themselves, others, and how the world works. Students' unexamined biases, assumptions, and worldviews can make it difficult for them to understand oppression and how various hegemonic forces leave some people discriminated against and underserved while other groups are privileged and positioned for success both in schools and in society.

As Dr. Johnson suggests in the quote that begins this chapter, teachers' identities and experiences shape their curricula and instructional decision making. Who they are in terms of their racial, ethnic, cultural, socioeconomic, gender, and linguistic background is perhaps one of the most important dimensions for teachers to consider when developing learning opportunities for students. This point may be contested by those who suggest that high-stakes testing and "scripted" curriculum guides prevent teachers from making decisions about what they emphasize in their teaching. However, by deciding what is germane and central to student learning opportunities, teachers still play an enormous role in what goes on in the classroom. Despite the structural and instructional limits caused by high-stakes testing, teachers bring their own perspectives and experiences into the classroom based on their own worldviews. Teacher identity is a critical facet of their work, and they should unpack how they make decisions for student learning.

INTRODUCING DR. JOHNSON

Dr. Johnson, an African American English teacher who lived in the Stevenson County School District, understood quite well how central her own and her colleagues' identities were to the learning opportunities available to their students. Having earned her doctorate from a large midwestern institution, she had a rich array of language arts subject-matter knowledge and was well equipped to connect with her mostly White students, although cultural and racial conflicts did emerge from time to time.

Dr. Johnson was the only African American teacher at Stevenson High to teach in the academic core; two others taught in the vocational/elective departments. Energetic and passionate, Dr. Johnson kept her students entertained and engaged in learning from the beginning of the class period to the end. She enjoyed reading, traveling, and, most of all, caring for her two children. Typically wearing slacks and a blouse, Dr. Johnson was well dressed and maintained a professional appearance.

FACILITATING STUDENT REFLECTION ON SELF, OTHERS, AND SOCIETY

There is value in facilitating student reflection of social realities regarding opportunity and privilege. Students need to understand how they are positioned in relation to others and how their worldview is shaped by forces both in and beyond their control.

Much has been written in the educational literature about the importance of teachers taking time to reflect on a range of matters, from subject matter and curriculum development to issues of race. Dr. Johnson used reflection, however, as an instructional tool in her classroom to facilitate discussion about the broader issues students face in society. For instance, she created opportunities for her students to reflect on how free they were to enjoy their social and economic status and to help them understand themselves in relation to others who did not necessarily enjoy the same economic status. These reflective discussions enabled her students to start thinking about their connections to those who are not in positions of economic privilege. In Banks's words, "Students need to understand the extent to which their own lives and fates are tightly tied to those of powerless and victimized groups."[2] And I would add that students need to understand that their own positions are a consequence of broader social and economic systems, which dictate and determine social and economic mobility in society. Students need to understand, as explained in chapter 1, that success and failure are determined by realities beyond merit.

Banks also suggests that when poverty exists, all in society are affected; students need to understand this, especially those who believe in a meritocracy. That is, students and adults who believe that people earn their positions in society and that hegemonic systems have little to do with socioeconomic status need to deepen their ideology and look at the evidence to help them broaden their positions and belief systems. Dr. Johnson thought deeply about the privileges she and her students enjoyed, a reality she considered important when making decisions for their learning. This point is particularly interesting if we consider the fact that the majority of her students were White and wealthy. She interpreted as central to their needs an understanding of how wealth, poverty, race, and culture work, especially in the broader society. She believed that her students needed to gain a level of self-knowledge and awareness before attempting to understand others. It is important to note that Dr. Johnson orchestrated such reflection to help her students understand power relations and matters of equity without making the students feel they were to blame for society's inequities.

She clearly created a safe and welcoming classroom environment in which students were given opportunities to think through the curriculum and draw connections to their own experiences and worldviews. I believe the creation of such inviting and caring contexts is critical for both high school and grade school students. Dr. Johnson would likely not have had the same level of success with her students in a less welcoming environment. She designed a space where her students felt empowered and where they were savvy and deliberate in exerting their voices and perspectives even as they disagreed with the multiple "texts" available in the classroom: the teacher, their classmates, books, and other curriculum materials.

I asked Dr. Johnson what she thought about when she was designing lessons for her students. She replied, "I try and go beyond the Eurocentric literature. Most of the contributions to literature were made by White men. The main thing I consider, then, besides my kids, is the importance of exposing the kids to writers who make up the world: the Hispanics and the Hispanic Americans, the Asians and the Asian Americans, the Africans and the African Americans." Dr. Johnson clearly had an idea of what she believed her students needed, and she was always thinking about whom she was teaching. As evident in her statement, she believed that helping students understand the role of ethnicity is critical. However, reflection on gender was also an important element in her teaching practice: "Women are also important because most of the writers were White men. I want my girls to read about women, too. I try to broaden their horizons. They are on their way out into the real world, and everybody they meet in the world might not look like the people here. To me, this is what's important in the decision making."

At the heart of Dr. Johnson's decision making for her students was opportunity. She facilitated their reflections to provide opportunities to think about important matters, which she worried they otherwise would not have—new experiences that could enlighten them about issues of race, ethnicity, culture, and gender. She especially wanted the female students to be exposed to women writers, a point that the research literature describes as a necessity for maintaining student interest and engagement. As feminist theorist bell hooks explains, girls and women too often are left out of classroom conversations and content.[3] Dr. Johnson still included the "White men"—the male authors who make up much of the traditional literary canon—but she also wanted the students to be exposed to women writers and writers from other ethnic groups. In sum, issues of culture were central in Dr. Johnson's thinking about students' opportunities for learning and reflection.

Dr. Johnson understood the importance of making lessons relevant to students and of learning from and with her students. She asserted: "If I were an Asian student, I would want my teacher to know something about Asian writers. It is important to make lessons relevant to students . . . these kids know so much nowadays, so you have to make the work fit into their scheme of thinking." While Dr. Johnson did not claim to know everything she needed to know about Asian writers, for instance, she was unwavering in her position that she was willing to learn about them and also to learn about Asian culture with and from her students. In fact, she believed that it is a teacher's responsibility to engage in this kind of learning about other cultures. As she asserted, "So, that means that I got to learn about Asians by asking the right kinds of questions, because you don't want to get too personal, but you want them to know that you [as the teacher] care about them enough to learn about their culture." Exposing the students to "the self" and "the other" was important to her given the fact that "many of these kids don't have any idea about how other people around the world live. They are sheltered. They are good kids, but they just don't *see it* [emphasis added]; so because for years I've been the only Black teacher they encountered, I try and plan and develop a set of experiences for my students that will make them better human beings when they leave."

Dr. Johnson's push for self-reflection and self-understanding as a way to enhance how one relates to others connected to how she thought about herself in relation to her students: "I work hard to make all my students feel like they are a part of the learning environment. *This might be because I haven't been made to feel like I am accepted in this school . . .* I have been hurt here, and I don't want my students to feel hurt for being different—you know, we need to celebrate our differences." Thus, Dr. Johnson understood that her own identity, experiences, and mind-set—the ways she interpreted her own (mis)treatment by others, mainly adults, in her school—played an enormous role in what she taught, how she taught it, and how she was able to relate to her students. Her decision to have her students reflect about justice and treating all people well regardless of their racial, ethnic, or gender background was clearly shaped by her own experiences and reflections about what she believed to be important.

Dr. Johnson felt she had not been "accepted" into her school because of a range of experiences, which are discussed below. In her words, "When they ask me to teach the seniors who[m] no one else wants to teach, I accept. That's right . . . I gladly accept because I bring out the best in them. And they [the students] see that I am different, and I have come to love myself for being different because wherever we go in life, there will be people who have problems with us." Thus, even at the mostly White and affluent Stevenson High School, there were students who were considered to be in the bottom tier, referred to as the "low group." There also were students considered gifted or the "top group," as well as those in the middle. Dr. Johnson enjoyed teaching the students considered the low group. She believed in creating opportunities for them to reflect about themselves, others, and society in order to be better equipped to thrive in the real world. Cleverly, she was able to help students think about localized situations of marginalization and to connect them to broader ones. As she facilitated learning opportunities through reflection for her students, she also worked to transcend and work through cultural conflicts that emerged in the classroom and school.

WORKING THROUGH AND TRANSCENDING CULTURAL CONFLICT

While cultural conflicts are inevitable in a range of social contexts in education, the ability of teachers to recognize those conflicts as learning opportunities is a promising component of developing knowledge to teach all students well. It is largely teachers' responsibility to bridge, work through, and eventually transcend cultural conflicts in order to get to the heart of the content/subject matter they are teaching.

The research literature often presents cultural conflict as tensions and inconsistencies that surface when White teachers teach culturally diverse students. Dr. Johnson's case demonstrates how cultural conflict can emerge between a Black teacher and White students and how they can work through those conflicts. Although there were many cultural differences between Dr. Johnson and her students in terms of beliefs and world experiences as well as race, she worked through and around powerful cultural conflicts that might seem inevitable when a Black woman teaches mostly White students.

In many ways, Dr. Johnson transcended cultural divides and created opportunities to connect with her students. Her success was evident in her students' participation and engagement in the classroom as well as their interactions with her in the hallways. But the power of her relationships with her students was made crystal clear when the graduating seniors asked her to present them with their diplomas at commencement each year. Dr. Johnson prided herself on the fact that she awarded more diplomas to graduating seniors than did any of her colleagues. Because the students selected their "most influential" teacher to award their diplomas, she interpreted the students' invitation as a sign that she was making a positive impact on them and their experiences.

Dr. Johnson clearly stood out as "different" in this mostly White context, and she was acutely aware of that fact. She had felt ostracized at times because she was quite vocal about issues of racial and cultural diversity, which she believed had made some of her colleagues and supervisors "uncomfortable." Dr. Johnson drew from her own experiences to connect to how her "low-group" students must feel as "seniors who[m] no one else wants to teach."

Dr. Johnson discussed her thinking about decision making and transcending cultural conflicts in terms of balancing the "self" with that of the "other." In a sense, she was stressing philosopher Cornel West's assertion that we cannot work for freedom [or social justice] on behalf of others until we are free and unbound ourselves.[4] The balance of self and other manifested itself in how Dr. Johnson developed lessons, the types of activities she developed to carry out those lessons, and how she tried to help her students understand their multiple identities and the many contributions of the people and places she presented in the curriculum. Connecting to these multiple identities was central in understanding her students' sense of belonging and acceptance in the larger school community. Her attempt to understand herself in relation to others and what her students were experiencing, was important to the kinds of relationships she developed;

the most successful of these helped her work through cultural differences that surfaced.

When transcending cultural conflicts, Dr. Johnson pushed her students to think about their own role in the school in relation to others. Her aim was to help them gain knowledge about how people may feel silenced or placed on the fringes of what society expects and accepts. As she explained, "These students will be stronger if they find a sense of belonging. They know that Dr. Johnson cares about them, and I'm not willing to let them get away with mediocrity." Thus, Dr. Johnson demonstrated that she cared about her students and had high expectations for them, despite the fact that many of her seniors were considered undesirable to teach. She asserted, "Just because they [the students] are not all on the football team or the most popular kids or the kids on the honor roll does not mean that they are not good students." Moreover, she built connections with her students and transcended cultural divides because she empathized with them: "I know how they must feel." She too has felt ostracized and marginalized, not only as a Black woman in society but also in her school. She used her thinking about herself and the students as a foundation in planning assignments: "I plan assignments like the self-portrait that allows them to think about themselves in positive ways. I also do self-portraits with them so they can see that I too am different and yet I'm OK. Kids like this, and they do it because they can relate. This helps me every time I [write a self portrait], so it probably helps them as well."

The content of her class could easily have been more general or have focused on other topics, but she was deliberate and mindful in helping the students make connections to and draw from their own experiences of marginalization. Dr. Johnson helped students think about themselves and their own marginalization in order to guide them to places of empathy (not pity) for others. Her decisions allowed Dr. Johnson to build connections with her students and to build broader perspectives about how the world works, for whom, why, and how. In essence, consistent with the research literature about good practice, Dr. Johnson's efforts helped her students link the head (affective) with the heart (cognitive).

Thus, Dr. Johnson avoided and transcended cultural conflicts by:

- Making explicit connections with her own and her students' experiences of feeling marginalized in the school
- Allowing students to see her as a real person
- Perceiving conflicts as opportunities to learn and develop
- Building relationships with students and developing lessons/experiences that helped them recognize their worth and intelligence
- Demonstrating her care for them, having high expectations of them, and not accepting mediocrity

Dr. Johnson further transcended cultural conflicts with her students by not allowing them to develop "White or cultural guilt" and by helping them see how all groups of people have been mistreated and have experienced hate in society. This point is elaborated on in the next section.

CREATING SAFE SPACE FOR OPEN DIALOGUE AND POSITIONING

There are many differences between teachers and students, and there are many similarities. It is in those spaces of commonality that curriculum and instructional practices can meaningfully connect with all those in a learning environment. Providing high school students the chance to examine their lives and worldviews safely in a space that is not antagonistic or hostile can be essential to facilitate open and honest dialogue and help students position themselves in classroom and broader discourses regarding difference.

Dr. Johnson also worked through cultural conflicts by helping students understand that they are not responsible for situations beyond their control. She provided opportunities for students to move beyond White and cultural guilt by exposing them to "hate against White people." She explained: "I want to teach them about hate and how hate is relegated to all groups of people, including the White race. I often discuss with my students how the Irish were mistreated. The Italians, you know, they were lynched and could only work in farming and agriculture." When Dr. Johnson exposed students to how their ancestors had been mistreated, they were more open to understanding how hate works and more willing to discuss its manifestation in current society. Ultimately, though, Dr. Johnson wanted her students "to eradicate hate. I want them to love themselves because when we hate ourselves, we hate others." She wanted her students to learn "more than what's in a book" and take action in a quest for social justice.

It is essential to clarify that in classrooms where the students are adults, such as in teacher education programs, tensions and uncomfortable conversations may be beneficial. The research literature suggests that classroom contexts with some hostility can serve as an additional tool in facilitating deep-rooted reflection, learning, growth, and change among adult learners—particularly when they are engaged with difficult issues such as race, prejudice, equity, sexism, and/or social justice. However, I agree with Dr. Johnson's approach and design for students in elementary, middle, and high school. The classroom settings needed to be supportive and safe for her students, especially if there was not a common school culture that supported tense classroom interactions as a pedagogical tool. From my observations, Dr. Johnson treated her students with care and concern, and they seemed to feel safe and supported in the social context, which allowed them to open up about difficult issues related to equity, wealth, and diversity in general.

To create a safe classroom setting, Dr. Johnson emphasized similarities between her students and herself, and, importantly, between her students and others in society. She did this to help students locate common spaces, sites, and experiences and to expand her students' realities. She explained: "Kids are into drugs; kids are, you know, smoking marijuana; they're not always being quiet when you tell them to be quiet. Homes are different. We have what they call a 'blended family.' We have divorced families. So, all of those things are important in kids' lives." These "important things in kids' lives" were where Dr. Johnson was able to draw connections and to build relationships with her students, which ultimately became central to avoiding the cultural conflicts that otherwise could have overshadowed learning opportunities. She continued: "My kids know that I was married and now I'm divorced, and my life goes on, and it's OK, you see? So, I guess part of it is showing the differences, but part of it is showing the similarities. We all hurt. We all cry. We all have bad days . . . when I show them the differences, I show them just how similar we are, too. So, being different is not bad, 'cause we are actually a lot alike. Does that make sense?" In essence, Dr. Johnson was able to demonstrate how she and her students were different and yet very similar at the same time.

While Dr. Johnson had the ability and skill to create safe and welcoming spaces for her students to engage in difficult discourses related to race and diversity, she also felt an added layer of pressure to both know and expose her students to multiple literacy worlds. She was a bit concerned that her students would never be exposed to certain writers or genres of literature without her exposure. Thus, Dr. Johnson came to know and represent multiple literacy worlds.

KNOWING MULTIPLE LITERACY WORLDS

Teachers of color sometimes feel that they have an additional burden to intimately know ethnically grounded literacy worlds as well as traditional literacy worlds.

As a Black teacher, Dr. Johnson explained that she had to know multiple literacy worlds in order to (1) expose students to literature they would more than likely not read without her direction and (2) maintain her love and appreciation for both Eurocentric and African and African American–centric literature. She noted that while she was expected to know traditional literature, she also read and deepened her knowledge of African American–centered literature. She added: "Culture plays a role. Because if you think about it, why haven't we, in our educational process, taught certain things [and people] in the classroom? I mean, if you look at White teachers—how many of them know about Toni Morrison? How many of them know about Terry McMillan? How many of them know about bell hooks? And they are not teaching that kind of stuff. bell hooks is a literary genius; she's more intellectual than many other writers, but *my White colleagues teach what they know*. They teach Hawthorne, you know, and it's a cultural thing. But with me, you know, we [Black teachers] have to know [and teach] Hawthorne too, and that makes me . . . flexible because we know both worlds." In essence, she maintained that teachers' identities are intricately tied to what they decide to teach and to the multiple worlds they come to know. Because of Dr. Johnson's identity, she reminded her students that "people have stories that are not a part of the White story."

Dr. Johnson believes that teachers teach what they know and who they are—that the worlds teachers know, live in, and negotiate influence how they conceive and represent curriculum matters both inside and beyond the classroom. In discussing her knowledge about multiple roles and the range of literature she has come to know, she suggested that she "knows" at least two worlds or realities. It became evident through my observations that Dr. Johnson actually knew multiple literacy worlds. For instance, she was as comfortable talking about Asian and African writers as about African American and White American writers.

Her notion of knowing multiple worlds points to what educational pioneer W. E. B. DuBois in his seminal text, *The Souls of Black Folk*, referred to as double consciousness.[5] Double consciousness suggests that Black Americans have at least two deep levels of awareness—they are African and they are also American. These levels of consciousness are sometimes at odds, but they are in communion as well. Tensions between what it means to be both African and American can make life complex and difficult. At the same time, their African consciousness allows Black Americans to operate at a deep level of awareness and understanding because it allows them to look at a situation from at least two intertwined perspectives.

Dr. Johnson maintained that she was expected to know more than her colleagues because of her African American identity, and she expressed how difficult it was to deal with these added expectations: "It's like Black teachers have to know more—we have to know about what's accepted and expected from a European perspective, and we are expected to be the expert on everything Black too. It's hard work."

Dr. Johnson realized that she needed to be able to teach the multiple forms of texts available in the classroom and the broader community. She recognized that text-based learning opportunities extended far beyond traditional definitions of what a text is. Moreover, she realized that she and her students would need to examine texts from various vantage points in order to build transformational learning opportunities and knowledge in the classroom.

TEACHING MULTIPLE TEXTS

It is important for teachers to recognize that they should be prepared to teach multiple forms of texts that range well beyond a traditional novel or textbook. Students themselves are texts, teachers are texts, and experiences in the classroom, school, and the broader society are texts. All these forms of texts need to be examined and explicated in order to complement and build on learning opportunities in traditional literary texts.

In this section, I attempt to capture some of the powerful qualities of Dr. Johnson's teaching. I describe how deeply Dr. Johnson understood the texts she taught, as well as their authors and the relevance the texts had for her and her students. The works that Dr. Johnson taught so brilliantly included:

- Traditional printed reading texts expected to be part of the curriculum, such as *To Kill a Mockingbird*
- Nontraditional printed reading texts that related to Dr. Johnson's own experiences, such as when she lived in Africa
- Traditional and nontraditional printed reading texts that represented her students' experiences both inside and outside the school, such as when students felt ostracized because they were not the most popular kids or the kids on honor roll

- Nontraditional human-experience texts through oral sharing, which allowed her to expose students to her own textual experiences and for them to share aspects of their experiences with her and their classmates

A Snapshot of Dr. Johnson's Teaching of Multiple Texts

Dr. Johnson prepares the class for the day's reading—Alice Walker's "Everyday Use," a short story that focuses on the cultural and historical legacy embedded in patchwork quilts and the art of quilting. She provides some brief information about Alice Walker and the story, which she calls "setting the stage." "You see," she explains, "Alice Walker is a brilliant African American woman who wrote the novel *The Color Purple*, which was made into a movie. Has anyone in this class read that novel or seen the movie?" Only two students raise their hands (all of the students are White). "I see," Dr. Johnson responds. "Well, let me tell you a bit about that novel before we move on." She spends about ten minutes discussing the time period of the novel and points out some of the major themes, after which she returns to the story at hand—"Everyday Use."

The students read the story aloud, with Dr. Johnson orchestrating the reading: she calls on students, one by one and by name—there is no choice in the matter—you either read or you are not participating, which means points are deducted. After a few paragraphs, Dr. Johnson breaks in with her own memories:

> I remember when I was a girl. My grandmother made me a quilt when I went off to college. I still have it today. That quilt is old and dingy now, but it'll be in my family forever because it means something to me culturally. I see that quilt as more than pieces of cloth sewn together. And I miss my grandmother—the food she cooked, and her smell, you know, all the things that remind us of the good times—when my sisters and I would play in her yard, and the clothes on the line outside flew in the wind. Those were some great times. And so, when I run across that quilt in my basement, I think back to those times and I get full [emotional]. Those are times for me to share about my sisters, my parents, and my grandmother with my [own] kids.

Not a person moves during Dr. Johnson's soliloquy—words cannot describe the calm in the room. Dr. Johnson continues:

And if my grandmother . . . could see me now as *Dr. Johnson*, her heart would be glad. I was a little Black girl who grew up right outside of [Ohio], and so, yes, it is deeper than just the cloth and the quilt and the fabric. It's about artifacts that we treasure and allow to become meaning makers to remind us—to remind us to tell stories to our children who I hope will tell stories to theirs—starting from a patch quilt. I cannot help but think about this as we read this story.

The bell sounds to dismiss class, but no one moves. It is obvious that this is an important and meaningful moment—not only for Dr. Johnson but for her students as well.

It is evident that Dr. Johnson relied on her memories of family customs and traditions as she interpreted the text of "Everyday Use." During the time I observed her classes, she consistently relied on her history, her multiple identities, and (in this lesson) on her experiences of quilting to bring the text to life. At the core of her transformative pedagogical decisions was her ability to share aspects of herself as a way to guide students toward deeper thinking, self-reflection and understanding. Her personal narratives allowed students to see the themes and experiences in a traditional text as relevant and real. Dr. Johnson often invited students to share similar experiences they had had with their grandparents or other family members—a tool she used to make connections to the multiple texts available in the classroom.

I asked Dr. Johnson to share with me why she chose to open up to her students about her family history, and she said, "I don't mind sharing my experiences with them. Some of them are hurtful, and others are times to celebrate. [My students] see me for a real person because I cannot present myself in any other way. They know this about me, and I am proud of that." It should be clear from the classroom snapshot above that Dr. Johnson taught at least two texts: a traditional printed reading text ("Everyday

Use") and a nontraditional text that showcased aspects of herself and her history. Another text that Dr. Johnson taught related to experiences that both she and her students had outside of the classroom and in their local community. One of her students, Dan, provided an opportunity for her to demonstrate her teaching of a nontraditional societal or community text based on his experience with an English language learner.

AN ENGLISH LANGUAGE LEARNERS LESSON

When I asked what she believed her students were learning from the curriculum and instructional opportunities available to them, Dr. Johnson explained that she attempted to help her students transfer the lessons from the classroom into the community as well as transfer community experience into the classroom. She shared this story about Dan, one of her students:

> During another class session [not the session on "Everyday Use"] Dan talked about being upset about the people who are coming into our district. I think he was referring to the Spanish or the Mexicans; I'm not sure what nationality. And Dan was saying that he was upset that this guy couldn't understand him in a convenience store. He said, "Why are these people moving here, and they can't even speak English?" And that gave me a chance to teach—to really get down and teach. I love it—because this kid was very passionate when asking, "Why are these people here?" And I told him that these people are doing things that we don't want to do. He was saying that he didn't like these people coming here, and I was saying that his family, his grandparents, great-grandparents, came from different countries. And they don't see that; that's all important to me because I think that sensitivity . . . I have a sensitivity to people who are not like my kids at Stevenson High School—that are not, you know, mainstreamed right away.

Dr. Johnson then related her comments to systemic power structures: "Any time you're part of the ruling class with power, it's likely that you don't see it. You're not as sensitive to minority groups, and that's OK. We have to learn these things from people who live them. It's not just Black and White. I've had many of my Asian students talk about things that they've heard or gone through, too. We all learned from the discussion that day [the "Everyday Use" lesson], even Dan."

Although captivated by Dr. Johnson's lesson on "Everyday Use," the students sometimes struggled to see her points. Given their youth, they had difficulty realizing how power works in the real world. Although Dr. Johnson had some power as the teacher, she was quick to demonstrate broader notions of power by pointing out the advantages her students had by virtue of their race, of their White privilege.[6] In fact, the power Dr. Johnson's students had was demonstrated when they complained about her teaching, and her classes were taken away from her (a point discussed below). Dr. Johnson's open approach and her decision to have a race/diversity-centered curriculum did not come without problems. The problems she encountered were most prevalent during her early years at the school, but they still seemed to affect her at the time of my study.

CONSEQUENCES AND DISCOMFORT OF DIVERSITY CONTENT

Teachers do not teach on secluded islands; they teach in a school environment that is shaped by people (other teachers, administrators, students, parents) with varying views on what is and is not appropriate and necessary to consider in curriculum and instruction. When a decision to focus on matters of diversity in the classroom is met with dissension, there can be serious consequences for a teacher.

Thus far, I have discussed several important aspects of Dr. Johnson's mind-set and practices, and the opportunities she attempted to provide for her students. As a Black educator working in a school with mostly wealthy White students, she believed that many opportunity gaps would have remained in their educational experience without the exposure she could provide. In particular, Dr. Johnson placed matters of gender, race, culture, and privilege at the root of her curriculum and instructional decision making because she believed they were important for her students. She taught her curriculum in part by facilitating student reflection, and she was able to transcend inevitable cultural conflicts by making powerful connections with her students and building solid and sustainable relationships.

Dr. Johnson's ability to transcend cultural conflicts was guided by the marginalization that she and many of her students experienced. She felt marginalized because she was so vocal about matters of culture among her colleagues; her students felt marginalized because they were not "the most popular kids." Moreover, Dr. Johnson developed relationships with her students felt marginalized because she was deliberate in allowing students to learn about her and her experiences. She also did not "blame" students for issues beyond their control. She was able to create a safe space in which students could grapple with difficult, sometimes controversial matters of diversity, be open to dialogue and critique, and avoid "White and cultural guilt."

I have explained that Dr. Johnson believed that she was expected to know both Eurocentric and African and African American–centric literature while her colleagues were expected to know only the former. In essence, Dr. Johnson stressed that her identity played an enormous role in what she taught and was expected to know in the classroom from a curriculum and instructional perspective; she transformed her curriculum to be responsive to students' everyday experiences and also to address what the students might experience after they graduated. The next section describes some of the consequences of Dr. Johnson's decisions to incorporate and centralize diversity into the curriculum and instruction.

SAME TEXT, DIFFERENT INTERPRETATIVE EMPHASIS

Although during my study, I saw only that Dr. Johnson was an outstanding teacher and the students seemed to respect her immensely, she shared with me that in the past there had been consequences to her diversity and equity-centered curriculum and instructional decisions. She explained: "I've become aware of how many of my colleagues look at various [curriculum] selections, and I'm not sure if they understand the whole message of what writers are attempting to do. What I want to talk about is basically how we teach a book called *To Kill a Mockingbird*—how we don't intently focus on the political, social, and racial aspects of that book." Then she gave a specific example: "There are two parts to that book. There is Boo Radley, and then there is that Tom Robinson situation. When I first started teaching here and I taught that book, my students would run down to the principal's office and tell the principal that I was prejudiced—they thought I was a racist."

She explained that students thought she was spending too much time on some of the broader social ills and situations, and her students were uncomfortable with this emphasis—especially when she first started teaching at Stevenson High. Dr. Johnson's experiences of being called a racist provide additional evidence that issues of race should be incorporated into teacher education programs and professional development opportunities. Dr. Johnson and Mr. Hall both experienced explicit situations in two very different learning contexts that required them to work through and address being called a racist. Her experiences of having students "run to the principal's office" to complain about her provide additional evidence of the importance of teachers' developing solid relationships with students—in all schools, not just urban or rural settings.

Searching inwardly, Dr. Johnson attempted to rationalize why her students complained: "Maybe I did spend too much time on the Tom Robinson aspect, but that's how they [the students] handled our discussions. They thought I was racist for exposing areas that made them uncomfortable. I was trying to get them to see how the female character falsely accused Tom Robinson [a Black male character] of raping that woman [a White character]." Dr. Johnson believed that too many students did not have opportunities to learn about the two important aspects of the book, especially that of the dangers of making assumptions: "And on the other side is how we make assumptions about people like Boo Radley. You know,

Boo never came out of that house—the house was all spooky and so on and so forth. And we make assumptions about people . . . my students didn't see all that. And as you know, I'm sort of animated in my classes, and they misinterpreted what was going on in there."

Dr. Johnson stressed that because the students had not previously focused on the nature of assumptions or on matters of race (or even, more broadly, diversity), they were not equipped to address those issues in her class. The students who complained about her teaching were White; the culturally diverse students in her class often saw the points she was hoping to make. She explained: "I didn't have any Black students in that class my first year, and I've found that when I do have Black students or Asian students or Hispanic students, they see what I'm trying to do and say because we live those experiences. It is my White students who don't understand, and I have to say that there are cultural differences that exist when you [a Black teacher] teach in a predominantly White situation. They [cultural differences] ought to be explored if we are doing what we need to do—preparing our kids for the real world." Dr. Johnson makes the point that there "are cultural differences" in predominantly White teaching contexts, although she believed that many of her colleagues did not think so. This reality, of course, is tantamount to Lewis's study outlined in chapter 1, which revealed that in White contexts, issues of race especially are dismissed as insignificant because there is not a critical mass of people of color in the social context.[7]

Dr. Johnson sought out the social and political themes in the class readings and used them to provide learning opportunities that would cause her students to think and act differently—perhaps in line with a social justice agenda. For many years she had presented lessons that focused on social and political matters in her classes, but she did so at the risk of being accused of being prejudiced and a racist, as she explained: "Many of the students took my teaching in this way as an attack on them. And, of course, there is a price we pay when you go outside of people's comfort areas. I was called into the office and questioned about it [from the principal]. And you guessed it—eventually my principal took those freshmen away from me. So, there is a price you pay for decision making and teaching in this way."

As is evident here, attempting to transform the curriculum in such a profound manner had its consequences for Dr. Johnson. Teaching in a predominantly White context with colleagues who Dr. Johnson suspected rarely thought about such issues likely intensified her being ridiculed and eventually having her freshmen classes "taken" from her. Teachers like Dr. Johnson must be prepared to negotiate, balance, and sometimes combat the pervasive counterproductive discourses and practices that are already in place in a social context, so that they can teach the content and provide related learning opportunities they believe to be appropriate related to issues of diversity (namely, gender, race, and culture inequities).[8] Dr. Johnson elaborated on the resistance she perceived from her students, colleagues, and other adults in the Stevenson community: "I think that it's due to the privileges of the White population here. Whether children or adults . . . there are privileges that they have been receiving that many of these kids don't understand."

ADMINISTRATIVE ACTIONS TO ADDRESS DISCOMFORT

Dr. Johnson explained that her mind-set and her decision to give her students opportunities to attend to deep-rooted assumptions were resisted by many of them, and as a result "that class was taken from me. These were ninth graders, and I don't teach ninth graders anymore; haven't for years now because they [the administration] felt like many of the students were right—that I was a racist. And that hurt me . . . I am not racist. I just wanted to *open eyes* [emphasis added]. I was anxious for the students to *see it* [emphasis added]." This experience has not stopped Dr. Johnson from working to eradicate "ignorance where culture and race" is concerned, and she provided such opportunities for her seniors. As she explained, "The older kids see it much clearer than the younger ones." In these senior courses, she again explicitly stressed issues that were important to her because of her experiences as a person of color and as a woman. From my view, there were at least two dimensions to the success Dr. Johnson had with the senior class. First, when Dr. Johnson began to teach in the mostly White context and was called prejudiced and racist, the students had not yet gotten to know her, and she had not yet developed the kinds of relationships with them necessary for connectedness. Second, her senior students were older, and from a developmental perspective they were perhaps better prepared and more willing to think outside of their comfort zones. Pushing her students to think outside that zone was important to Dr. Johnson because she wanted her students to be prepared for college: "So they get a taste of it, and I can openly tell them that I want them not to go away to college not having experienced other people's cultures. But I found that [with] a lot of my ninth-grade students, it was like they were in denial, and I think that it had to do with maturation."

It was evident, though, that Dr. Johnson was not as frustrated with her ninth graders as she was with how the administration handled the complaints about her: "What surprised me was . . . not so much the kids; it was my administration that didn't understand because I was constantly being called down to the office and told that the students said that I was a racist for teaching certain books in certain ways." She persistently had to justify what she was teaching and why, and she did not feel she was supported by the administration, which she found frustrating and disappointing. Over time, however, she saw that the pendulum shifted a bit, and teaching the more controversial aspects of books had become more acceptable because White teachers had begun to do so at Stevenson High. Dr. Johnson said, "You see, they [the administration] see the worth so it's accepted and even expected now. But they [White teachers] are not [necessarily] teaching the social, political, and historical aspects of that book . . . Racism is a major theme that has been blatantly overlooked by most teachers here—how we treat people."

In sum, there were serious consequences related to the curriculum Dr. Johnson decided to teach and how she taught it when she first entered the Stevenson school district. Nevertheless, she exhibited a level of stick-to-itiveness in the face of serious challenges and adversity that many teachers likely would have found unbearable. The consequences of such interaction and perceptions of colleagues and administration could cause a teacher to revert to or fall in line with the common discourses and expectations established in a school (see Buendia, Gitlin, and Doumbia for more on this).[9] However, those experiences, although hurtful, did not stop Dr. Johnson from offering "eye-opening" experiences to her students through the curriculum. She had to present these opportunities to her seniors rather than the freshmen, but they were an integral part of what she felt she needed to cover with her students, and so she continued to do so.

A TEACHER'S TRANSFORMATIVE CURRICULUM AND TEACHING

Dr. Johnson worked through and transcended cultural conflicts in her mostly White school context, and she maintained a diversity-oriented curriculum even when she was called prejudiced and racist by students and even when her ninth-grade classes were taken away from her. She helped her students think about themselves and how privilege, power, and marginalization were prevalent at many levels—in the school, in the local community, and in the broader society. Dr. Johnson helped the students understand their economic, racial, and ethnic privilege while simultaneously facilitating their reflections on their own experiences of historical marginalization. Transforming the curriculum also meant that students were exposed to knowledge about others—from other cultures, races, and gender groups.

Dr. Johnson felt it was essential to create a classroom culture in which she could talk about issues of power and privilege without making students feel as if she were attacking them, their parents, or their ancestry. From her perspective, all ethnic groups had been discriminated against at some point in history, and she connected with her White students by pointing out that most of their ancestors at one time had experienced discrimination. Moreover, when a student complained about the increased number of English language learners who were moving into their district, she reminded him that they (their parents, grandparents, and great-grandparents) had immigrated to the United States from other countries as well at some point in history. Developing a safe and welcoming space to reflect about themselves, others, and macro-level societal matters allowed her seniors to let down their guards and to think about matters of power, equity, privilege, and discrimination beyond a Black-White divide. She was deliberate in her practices to focus on issues of gender, issues of immigration, and broader themes such as the social construction of assumptions that move far beyond those of Black and White.

In this case, it appeared that "the school culture and social structure are powerful determinants of how students [and teachers] learn to perceive themselves [and others]. These factors influence the social interactions that take place between students and teachers and among students, both inside and outside the classroom."[10] Dr. Johnson's perception of the support—or lack thereof—that she received from her colleagues, the school community, and the broader community seemed to have a profound influence on her. Being called to the principal's office to be questioned about what she was teaching her freshman students could easily have made her want to retreat from such scrutiny. However, she persisted and persevered. The question is: why and how do some teachers persevere in the face of adversity while others do not?

Although teachers of color may consider racial and cultural conditions and experiences appropriate and relevant to include in the curriculum because of their personal experiences, the pervasive belief systems, goals, and discourses of a school can derail this desire to provide a more nuanced set of opportunities for students. Early in her career at Stevenson, for example, Dr. Johnson paid a price for the opportunities she attempted to construct for her students. Teachers of any ethnic background may struggle in unsupportive contexts, and whether or not Dr. Johnson's colleagues were supportive of her pedagogical strategies is not as important as Dr. Johnson's *perception* of their lack of support. Nevertheless, Dr. Johnson had earned a doctorate from a major research institution, and she had traveled the world, even living in Africa at one point with her ex-husband.

Her exposure and previous experiences to a wide range of information likely contributed to her persistence even during difficult times. Teachers who cannot rely on such a wide body of knowledge and experience likely would find it more difficult to persevere in their quest to disrupt and expand on established mind-sets, discourses, and practices.

As evident in this research, who teachers are as racial and cultural beings often surfaces in their choice and presentation of their curricula. How a teacher perceives himself or herself and what that person stands for is reflected in what and how a teacher teaches. Moreover, this case suggests that teachers' identities, experiences, and stories often emerge in their work with students. Thus, teaching is almost always a personal and political endeavor.[11]

Dr. Johnson felt a professional and moral obligation to prepare her students for a diverse world and to help them not be color-blind or in denial about our diverse society and world. Teaching and learning are preparation for life. As Banks explains, "The world's greatest problems do not result from people being unable to read and write. They result from people in the world—from different cultures, races, religions and nations—being unable to get along and to work together to solve the world's intractable problems such as global warming, the AIDS epidemic, poverty, racism, sexism, and war."[12] Surely all students, not only those outside of the mainstream, need and deserve learning opportunities that provide the knowledge, skills, awareness, and understanding necessary to combat these and other social problems and perhaps experience the world more fully.

4

Black Male and Female Teachers, Diverse Urban School

Recognizing Assets in Unexpected People and Places

The reason I know what is happening in their world is that I live in their world. I have a fourteen-year-old; I have an eleven-year-old; I have an eight-year-old. I know the world they came from with my eight-year-old, and I know where they are with my eleven-year-old . . . I know where they are going with my fourteen-year-old. Because I teach in middle school, I am right around eleven- and twelve-year-old range [students] . . . If I didn't have children their age, I would have to learn about what's happening with them. It's my job to do this.

—Mr. Jackson, urban middle school math and science teacher

You are going to be the social worker; you are going to be the parent; you are going to be the friend.

—Ms. Shaw, urban middle school social studies teacher

IN THE QUOTES ABOVE, Mr. Jackson, a Black math and science teacher, and Ms. Shaw, a Black social studies teacher, stressed two important dimensions of their mind-sets and their practices at their diverse urban school, Bridge Middle School. Mr. Jackson shared how he relied on his own children to help him stay connected to and gauge what was going on with his middle school students. While he admitted that he was at an advantage because his own biological children spanned the age of his students in his classes, he asserted that it was still a teacher's responsibility to learn about what is happening with students in order to teach them successfully.

Ms. Shaw reminds readers that teachers need to assume multiple interrelated roles when they are teaching. Although the role they play will vary according to the social context of their work, Ms. Shaw was firm in her position that teachers will assume roles far beyond the classroom, especially in urban and highly diverse schools. Mr. Jackson and Ms. Shaw both taught in the same school as Mr. Hall, who was the subject of chapter 2.

In chapter 2, I shared how Mr. Hall, a White science teacher, developed over the years by listening to the voices of his students and being responsive to their requests, needs, and actions. For example, Mr. Hall developed meaningful relationships with his students and got to "know" them because they insisted that he needed to do this. Moreover, Mr. Hall started to think about matters of race and diversity, although he began his work avoiding such an emphasis. At the beginning of his work at Bridge, he declared that his goal was to do one thing: "teach science." Through his experiences and interactions with his students, he came to understand what was really essential for success in the classroom—he realized that he could not teach science until he came to know and understand *to whom* he was teaching science.

In chapter 3, I provided a picture of Dr. Johnson, an African American high school language arts teacher who developed transformative learning opportunities for her mostly White and wealthy students at Stevenson High School. Dr. Johnson was able to work through and transcend cultural conflicts, and she developed powerful relationships with students by building on experiences in and out of school that both she and her students encountered. Although she was met with resistance and had not felt supported in the school at times, Dr. Johnson was resolute in her decision and her desires to develop and implement curriculum and instructional opportunities that exposed students to matters that are often ignored in mostly White contexts, such as those dealing with equity, diversity (race in particular), and discrimination as well as White and socioeconomic privilege. Moreover, she discovered that it was necessary for her to provide a safe, welcoming, and comfortable space for her high school students in order for them to remain open to the multiple themes explored in the classroom. She helped the students understand that all groups of people experience hate and discrimination, and Dr. Johnson was cognizant of her goal for her high school students not to feel White and cultural guilt. From a developmental perspective, this seemed important, although older (college) students may find that a more assertive approach, where students are sometimes guided to feel uncomfortable about difficult, taboo, and controversial issues, is necessary. Although Dr. Johnson was successful in her work at Stevenson High, she had experienced adversity, especially when she first began teaching there. Some of her ninth-grade students interpreted her curriculum and instructional practices as prejudiced and racist. As a result, her freshman classes were taken from her, and she was assigned a new set of courses with high school seniors. However, her instructional and curriculum goals remained the same: she continued teaching with a diversity-centered focus.

In this chapter, I showcase the mind-sets and practices of two teachers as they designed learning opportunities for students at Bridge Middle School. Mr. Jackson embraced opportunities to use music and hip-hop culture to build relationships with students and develop lessons. Ms. Shaw provided opportunities for her students to develop a sense of agency and authority and contribute to the local community. Understanding how important community was meant that she was not solely emphasizing test score results.

INTRODUCING MR. JACKSON

When I met him, Mr. Jackson had been teaching for seven years. At school, he always wore a shirt and tie, usually a suit jacket as well, and could typically be found standing in front of his door between classes. He often reminded students (both those he had taught and students not in his classes) to "be mindful of the time" and not to be late for class. He had a deep love and appreciation for music—jazz, pop, rhythm and blues, classical, and hip-hop—which filtered into his teaching. Music was almost always playing softly during his classes.

Married with three children, Mr. Jackson was engaged, even immersed, in popular culture. He watched music videos, listened to "hip" radio stations, and played video games. It was rare that students used language he did not understand. Although well versed in slang, he could quickly code-switch to more conventional language when necessary. His interaction with students was never forced, and he seemed to naturally stay current and relevant with his students.

SIGNIFICANCE AND INSIGNIFICANCE OF RACE

Race is always a salient factor that educators should consider, but having the same racial background as students will not necessarily sustain teachers in the classroom when they do not have the knowledge and skill to teach all students equitably.

While I have argued throughout this book about the significance and relevance of teachers' racial consciousness and development as they construct learning opportunities for their students, Mr. Jackson added a different spin on the issue. When I first began observing his classes, I assumed he was able to connect with his students primarily because he was Black. Indeed, I wondered about the nexus between his success and his status as a Black male teacher in a diverse urban classroom, with large numbers of Black students in his classes. I asked him, based on his experiences at Bridge Middle School, whether he believed being a Black man gave him an advantage, in that the majority of his students were Black. He replied, "Yes and no. I hate to be ambiguous like that, but . . . yes, initially, because they can relate to me because of my ethnicity . . . Initially. *But the effectiveness comes from my style, how I teach, and how I manage* [emphasis added], and any person of any race can do that if trained properly. Any gender can do that."

I observed how one African American student, Ryan, would be disruptive and disengaged from the beginning to the end of a different class, then walk into Mr. Jackson's classroom and act completely the opposite. While Ryan seemed to yearn for attention in the classroom in general, his actions to gain recognition moved from completely disrespectful and intolerable in one classroom setting to respectful and welcoming in Mr. Jackson's. Ryan was unquestionably a different student in Mr. Jackson's classroom. Mr. Jackson was stern in his position that he initially garnered respect, and students seemed to be drawn to him based on phenotype: when his students saw a Black teacher and perhaps a Black male, they were willing to give him a chance to teach them. However, Mr. Jackson came to believe that it was his teaching style and the ways in which he managed learning opportunities that made the difference. Thus, Mr. Jackson believed that a teacher from either gender or any racial or ethnic group could be successful in an urban and diverse school. What mattered for Mr. Jackson was *how* they taught.[1] This point is not only substantiated in the literature, it is also confirmed by Mr. Hall's success, portrayed in chapter 2.

Mr. Jackson expanded on his thinking regarding the significance of his race and gender to his practices: "So, I say yes, [race and gender are significant] because initially they [students] get attached to me, but that is only the start of the race. You can have another guy come in with the same ethnicity, and they may become attached to him at first, but if he is not being consistent, if he is not being fair, if he is not doing everything you are supposed to do, he is not going to be effective." He said that teachers must earn students' respect, and noted that students are sometimes not willing to allow a teacher to teach them if they do not have a deep connection, deeper than just shared race and gender. In Mr. Jackson's words, "I have seen several men with the same ethnicity come in and couldn't quite cut it. But initially [students said] 'he was cool; he's a good guy; he's cool,' but then—if you are not being fair, if you are not being consistent, and if you are not effectively managing the classroom, you are not going to be very effective to the whole, maybe a small group—but not the whole." Mr. Jackson was clear that a teacher's knowledge base and skill would ultimately be the sustaining factors that made the difference in the classroom and would surpass surface-level connections that could initially connect a teacher with students. In his view, "If somebody comes in from a different ethnicity—even if they don't feel like they have a sense of belonging with them—if they come in and [are] consistent and fair and stress everything, they are going to be successful, I believe."

STRESSING THE VALUE AND RELEVANCE OF LEARNING

There are competing positions about students' value of and interest in learning in urban and highly diverse schools. Some research suggests that students in these schools do not value learning, while other research points to the importance of context in making such claims; indeed, the sociocultural context of some urban and highly diverse schools fosters a valuing of learning, while other social contexts may not.

Given the divergent views on student motivation for learning in urban and highly diverse schools, I was curious about the kinds of challenges Mr. Jackson faced as he tried to design and implement learning opportunities at Bridge Middle School. He said he continually struggled to help his students find the value and relevance of learning and the value of school, and to do so he attempted to help them visualize how learning and school could help them do what they *aspired* to do in their lives outside of school, both currently and in the future. He believed that he needed to provide opportunities for his students to see themselves as capable of success in the classroom and beyond. Too many of his students did not recognize their own genius, and he needed to help them see themselves as both capable and worthy of academic, social, and educational success. In short, many of his students did not see "successful student" as part of their identity. Informally, I questioned one of his students, a Latina seventh grader, about what she wanted to do in her life postgraduation. At first I wondered if the student had spent much time thinking about her life after graduation yet, in light of the fact that she was in seventh grade. The student shared rather emphatically with me: "I plan to go to culinary school. I'm in this math class because I have to be. It really won't matter much to me later when I start stacking my papers [earning money] cooking for celebrities." The student clearly had not come to see how learning mathematics in seventh grade would be important in her future work as a chef "cooking for celebrities."

Because students often cared most about impressing their friends and were often more interested in what was happening in other areas of their lives, especially the social areas, Mr. Jackson realized that it was important for him to help students see school as a "hip" and "cool" place to be even as he worked to convince them that learning was salient to their current and future experiences and opportunities.

Mr. Jackson believed that "the biggest struggle in most urban schools is getting over the 'it's not cool to learn' factor. Once you break those barriers and you get your classroom management in check, everything rolls pretty smooth[ly]. But that [the idea that school is not cool] is a microcosm of our society." Mr. Jackson observed that there was a hierarchy of priorities in society and at Bridge Middle School, and academics were not at the top of the structure. He felt that entertainment was number one in the broader society, and noted, "It's like that in the school system. The biggest struggle would be getting . . . the children to understand how important education is and that it is OK to act cool and be smart and intelligent" at the same time. Creating opportunities for students to think seriously about school and education may be an unexpected focus for a math and science teacher, but like Mr. Hall, Mr. Jackson understood the complex interplay between motivating students to want to learn and teaching mathematics and science. He considered it a critical part of his job to get all students motivated and interested in learning, and he admitted that it was sometimes a struggle to think of creative and relevant ways to do this.

The research literature provides a range of views on the idea that students in urban and highly diverse settings do not find value in learning or education. Some research suggests that students of color in these contexts, such as African American or Latino/a students, or English language learners do not value learning, or they see academic achievement and success as "uncool" or as achievements for White students to enjoy.[2] Another line of research counters this position, suggesting that students of color from urban and highly diverse settings *do* value learning and education. This literature says students' interests and what they value depend on their social environment and their interpretations of what is acceptable and appropriate for them in their space.[3] This latter line of research offers a counternarrative to the research that asserts that urban and diverse students devalue school and that they see academic success as "acting White." Either way, there was a power structure among the students at Bridge Middle School.

POWER STRUCTURES AMONG STUDENTS

Implicit social and academic power structures exist among students in schools. Some of these power structures are conceptualized by adults and are shared by students. Other power structures are constructed by students themselves. Understanding these power structures and how they operate and are enacted can help educators bridge the space between social facets of the school environment with academic aspects.

In the previous chapter, I discussed how adults at Stevenson High School, a predominantly wealthy and White school, had created an academic power structure in which students were classified into high, middle, and low groups. A similar social power structure existed among the students in an urban social context, Ballou High School, which was captured by journalist Ron Suskind in an important book: *A Hope in the Unseen: An American Odyssey from the Inner City to the Ivy League.*[4] The book provides an account of Cedric, a high-achieving African American student, who beats the odds and succeeds in one of the poorest inner-city neighborhoods of Washington, D.C. Cedric matriculates and transitions from Ballou High School to the Ivy League of Brown University. Suskind describes the social power structure among the students at Ballou in three levels: (1) those who were high achieving were at the bottom; (2) successful and gifted athletes were in the middle, as there was a level of effort and achievement that went along with playing sports; and (3) drug dealers and gangbangers were at the top.

My experiences as a high school English teacher in a mostly Black, high-poverty school several years ago told a very different story. The valedictorian and salutatorian were usually African American, and while student athletes and those who might be classified as troublemakers certainly were held in some esteem, most of the students did not reject academic success and achievement. Among the students, the valedictorian and salutatorian were praised, not teased, for being successful. Moreover, students did not, from my experience, relegate academic success to "acting White." I share my experience as a high school English teacher to reiterate the point that different social contexts will reveal different results related to how students in urban and highly diverse contexts interpret academic success and achievement.

At Bridge Middle School, according to Mr. Jackson and based on my observations, the athletes and cheerleaders were often held in the highest esteem among their peers. Because of their high esteem among the other students and the social power structure, Mr. Jackson worked to get the popular kids on his side to develop a classroom culture that stressed the importance of learning and doing well in school. He relied on those at the top of the student-constructed social/power structure to help recruit their classmates to appreciate and value learning in the classroom. He attempted to bridge what it meant to be "cool" and to be smart. Mr. Jackson believed that the majority of students—even those who might not normally be actively engaged in learning—would get connected as well when they witnessed their "cool" classmates involved. Many students did in fact follow their classmates' leads.

In essence, Mr. Jackson encouraged his students to value learning by targeting the most powerful students to serve as role models. He believed he needed to use such power as an anchor for the engagement and learning he hoped would result. He said, "I try to target the coolest. I try to target the toughest. I try to target the most popular students, and I get them to understand and follow my vision. And once I get them, the rest of the class usually follows." It is important to note that Mr. Jackson was not trying to manipulate the students but, rather, help them develop a critical consciousness about what they were learning and of its importance. He could not stress enough the power and influence his students had on each other.

However, because Mr. Jackson felt confident that his students were constructing their own picture of him and his decisions and fairness in the classroom, he constantly referred to the idea that he had to be consistent with his expectations: "I don't care what your [power] status is—you are going to get consequences. I don't care if you are the big linebacker bully in the school or if you are the quiet little girl who is eighty pounds and never does anything. I want you serious about your work [engaging in learning]."

To recap, in many respects, students' peers were *much* more important to them than their teachers or even their parents. The most popular students at the school possessed a great deal of power and influence; Mr. Jackson understood that he had to understand the social power structure and had to get those "powerful" students on his side for the sake of learning and relevance in the classroom. He shared his strategy: "You have to get the people who have the most influence—the peer influence is very big in their [the students'] world, very big. So if you get the toughest kids, the strongest kids, the most powerful kids, you get them to 'buy in,' then you have got it [for the entire class]." In class, it was obvious that Mr. Jackson had gotten this buy-in—even the students who were considered the most popular and/or the toughest seemed to be actively involved with learning. Perhaps Mr. Jackson was successful in this regard because he deliberately and assertively sought out those at the top of the social hierarchy to promote the value and relevance of learning in the classroom community.

CONSTRUCTING IMAGES AND PERCEPTIONS AS REALITY

At times, educators may believe that students are wrong about how they have constructed the world—particularly about what happens during a classroom event such as when a teacher corrects some off-task behavior. However, educators must realize that our perceptions become our reality and that we rely on our past experiences to help define what becomes real to us.

Throughout my time observing Mr. Jackson's practices and learning how he thought about his work, he consistently pointed to image and perception, both among students and between the teachers and students. For Mr. Jackson's students at Bridge Middle School, perception *was* reality. He knew that students were watching what happened in the classroom: how he handled situations, whether he called on the same students all the time, who he asked to help him in the classroom, or how he handled disruption from one student to another. He needed, in his words, to be "fair, firm, and consistent," and he recognized that students' perceptions of what he did and how would play a critical role in how and whether they would be willing to attend his class and complete their classwork.

Mr. Jackson wanted his students to have a positive image of him and what was going on in the classroom, and he did not want any of them to feel that one student was more important than any other. They were *all* his kids, and he wanted them all to maximize their potential and succeed. Like Mr. Hall, Mr. Jackson believed that he was somewhat of a mentor to his students and therefore always needed to take the high road and do what was right, no matter what occurred. Probably because of his relevant and cool demeanor, students seemed to look up to Mr. Jackson; he had earned their respect.

The fact that Mr. Jackson saw himself as a mentor to his students likely played a role in his decision to wear a shirt and tie each day. He believed that his attire was an important part of his image and power as a teacher and that his students needed to see him in a certain light. In Mr. Jackson's words, "Teachers should dress for where they are going, not necessarily where they are currently." This statement really connected to one of the main missions of his teaching: *he wanted his students to envision life beyond their current situations.* The students' current situations were sometimes bleak; however, he wanted them to realize that they did not have to accept negative circumstances without fighting to change them.

The idea that students visualize themselves beyond their current situation was profound, because many of Mr. Jackson's students' experiences were limited to their local communities and circumstances. One White male student who I learned was living in poverty told me that he had never traveled outside his immediate community of Bridge Middle School. When I shared with him that my wife and I had traveled to a mall on the south side of the city over the weekend during one of my visits, he said he had never been to that mall and had never seen other parts of the city—let alone traveled outside the state. I learned, for example, that several of the students at Bridge Middle School had never gone on a vacation with their families and did not know anyone personally who worked in corporate America. Educational historian Vanessa Siddle-Walker explains that before desegregation, teachers taught their students as if they were already living in desegregation.[5] They prepared their students for life beyond what they were currently experiencing. Similarly, the notion of seeing life beyond the present was a central element of Mr. Jackson's teaching. He aspired to become a principal and dressed for where he was going in his career, not necessarily for where he was. Part of the image Mr. Jackson wanted his students to embrace was of him as a man who was headed for promotion and a higher level of success.

Student image and perception were consistent themes of Mr. Jackson's mind-set and practices because he understood that students were both constructing images and perceptions and talking to each other about these images and perceptions (whether Mr. Jackson believed they were accurate or not). Images and perceptions were being constructed, then, both individually and collectively as the students in the school were making sense of what Mr. Jackson and other teachers were doing in the school community. Mr. Jackson understood the importance of image and perception construction among his students because he immersed himself in their worlds in order to more deeply understand them, develop relationships with them, and teach them.

IMMERSION IN STUDENTS' WORLDS

Getting to know students means that teachers might have to move into a space that capitalizes on what is going on in students' worlds. Through immersion, teachers learn what is happening with students, what their interests are, and how students spend their time outside of school; they then use such knowledge in their classroom decision making.

By immersing himself in students' experiences both inside and outside of school, Mr. Jackson deepened his connections to his students. It is important to note that Mr. Jackson was not perceived as intrusive when he pursued information about his students' lives. To the contrary, his queries into what was happening with his students stemmed from his genuine interest and concern for what was important to them. He allowed them to lead in helping him understand their experiences. Dr. Johnson, portrayed in chapter 3, also stressed how important it was for her to not be too intrusive when she attempted to learn more about Asian (American) culture at Stevenson High School. Mr. Jackson's efforts to "remain current" in what was happening in the students' worlds helped him bridge the inevitable cultural divides between him and his students. Although Mr. Jackson was African American, as were many of his students, there was still ample room for conflict due to a range of differences between them.

Ultimately, he believed that he needed to immerse himself in the worlds of his students to design learning environments and develop instructional practices that connected to his students and that did not appear "foreign" to them. I have come to understand that the examples a teacher employs in a lesson, the nature of questions posed, how students are allowed to express themselves, and whose knowledge is validated (or not) in the classroom are all related to cultural connections that can have a huge bearing on students. Where instructional approaches were concerned, Mr. Jackson advised, "implement things from their world into their academic setting. So, if I am doing math problems, I am going to have problems with stuff that comes out of the rap world or the video game world . . . Just recently, our basketball team was doing really well, and I used the players in the math assignments, and that gets them [the students] engaged." It's important to note that Mr. Jackson was not talking about merely incorporating "their world" experiences from time to time in the learning that took place. Rather, he was referring to "keeping their worlds" at the center of the curriculum and teaching. From my observations, his students looked forward to word problems with real-world relevance. They would often correct Mr. Jackson's errors about the number of points a player scored in a game, which might seem insignificant or irrelevant to others but was a big deal to the students because it was their reality, their world, and they wanted the examples to tell the truth.

I wondered how Mr. Jackson was able to stay so current with what was happening with his middle school students in order to "implement things from their world into their academics." Mr. Jackson was able to recite versions of hip-hop songs, list names of the most popular professional athletes, and recognize the latest movies that were out in the theaters. He was, in a sense, immersed in popular culture. Mr. Jackson explained why he was so connected to the pop culture world of his students: he "lived" in their worlds through his own children and had a sense of where his students were developmentally because of the age range of his children. But there was another reason for his connection to his students' culture, as he went on to explain: "I am a DJ—I like the rap music myself. I play rap music [outside of school]. I feel like a kid at heart sometimes, so I kind of stay in touch with them in that way too." So Mr. Jackson knew the codes that many of his students were speaking and enacting in the hallways or during downtime in the classroom. The language commonality code provided for natural interactions between Mr. Jackson and his students, although the students seemed to transition from speaking in slang or more casual language to more "academic" language without his having to remind them. There was, without question, mutual respect between Mr. Jackson and his students. The students did not take Mr. Jackson's connection to hip-hop or pop culture as an indication that he was a peer. To the contrary, they respected him because in their eyes he had earned it.

One could argue that Mr. Jackson was at an advantage in teaching his students at Bridge Middle School: (1) he was African American, (2) he was male, (3) he had children around the same age as his students, and (4) he enjoyed many of the same things that his students did (hip-hop, video games, and sports, in particular). It is important to note that Mr. Jackson did not believe that it was impossible for other teachers to immerse themselves in students' worlds, even if they did not share one of these four characteristics or qualities. In fact, Mr. Jackson asserted that it is the teachers' responsibility to do so. Mr. Jackson believed that by learning about the world of their students, teachers could enhance the learning that took place in the classroom. In his words: "You have to immerse yourself in their world in some form or fashion. I am just lucky to come from the world that I teach in. I came from that world. I truly live in that world, so I am immersed already in my natural life. So if I were in a system where the students came from a different world, I would just have to immerse myself in their world." Mr. Jackson asserted: "You have to understand their desires, wants, and needs and dislikes . . . You have to implement that in your academics because *if they are not interested, then they are not going to learn*" (emphasis added). Clearly, there was a direct connection between the immersion of this teacher in the students' world and the learning opportunities that were available in his classroom.

As mentioned, Mr. Jackson had a genuine interest in and affection for music and hip-hop in particular, and he used this asset in his teaching. He believed that all teachers should use what they possess (themselves) as assets, as well as allow students to use what they have in the classroom as assets. As a DJ and father of three, one asset that Mr. Jackson brought into the classroom was a knowledge of and interest in hip-hop music.

MUSIC, HIP-HOP CULTURE, AND LEARNING

Teachers need to understand the music, hip-hop culture, and learning nexus, especially if their students are immersed in music and the culture of hip-hop. Understanding the connections, whether teachers agree with the genre of music or the hip-hop culture or not, can serve as a foundation for teaching and learning opportunities.

Some type of music was almost always playing in Mr. Jackson's classroom, and at times, students from other classes would stop by and look in, just to see what was being played on any particular day. The immersion of some youth in what is known as hip-hop culture makes it necessary for teachers to understand it and to build from it in the classroom.[6] There are particular ways of living associated with hip-hop culture that researchers find to be relevant to the knowledge base of teachers if they are interested in deepening their understanding of youth who operate in and through cultural frames associated with hip-hop. Urban teacher education researcher Jason Irizarry explains how drawing from hip-hop culture, rap music, and youth culture can inform teachers about working with students, especially Latino/a students, English language learners, and African American students. His study provides "examples of how a group of teachers in urban schools [embodied]" cultural characteristics associated with hip-hop culture that served as a bridge to connect teachers and students.[7] Some teachers prefer working in resistance to all forms of hip-hop culture rather than using it as a means to connect with students and to scaffold learning opportunities in different subject-matter domains. Consequently, students are often in opposition to a more mainstream culture that teachers may possess. The idea is that teachers and students locate common cultural connections to optimize instructional and learning opportunities in a social context.

When asked about the relevance and reasoning behind his implementation of music in the classroom, Mr. Jackson said: "Well, it's nothing new. It was actually used in ancient Egypt where they used drums and instruments in the classroom. I do it for a couple reasons. Number one reason is kind of selfish—I like it . . . it's like people like to go take smoke breaks or eat chocolate—I like to listen to music. And, it soothes me. It's usually jazz, sometimes some soft rock, [or] some soft R&B, but it's usually jazz, occasionally classical." He had also done some research about music and learning in the classroom. He shared his findings: "The research states that when you play soft music, it calms students down and if you continue to play it, it kind of works as association—when students take tests, and you play the same songs [as what was played when covering the material], they can remember something about the assignment [or content] through the sound of the song—through association." So, he was adamant about the place, relevance, and appropriateness of music in his classroom, having learned about its benefits through reading as well as his own experiences with his students.

It appeared that the students enjoyed the class, especially the incorporation of music, perhaps because the teacher offered something different from what typically happened in too many classrooms across U.S. society where students come in, sit down, listen to the teacher, are told what to do, have very little voice and input in the classroom, do work sheets, and are dismissed.[8] I would hear students in the hallway or in the cafeteria report that they were ready to "get to Jackson's class." They were eager to find out what was going to happen on any given day, and they especially wanted to hear the music.

One learning opportunity the students really enjoyed was what Mr. Jackson called "Science Feud," a game that served as a form of review for upcoming examinations. During these "feuds," Mr. Jackson would play music that students could dance to—music that was relevant and responsive to students' interests, such as hip-hop. And the students loved it! He explained the structure and relevance of the game, which to me was not that innovative. Like the popular game show *Family Feud*, students would answer questions about some dimension of science that had been covered in class. The "hook" was not that Mr. Jackson played music during the game or that he was conducting a review, because he constantly had music playing in the classroom, and it was expected that he would enact some form of review for math and science exams. The hook was the *particular type* of music being played. It was the kind of music the students wanted to hear—the same music they listened to during their free time at school and outside of school. Of course, the music that he played was free of profanity and vulgarity.

After dividing the class into teams, as the students walked up to the front of the room to answer a question during Science Feud, Mr. Jackson played music that the students enjoyed, typically rhythm and blues or hip-hop. Sadly, many students are forced to sit in classrooms without any real meaning or connection to what they care about, whether that is music or other interests. For Mr. Jackson, the classroom was not a place to develop complete opposition to students, but one where students could find connections and relevance to their interests outside of school. The popularity of the Science Feud outlasted the students enrolled in Mr. Jackson's class. He described how "the sixth graders I had who are now in seventh or eighth grade . . . still come by when I have it going on, and they say, 'I wanna play, I wanna play.' They like it." Mr. Jackson told me that while the students enjoyed playing the game because they wanted to listen to the music, they actually studied the material and tried to answer the questions correctly. The hook was playing the type of music during the activity that the students appreciated and found relevant. In essence, the students felt they could relax a bit while still working hard to answer the questions on the content that had been covered.

POP CULTURE, TEACHING, AND LEARNING

Popular culture informed Mr. Jackson's mind-set and practices, and I suggest that other teachers can utilize popular culture to become more tuned in to students' interests in ways that can benefit their classroom instruction and help them build connections with their students. Examples of popular culture that students may be involved with and that teachers should be aware of include the following:

- *Music:* Students enjoy listening to all kinds of music, including rap, rhythm and blues, jazz, country, and classical. Some students are even aspiring (or already successful) musicians and musical artists.
- *Movies:* Students enjoy a range of movies, including comedy, horror, drama, romance, and suspense. Some students even aspire to become professional actors and actresses and are consumed by not only the messages in the movies but also the mechanics and technicalities of moviemaking and/or directing.
- *Sitcoms:* Students also like to watch weekly television shows. They are often faithful to certain sitcoms or dramas that allow them to connect with characters and story lines.
- *Reality shows:* Television stations, such as Music Television (MTV), Bravo, Black Entertainment (BET), Oxygen, and Country Music Television (CMT), increasingly feature reality shows that allow students to follow "real" people through authentic experiences, such as dating and competitions of all kinds.
- *Video games:* Games allow students to engage in competition, either with themselves, the gaming system, or friends. They also allow students to engage their imaginations and improve their performance over time, using either a personal computer, laptop, or other gaming systems connected to their television.
- *Magazines:* Comic books, *Teen* and *Seventeen* magazine, and *Cosmopolitan,* for example, are important and relevant to some students. These magazines sometimes provide extra information about other forms of pop culture, such as what is happening on a sitcom or in the life of a reality television star.

Many students are much more interested in pop culture than in their school subjects. Linguist and language and literacy researcher James Gee reminds us that students will engage with pop culture—music, sitcoms, video games, comic books, and magazines—for hours and hours but will rush to finish their homework or not complete their homework at all.[9] Moreover, Gee, along with other language and literacy researchers, such as Jeffrey Duncan-Andrade and Ernest Morrell, provide additional insight into the kinds of information that popular culture can provide, which educators can learn from and build on in the classroom.[10] Gee stresses that video games are complex, and students actually respond to the challenge as they learn what it takes to play them. Yet in the classroom, students sometimes avoid engaging with difficult learning tasks. So what is it about video games that students are drawn to that can assist educators in designing complex learning opportunities in the classroom?

According to Gee, video games give players/students an opportunity to build a strong sense of identity. For example, players can typically choose a game or select a "man/woman" or player to play with during a game. Later a player is allowed to select another "man/woman" or player if he or she is not satisfied with the performance of the previous one. In this way, students develop an identity and are allowed to rebuild, reconstruct, or rework their identity when necessary. The opportunity to select another player is also advantageous when players "mess up" or are eliminated from a phase of the game. The idea is that players have multiple chances to succeed and move to higher levels in the gaming world (a point that will be explored in more depth later).

While teachers may resist the notion of actually "gaming" given their schedules and interests, they may find that the games allow them to relax. Also, teachers may find that when they coach a sport or serve as the faculty sponsor for a club, they are able to develop relationships with students that allow them to challenge students to succeed academically. For instance, Mr. Hall, in particular, demonstrated the power of playing one-on-one with one of his more difficult students and how that gesture opened the door to their relationship; the student began to engage more in the classroom and both Mr. Hall and the student benefited.

Gee also stresses that video games allow players to produce and create, not just consume, knowledge and information. This idea is consistent with the philosophical and theoretical ideas of Freire, who insists that learners bring a wealth of knowledge into the classroom that should be used as a foundation to construct and assemble knowledge.[11] In this sense, teachers should strive to empower and work *with* students in learning, not adapt a position that they are just pouring knowledge into students. This approach is what Freire refers to as a "banking" approach, where "the scope of action allowed to the students extends only as far as receiving, filing, and storing the deposits" they receive from teachers, who are considered the depositors of knowledge, while students are those who must be taught, or the consumers of knowledge.[12] McCutcheon maintains that teachers are not the only, or even the main, arbiters of knowledge. Students, too, are knowledgeable and should be allowed to construct, create, and produce knowledge in various learning contexts.[13]

Gee also stresses that video games allows players (learners) to engage in deeply complex problem solving. The idea is that learners must figure out multilayered matters of complexity in solving problems, which are typically based on what players have learned and been exposed to in previous phases of the game. Students usually enjoy the challenge of trying to figure out complex problems as they build on previous knowledge and experiences. Gee also asserts that video games allow students to explore and take risks without huge consequences. For example, in many games, players are allowed to start from where their last game ended, and video games always provide players with more than one "life" to live. In other words, once a player is defeated or makes an error in a game, the game does not necessarily end. There are additional opportunities for players to solve the problem or defeat an opponent, for instance. Thus, the lesson here is that students need multiple opportunities for success in the classroom, and they should be allowed to create, construct, recreate, and reconstruct their identities as they grow, mature, and develop in knowledge, ability, and skill. Students should be allowed to give their best effort to a task and feel confident that there will be opportunities for them to keep working at it without fearing that they will fail or be considered a failure—note my purposeful distinction between the two, (fail versus failure).

Gee also explains how video games are designed to guide students through various phases and dimensions of life and learning. For instance, preliminary knowledge, information, and experiences come early in the game; more elaborate and sophisticated knowledge and experience build on this information, moving to more complex forms of knowledge, expertise, and experience. The importance of building knowledge and scaffolding learning opportunities is obvious; teachers should be mindful of how they construct earlier phases of learning, then carefully craft later learning to build on those early phases.

Music is another popular cultural phenomenon, and students are able to express their preferences through the type of music they enjoy. The idea of choice is an important principle that is transferable to teaching and learning. By allowing choice, teachers can provide students with opportunities to make some decisions in the learning process. Music allows listeners to locate common identity markers with artists and song lyrics; it can provide relevant real-life lessons and also allow students to fantasize and use their imagination and creativity—all of which can be effective in the classroom.

In listening to the type of music that students listen to, either on the radio or through other media, teachers learn what students like. They use this knowledge to build lessons or just to demonstrate that they have actually heard a particular song or genre of music that is popular with their students. As Duncan-Andrade and Morrell declare: "Turn that radio up, teacher!"[14] Students are often fascinated to learn that teachers have even heard of some of the most mainstream artists, such as Jay Z, Beyonce, Taylor Swift, Common, Queen Latifah, Rascal Flats, Usher, Carrie Underwood, Justin Bieber, Trey Songz, or Will Smith.

Like video games and music, sitcoms can provide important insight into teaching and learning. They also can provide strong contextual grounding: when a program begins, actors (or teachers) must be prepared to capture the attention of the audience (students). Capturing the audience's attention immediately is crucial for both producers of television and teachers in a classroom. Sitcoms must contextualize a story or message quickly and keep viewers engaged because they have only thirty minutes to set the stage, provide the details, and resolve the story—in other words, they need to hook the audience, much in the way a teacher needs to hook her or his students' attention. Like a sitcom, teachers should also create a guiding narrative that persuasively links the different elements of the lesson covered. If successful, a sitcom will have viewers who want to discuss the story with friends and family members, and the audience will eagerly await the next episode. Would it not be refreshing if schools were places where students yearned to be and eagerly anticipated what was coming next?

Television shows of interest to students may include sporting events or weekly sitcoms. Teachers may find that they already possess some similar interests in shows, such as pivotal sporting events like the Super Bowl, NBA playoffs, Stanley Cup, March Madness, golf's Master's Tournament, the Olympics, and the World Series. What I have come to learn is that even when teachers have only a marginal interest in or knowledge of a television show, this link can provide a powerful window for teachers and students to connect.

Engaging in popular culture and learning about ways to connect lessons from popular culture into teaching and learning have potential to assist educators. However, I understand and agree with Duncan-Andrade and Morrell when they remind us that some culture is considered "high" and acceptable while other forms are considered "low."[15] Hip-hop and popular culture can be considered as low—culture that is insignificant and irrelevant to the kinds of high cultural experiences valued in learning environments. Thus, educators can struggle to see the relevance of and possibility for using music, for instance, as a cultural experience to connect with students in terms of curriculum (what they teach) and instruction (how they teach it). The reality that teachers and others see certain kinds of music and certain types of culture as high or low is infiltrated with isms and phobias—too many to name. Duncan-Andrade and Morrell queried, as do I: will schools continue to be places where students do not want to be, where they do not enjoy learning and find relevance, or will they ever be places where students really find value and relevance to their lives and experiences?

LEARNING ABOUT STUDENT INTERESTS

Developing knowledge about student interests can be essential to the kinds of learning opportunities that are relevant to students and allow them to make meaningful connections to areas of their lives that matter most to them.

Teachers may wonder how they can learn about student interests generally, not only in popular culture. It was evident that Mr. Jackson had learned how to gauge his students' interests. Other teachers who are serious about understanding student interests should consider the following techniques to gain knowledge and perspective that can be used in the design of learning opportunities in the classroom:

- Ask students about their interests by actually engaging in one-on-one and group conversation and discussion.
- Develop assignments that allow students to share their interests.
- Engage in reciprocity where teachers also share some appropriate interests with students; teacher sharing can increase the likelihood that students will feel comfortable enough to share some of their interests.

These three suggestions are excellent examples of how educators learn about student interests. It is critical, however, that teachers try not to judge student preferences in music and/or movies with questions like, "How in the world could you enjoy listening to *that*?" As Mr. Jackson learned, teachers can

- Make explicit connections between their interests in pop culture and the curriculum as well as instruction.
- Demonstrate that they have heard a song or seen a movie of interest to students. Such a demonstration can serve as a conduit for building relationships with students because students can see the teacher as a real person who actually listens to the radio, watches movies, or perhaps plays video games; some students find it difficult to perceive their teachers as "real people" who share some of their interests.

- Create opportunities for students to analyze and critique appropriate movies, music, and sitcoms through the curriculum.
- Ask students to find "companion" pieces that compare, contrast, connect, and contradict the canon or traditional forms of writing in American literature or British literature. Or use music or movies to illustrate and expand on content in other disciplines such as science, social studies/history, art, or mathematics.

In the next section, I shift the discussion to Ms. Shaw, who also diligently cultivated relationships with her students—but not through music. She worked to instill a sense of higher purpose in her students and empowered them to improve their lives and their communities.

INTRODUCING MS. SHAW

Ms. Shaw was always immaculately dressed. She frequently wore a stylish scarf to accent her attire, which was often a linen suit because it complemented the student uniforms in the Bridge School District. Ms. Shaw was teaching from the moment the class started until the students walked out the door. Her students were always engaged in some project, discussion, or writing assignment. Furthermore, I never walked into Ms. Shaw's classroom when she was not at the front of the room. She never sat at her desk, which was in the back corner. She was a master storyteller, and students seemed to hang on her every word. On a rotation basis, Ms. Shaw taught the following courses: civics, reading in the social studies, and multicultural education in the United States. She had been teaching for thirty-five years, and she had attended Bridge Middle School herself as a child.

TEACHING AS MISSION AND RESPONSIBILITY

Some teachers see their work as involving more than conveying information or facilitating learning opportunities. They perceive their work as educators

as what they were "called" to do, and thus they believe they have a responsi-
bility to their students and to the profession.

While Mr. Jackson had a deep passion for popular culture, Ms. Shaw had a much more traditional mind-set and approach to her practice at Bridge Middle School. She believed it was her responsibility and mission to teach and to help students build a skill set to facilitate their social success once they graduated from Bridge Middle School and eventually high school. She also wanted her students to develop a mission-minded approach to their decisions and actions. By mission-minded, I mean that she wanted her students to think about a broader collective purpose and about their calling in life. Ms. Shaw wanted her students to develop skills that would allow them to contribute to something beyond themselves. Ms. Shaw made it clear that it was part of her role, responsibility, and calling to empower her students to serve and to change their communities.

She attempted to empower her students to develop a critical consciousness about some of the social realities in the Bridge community that they were not necessarily aware of. She felt very strongly that there was a need for her students to develop a mind-set to serve their communities and find ways to change and improve it. Ms. Shaw, like Dr. Johnson, shared personal narratives throughout her lessons to help the students understand the content she was attempting to cover. In an interview, she shared: "Now I am almost sixty . . . when we were taught in teacher training, we had a mission. Our mission was to go out to serve . . . to reach and to help the generations." She believed that reminding students that they were on earth to make a contribution to humanity and to think about their "purpose" and contribution to society beyond their current situations and experiences was essential to their success. Encouraging students to think beyond their present mind-set and experiences became a major feature of what she perceived as her responsibility to her students. Helping students see life beyond themselves and the present was also a consistent theme of Mr. Jackson's mind-set and practices. In essence, Ms. Shaw wanted her students to recognize that they were part of a larger community (beyond Bridge Middle School) and needed to think beyond themselves when making decisions.

It was clear from my observations that Ms. Shaw believed that she was called to the work of teaching, and she attempted to cultivate relationships with all the students at Bridge Middle School. For instance, during a class period I observed, Christine, a student in Ms. Shaw's fifth period, walked into Ms. Shaw's second period with an "assignment sheet" from in-school suspension (ISS). Christine looked perplexed and sad, and it was obvious that she had been crying. Consider the following interaction I observed between Ms. Shaw and Christine:

Christine: Ms. Shaw, fill this [the assignment sheet] out. They [the administration] put me in ISS. [Tears started to flow.]

Ms. Shaw: Christine, what's going on?

Christine: I just don't like her [referring to one of her other teachers].

Ms. Shaw: Well, Christine, you will meet a lot of folks in your life you don't like. You've got to learn to work with people you don't like. It's going to be all right, though, because you are smart, and you've got to let that situation roll off your back.

Christine: I knew you were going to say that, but I still don't like her.

At this point, Christine still looked like she was deeply troubled and hurt either by being sent to ISS or by the situation she experienced with the teacher, whom she declared that she "does not like." As Ms. Shaw was gathering "assignments" for Christine to occupy her time in ISS, it appeared that she noticed the troubled look on Christine's face. It seemed that Christine was taking the situation very seriously and that it was causing her emotional distress.

Ms. Shaw: OK, Christine, sit down. Just hang out in here with me for a while. You don't need to go to ISS in this state. How is your sister doing? You know I have taught all your older sisters, and you all are smart girls. What would your sister Tonya say if she saw you all upset like this?

Christine: She would tell me to calm down.

Ms. Shaw: Exactly. Just shake this situation off, Christine. It is so not the end of the world. You will bounce back from this. How is Tonya doing?

Christine: She is fine. She just got married.

By the time Ms. Shaw finished posing questions to Christine about her sister and reassuring her that she was indeed "all right," Christine had calmed down. In fact, by the end of her exchange, Christine looked like a completely different person. She was now ready to move forward with her punishment in ISS. When I talked with Ms. Shaw about the interaction, she said she worried that, had she allowed Christine to leave her room in the state she was in, she would have run into even more problems. She felt responsible for Christine and invited her to hang out in her room until Christine was in a space to move forward. Again, she saw her work as a teacher as her mission and calling. In addition, as students made decisions and as she taught them, she reflected on the intricate and complex nature of race and its role.

REMEMBERING RACE

Although we have made significant strides in U.S. society (and consequently in schools), race is still a salient issue in society and in education. Remembering race, predesegregation, allows teachers the opportunity to gauge how far we have come but also reminds us how far we need to go in education.

Ms. Shaw also talked explicitly about race and its relevance in her practices at Bridge Middle School. In the classroom and during interviews, she reflected often on her own experiences as a student and teacher predesegregation, and she discussed how her mind-set had been shaped by the "Black community." She explained that "Black culture" had fostered a sense of community commitment, and she was taught that she should use her increasing individual influence and success in ways that contributed to society. This broader emphasis on community and change was evident in the kinds of experiences she wanted to construct for her students. Ms. Shaw's ability to think deeply about herself and her own experiences, and about how her identity construction helped ground her desires and instructional designs for her students, was consistent with the ideas Dr. Johnson emphasized.

As she related, "In the Black culture, that has also been our mission [to serve and to change/improve communities]. It was our mission and responsibility in our families and our churches and our homes . . . [When I was in grade school] we heard that in different ways . . . we heard that in sermons, [at church and] we heard it at home." Ms. Shaw regretted that a community-focused discourse did not necessarily permeate the various institutions her students would frequent: school, churches, homes, and so forth. As an ideal, she desired that her students would be focused on human and community improvement rather than on materialism and individualism (a point I will address in more depth later in this chapter).

Moreover, Ms. Shaw said her decision to design and promote a community-based orientation in her work was precipitated by the fact that she had been helped throughout her life, especially in the Black community: "And so, as I became a teacher, somebody helped me along the way; somebody showed me, and then they corrected me." As a teacher who had spent many years at Bridge, Ms. Shaw perceived all the students in the school as "my kids." She would "correct" students in the hallway or the stairwell if necessary. When I observed her correct students not in her classes, the students, who all knew her name, changed their behavior immediately. It appeared that she had gained respect from students in the Bridge school community, not only those in her classes. There was a clear theme of community improvement to Ms. Shaw's mind-set and practices as she made connections between what was happening in her life at school and what was happening to her in other spaces, such as at home, in church, and in the community.

She seemed to have a recurrent view that as an African American, her goal was to serve and improve the situations that were "unfair" and "unjust." This community emphasis was consistently reinforced in her classroom. For example, she would ask the students to think about what could have been done to improve people's situations in the past and what could be done in the present. Her class discussions were very focused on aspects of history that forced students to make explicit links to current-day situations, rather than on remembering a host of dates and names. Her focus seemed to be on skill development such as critical and analytic thinking and helping students think about important historic and current social ills, such as those related to race. Overall, though, she seemed to worry that her students had forgotten about the historic role of race in society and how racism could still manifest in their experiences. She wondered if the students were prepared for the racialized experiences they would inevitably face, especially as they moved into adulthood. In addition, she wanted her students to move beyond a focus on materialism to one more connected with service for humanity.

MOVING BEYOND MATERIALISM

Society's intense and relentless focus on material possessions can complicate priorities and create a desire for personal wealth, distracting students from more germane and important goals, such as using their resources and assets to assist others.

Ms. Shaw believed that all of her students needed to be more community focused, and she drew from her experiences as an African American to discuss why community was so important. It is important to note that she felt all her students needed to be more community focused, not just her Black students. Her references to race, though, allowed her to reflect on her own experiences growing up during a time when you "had to be" concerned about aspects of life greater than self. In addition, it was evident that her commitment to service and her efforts to promote it through her teaching were so prevalent in her work because she had attended Bridge Middle School herself and had at one time lived in her students' community. Combined with her emphasis on community and what she called her "African American culture" was her concern that students were interested in material possessions, not necessarily the knowledge and skills that had potential to improve something greater than themselves as individuals.

Ms. Shaw was committed to helping her students realize that life was about more than what one could acquire materially. She felt it was her mission and responsibility to help her students realize that they too were "responsible for their communities," and she challenged them to make changes in their communities when they witnessed something that was unfair, unjust, or simply wrong. Through the many stories she shared, her students came to realize that because Ms. Shaw had experienced life before desegregation and had experienced racism firsthand, she did not want them to take for granted all the sacrifices people before them had made on their behalf. She explained that people had died for the privileges that they were able to enjoy currently, and she believed that some of her students did not realize how close we as a country still are to desegregation and to broader, more systemic forms of discrimination, racism, and sexism. Thus, her decision to highlight community over material possessions was often couched in her reflections about times when she had substandard materials, such as "Black-only facilities and resources, used textbooks," and dilapidated educational facilities. When students did not handle their educational materials properly, she would remind them that at one point in U.S. history, Black students had only "hand-me-down" and out-of-date books.

Ms. Shaw was also deliberate in introducing her students to people from the Bridge County area and beyond who had made tremendous strides forward in their careers and communities. In other words, Ms. Shaw believed that life was not only about succeeding personally but also should have "purpose for the masses." She explained to her students that they needed to contribute to community so that it could succeed as well. She shared the experiences of then senator Barack Obama, Ruby Dee, Dr. Bobby Lovett, Reverend Andrew Young, and others. Ms. Shaw wanted her students to learn about these individuals because it allowed them to recognize their historical "journeys" and how their own journeys were inextricably tied to those they discussed in the classroom. She believed, similar to Mr. Hall, that students sometimes see the end result without recognizing that many people we celebrate have gone through hardships (including deep-rooted poverty and abuse) to get to where they are. Material possessions, she would explain, are the rewards of hard work and dedication, but many of these individuals had service as their mission, not things.

Like the other teachers in this book, Ms. Shaw saw it as her responsibility and mission to accept and serve in multiple roles. Thus, she was concerned that her students cared more about what some called "bling" than about issues that concerned the broader human condition. She believed that the media had actually "harmed" students and seduced them into concentrating on the wrong things. Such a position ran counter to Mr. Jackson's view of the role, influence, and relevance of popular culture.

ACCEPTING AND SERVING IN MULTIPLE ROLES

Although they may not yet realize it in teacher education programs, whether traditional or alternative, teachers will assume and serve in multiple roles— beyond a content-area teacher—to connect with students and meet their many and varied needs. In their practices, teachers learn that they either accept the multiple roles that students need and come to expect or work to circumvent them. Successful teachers, though, seem to understand that teaching involves much more than classroom instruction, requiring them to serve students in myriad ways and in a range of meaningful roles.

When thinking about her role in the school, Ms. Shaw embraced the idea of assuming many roles in working with her students: "There are some teachers who are saying, 'That's [serving in multiple roles] not our job,' but it becomes your job because somebody's got to take on that role [the different roles required to support students] for the students. A lot of things I didn't understand either . . . when people told us when I started teaching that you are going to be the social worker; you are going to be the parent; you are going to be the friend . . . when they said all that stuff I said 'sure,' . . . but I see that I've become that. And I can either take that role, or I can say . . . I am out of here." Thus, students enter the learning context with needs to be met, many of which teachers must address and fill. As a teacher whom one of her students referred to as her "mama," Ms. Shaw had come to assume multiple roles in her practices in order to bridge opportunity gaps, although she did not understand the multitude of these needs as a student learning to teach. In her practice with students over the years, she explained that she has taken on roles that she never thought she would need to assume as a classroom teacher.

Like all the teachers showcased in these case studies, Ms. Shaw understood that relationships were critical to her success as a teacher. When students see teachers in a role that "fits" or is responsive to one of their needs, they are willing to trust the teacher enough to learn from him or her—to push themselves to engage in materials that may have seemed difficult otherwise. Thus, the fact that Ms. Shaw performed roles that filled voids in some students' lives propelled students to open up to her and enabled her to build relationships with her students that might not have been possible otherwise.

Based on my observations, Ms. Shaw taught the students life lessons, and these life lessons often emerged from what she came to know in her own story. She made explicit connections to her students' lives outside of the school context—connections not only to their current lives but also to their lives in the future. For instance, Ms. Shaw explained to the students the importance of honesty, what was necessary to secure a good-paying job, and the importance of building and "securing" social security. In an interview she asserted: "I do want them to work, so they can get some Social Security money in the system . . . who is going to take care of you for the rest of your life? And who wants to?"

She spoke candidly with students about what happens when people do not develop knowledge and skills, and in many ways she assumed roles that allowed her to teach life lessons beyond the stated and expected curriculum. She shared real consequences with her students, which allowed them to think about realities they might not have considered without her insight. Because she was at an age where she could retire, she was attempting to provide a window for her students that allowed them to visualize what was possible as well as what the challenges could be if they were not conscious and conscientious about the decisions they made. In this sense, Ms. Shaw assumed the role of mentor or counselor because she wanted her students to think beyond their current situations and to imagine life when they could receive Social Security in retirement.

It is important to note that Ms. Shaw attempted to demystify and break down some of the anxiety many of the students may have felt about preparing for their futures. However, she was unyielding about sharing information that could impact students' current and future lives. She refused to present everything as "easy," and she explained to students that they would experience difficulties in their lives, some of which would be the consequences of matters far beyond their control. For instance, she shared with her female students that they could possibly earn less than their male counterparts in their professions. Expressing to students that they were not immortal and that life would bring challenges that they would need to be prepared to work through by building the appropriate knowledge, skills, and attitudes was something that the students seemed to appreciate.

In short, Ms. Shaw wanted her students to take their learning and lives seriously, and she was very direct with how life could be if the students did not engage, work hard, and serve. In this sense, she was no-nonsense. During my entire time studying at Bridge Middle School, I never saw Ms. Shaw send a student out of the classroom, and I never observed a student being disrespectful. The students worked, and she expected them to produce high-quality work, or she would force them to redo the assignment. I am not sure how many middle school teachers would focus their students on Social Security as a priority, but Ms. Shaw attempted to paint pictures for students that could help them think about where they were headed, demonstrating multiple options and pathways that could end with personal and community success or failure. In this way, Ms. Shaw acted as an "other mother" (see the important work of Foster and Irvine), a point that will be taken up later in this chapter.[16]

While Ms. Shaw provided concrete examples of how life could be for students in the real world, she was also careful to explain that they would not have all the answers: "They understand what their purpose here is. 'I am not here to entertain you. I am here to help you and direct learning and guide your learning.' I keep telling them I don't know everything because now there is so much information that we'll never know. So, they understand. But, I'll tell you what, I know how to learn the answer, and I'll show you how [to find the answers to problems]. So I make that clear. So I'm not all-knowing." In her role as an "other mother," she helped her students understand that they must become lifelong learners and work to discover the information that they do not know in order to succeed and solve problems. Such learning opportunities are important for students who may struggle to understand why they are on earth and what they are supposed to be doing here.

Consistently, Ms. Shaw also encouraged her students to take pride in themselves and in their school. She particularly urged her female students to take pride in themselves as young women and to think about their futures, as she wanted them to become independent and empowered to reach their goals. She stressed to both gender groups the importance of attire and appearance, and urged them to take pride in how they dressed and carried themselves because they were representing not only themselves but also their school, their parents, their ancestry, and her as their teacher.

SELF- AND SCHOOL PRIDE

When educators invest in students, empowering them to believe that they are important contributors to the broader school social context and helping students realize that they represent bodies, institutions, and people beyond themselves, students may be more willing to build pride in their school while simultaneously assembling and enhancing pride in the self.

Ms. Shaw was committed to building school pride at Bridge Middle School and to helping students build a sense of personal pride. This was important to her because many of the teachers and students in the school saw themselves as a family. One recurrent question in Ms. Shaw's classes was, "What is good citizenship at this middle school?" She wanted her students to treat others well and to reflect the positive attributes of the school when they went out in the community. Ms. Shaw believed they needed to revive and return to some of the core values that were evident before desegregation, when she was a student at Bridge Middle School: "In urban schools, we are going to have to go back—you know, in the sixties we were making so many gains, and there was so much self-pride—why? *Because we were proud of what was on the inside and not on the outside.* We have to go back to our core values. Love and respect for one another, integrity, humility, self-discipline, honesty. *And it's not that they don't have that, it's just that it can be lost in a world where 'stuff' matters more than people.* [emphasis added]"

To be clear, Ms. Shaw was not criticizing or blaming the students for a lack of character or integrity. Rather, she pointed to a society that often pushes and rewards materialism and "stuff" over people's hearts and minds. Indeed, Ms. Shaw stressed that school and self-pride was essential, and conveying this belief was one of the primary goals in her teaching. Her students seemed to buy in to these ideas, as Ms. Shaw regularly reminded them of the importance of doing what's right, even when others do not. For instance, she stressed to students who were having disagreements that they must not allow the conflicts to define who they were and who they were becoming. For her, doing what was "right" mattered more than retaliating against someone who had in their view "mistreated" or "disrespected" them. Ms. Shaw clearly assumed roles and shared information with students far beyond what was expected of her in the curriculum, because she believed that part of her role was to help students build pride in themselves as well as in the Bridge Middle School community. School pride, in her opinion, would translate into students having pride in their home communities.

BLACK TEACHERS AND TEACHING

Mr. Jackson and Ms. Shaw attempted to address opportunity gaps among their students at Bridge Middle School, although they did not discuss their efforts in those terms. Dr. Johnson, too, was addressing opportunity gaps, although her setting was very different from the context that Mr. Jackson and Ms. Shaw experienced. Their mind-sets and practices were consistent with and extends an established body of research about Black teachers and their teaching. Much has been written about Black teachers—their experiences, their curriculum development, and their teaching in public school classrooms, both pre- and postdesegregation.[17] For example, Siddle-Walker makes the following observation in her analysis of African American teachers during segregation:

> Consistently remembered for their high expectations for student success, for their dedication, and for their demanding teaching style, these [Black] teachers appear to have worked with the assumption that their job was to be certain that children learned the material presented.[18]

The Black teachers presented in the research literature worked overtime to help their students learn. Although teaching during segregation, these teachers were preparing their students for a world of desegregation.[19] Siddle-Walker's research is consistent with the mind-set and approach of Mr. Jackson and Ms. Shaw. They both were preparing students for experiences they currently could not even imagine they would encounter. Moreover, as educational administration researcher Linda Tillman explains, "These Black teachers saw potential in their Black students, considered them to be intelligent, and were committed to their success."[20] They saw their roles and responsibilities as reaching far beyond the hallways of their schools, and the teachers had a mission to teach their students because they realized the possible consequences for their students if they did not teach them and if the students did not learn.

Research suggests that "Black educators are far more than physical role models, and they bring diverse family histories, value orientations, and experiences to students in the classroom, attributes often not found in textbooks or viewpoints often omitted."[21] Thus, Black teachers (like teachers from other racial and ethnic backgrounds) in a sense are texts themselves, and the pages of their texts are filled with histories of racism, sexism, and oppression, as well as strength, perseverance, and success. These "texts" are rich and empowering, and they have the potential to help students understand the world and change the world.[22] This is evident in Ms. Shaw's stressing that she was unyielding in her goal to have her students change and improve the world. Historically, Black teachers have had a meaningful impact on Black students' academic and social success because they deeply understood their students' situations and their needs, both inside and outside of the classroom, in no small part because they lived in the same communities. However, it is important to note that Black teachers are successful not only with students of African descent but with those from other racial and ethnic backgrounds.

The research suggests that Black teachers maintain high expectations for their students,[23] and they empathize with rather than pity the students who are not succeeding academically and socially.[24] Also, the research literature suggests that many Black teachers do not accept mediocrity, and they *insist* that their students reach their full capacity. Having such high expectations gives students the best chance to mobilize themselves and their families and communities. Moreover, these teachers understand that allowing students to just get by could leave them in their current (negative) situation or even worse.

The care and concern of Black teachers has been described as "other mothering" or "other parenting" in that teachers take on a parental role, as did Mr. Jackson, Dr. Johnson, and Ms. Shaw.[25] The research literature stresses that Black teachers, especially in mostly Black and urban schools, adopt and display a surrogate parental role for their students. In other words, the teachers want the best for their students—just as they would want for their own biological children. Students can sense teachers' commitment and care for them. Students recognize when there is unnecessary distance between them and their teachers. Students may question: "Why should I adhere to this teacher's requests and desires when she or he does not really care about me?" Students often act defiantly in order to distance themselves from what they perceive as uncaring and disrespectful teachers. This may continue until teachers and students negotiate the level of care and commitment necessary for all to succeed in an academic environment.

In figure 4.1, I provide a summary of some of the major features of Mr. Jackson and Ms. Shaw's mind-sets and practices as they attempted to

FIGURE 4.1

Summary of teachers' mind-sets and practices to address opportunity gaps

To address opportunity gaps, the teachers in this chapter:

Stressed the value and importance of learning: Teachers explicitly conveyed the importance and value of education and learning to students. They helped students understand and embrace the reality that one can be smart and intelligent and, at the same time, cool and hip.

Immersed themselves in students' lifeworlds: Teachers attempted to understand what it meant to live in the world of their students through music, sports, film, and pop culture. They incorporated this knowledge and understanding into the learning opportunities in the classroom.

Incorporated pop culture: Teachers understood the multiple layers of popular culture that students were interested in outside of school. They incorporated this understanding in developing relevant and responsive lessons for students.

Did more with fewer resources: Teachers did not allow what they did not have to hinder their efforts, goals, and visions for their students. They did whatever it took to succeed and for their students to succeed; they never gave up, even when resources were scarce.

Rejected deficit notions: Teachers concentrated on the assets that students brought into the classroom and built on those assets in the learning contexts. They also understood their own assets as teachers and used those as a foundation to bridge opportunity gaps in the classroom.

Understood equity in practice: Teachers understood the difference between equality and equity. They worked to meet the needs of individual students and realized that their curriculum and instruction might not be exactly the same among all students at all times but would depend on the particular needs of each student.

Built and sustained relationships: Teachers understood that students needed to get to know them and that they needed to get to know their students. They saw their teaching as members of a family affair and viewed their students as their own family. In other words, they engaged in "other mothering" and "other fathering."

(continued)

FIGURE 4.1 *(continued)*

Summary of teachers' mind-sets and practices to address opportunity gaps

Understood power structures among students: Teachers understood that there were power structures among the students. They recruited popular students to embrace the vision of learning and engagement in the classroom in order to get other students engaged and motivated to learn.

Understood the self in relation to others: Teachers assembled knowledge and understood points of intersection and convergence between themselves and their students. They used this knowledge and understanding to build and sustain relationships in the classroom.

Granted students entry into teachers' worlds: Teachers allowed students to learn things about them and made connections to demonstrate the commonalities that existed between students and teachers. They shared stories with their students and allowed them to share theirs in order to build community, collective knowledge, and points of reference.

Conceived of school as a community with family: Teachers conceived of school as a community that was established by all those in the environment. They allowed students to have voice and perspectives in how the community would be defined. Teachers respected and cared about those in the community as if they were family members.

Dealt with the presence of race and culture: Teachers rejected color-blind, culture-blind, and diversity-blind ideologies. They saw themselves and their students as racial and cultural beings and used that knowledge in working with students and in teaching them.

Perceived teaching as mission and responsibility: Teachers cared deeply about their students and developed mission-minded approaches that allowed students to reach their potential. They saw teaching as their calling and took it personally when students did not succeed academically.

Developed critical consciousness: Teachers critiqued the knowledge and information available. They consciously fought against injustice; they spoke out against inequity both inside and outside of the classroom and empowered students to do the same.

address and close opportunity gaps at Bridge Middle School. Moreover, the figure captures some of the findings regarding effective teaching already established in the research literature.

5

White Teachers Learning to Teach

Bittersweet Challenges—
and Possibilities—
in Teacher Preparation

I HAVE BEEN DELIBERATE in my decision to conclude my discussion of teachers' mind-sets and practices as they relate to student opportunity gaps by focusing on teachers, mostly White educators, who are learning to teach. Teacher education researcher Christine Sleeter poignantly asserts that we who work in teacher education should "research backwards" to gain insight into about preparation of teachers.[1] By "researching backwards," Sleeter suggests that we focus on promising and successful teacher practices in P–12 classrooms, and then adjust and transform the teacher education curriculum, pedagogy, and related learning experiences (such as student teaching) accordingly. A persistent challenge in addressing and hopefully closing opportunity gaps in P–12 classrooms has to do with how teachers are educated, whether in traditional or nontraditional teacher education programs.

Teachers education—where teachers are prepared to meet the instructional needs of all their students—should be thought of as an ongoing imperative.[2] Like educational experiences in other fields, such as social work, medicine, or engineering, teachers' learning does not (and should not) end when they graduate from a teacher education program.[3] Learning continues inservice, while teachers are actually working in P–12 classrooms. The cases presented in the preceding chapters have provided what I hope are powerful insights into the complexities that real teachers and students face in addressing opportunity. In this chapter, I turn to challenges teacher education confronts in preparing teachers to develop (1) the mind-set to understand opportunity gaps and (2) practices that will address them. Of course, the opportunity gaps that I have discussed and consider so important for all students are those related to diversity and teaching.

In the first part of this chapter, I draw insights from six White teachers learning to teach for diversity and opportunity. Based on my work over the last decade, I believe these teachers provide a representative sample of the kinds of challenges and promise that teacher education must engage, with a focus on the diversity-opportunity connection. I then discuss the complex roles that teacher educators play in the education of teachers. I assert that we need to look carefully at who teaches in teacher education and how and if they address the opportunity-diversity convergence in their education of teachers. I also outline some structural and systemic challenges that we in teacher education sometimes face, and how those challenges can block efforts to implement and reform teacher education programs.

CHALLENGES IN TEACHER EDUCATION

Both traditional and nontraditional teacher education programs face many serious challenges, some of which are substantiated while others are not. At the heart of many of the criticisms of teacher education are these arguments:

- Teacher education programs are not rigorous enough.
- Teacher education programs do not provide enough subject-matter knowledge for teachers to convey that content successfully in the classroom.

- Teacher education programs have not shown sufficient evidence that teacher "training" actually correlates with P–12 student outcomes— mainly scores on standardized tests.
- There is too much variation among different teacher education programs in their coverage of content and necessary practices that teachers should acquire.

A recurrent national debate among many in teacher education concerns the type and structure of programs that prepare teachers for P–12 teaching—traditional or nontraditional. For instance, studies suggest that particular teacher education programs (university-based versus alternative) are better than others, based on P–12 students' performance on standardized tests, teacher persistence and attrition rates, and teachers' self-efficacy (see, for instance, Darling-Hammond, Chung, and Frelow).[4] This debate is serious, but it appears that at present neither structure (university-based or alternative) is going to vanish. Thus, because teachers will be trained through different teacher education structures, it seems that our energies should be focused on developing these structures in ways that enable each program to maximize preparation for P–12 teaching.

INTRODUCING THE TEACHERS

The six White female teacher candidates (hereafter *teachers*) provide information about the challenges of preparing teachers, particularly how to empower them with the knowledge and skill to address opportunity gaps and diversity. Their backgrounds and experiences are representative of the kinds of perspectives that I have come to know as a teacher educator, having worked in different teacher education programs over the last nine years. For instance, I have taught in at least three traditional teacher education programs and have conducted dozens of professional development workshops for practicing inservice teachers; most of these workshops centered on issues of opportunity and diversity. Some of the data I share emerged from a course I coplanned and cotaught with a colleague,

Margaret Smithey, several years ago.[5] While my colleague and I engaged in some research regarding our teaching experience in the course about diversity, I alone conducted and analyzed the interviews with teachers. In some cases, I share that data in this chapter.

The teachers showcased in this chapter represent an important range of diversity. Rather than attempting to provide individual characteristics of each teacher, I focus instead on common themes that emerged among them. It is important to note that I do not mean to suggest that all White teachers are the same. Teacher education researcher Judson Laughter reminds us of the danger of treating all White preservice teachers as a monolithic group.[6] His research reveals significant diversity among White teachers, and he cautions against developing frameworks and designs that do not consider the variation among White teachers. Thus, those of us in teacher education must look beyond basic stereotypes to determine who White teachers are and what their challenges and successes happen to be. A more nuanced view is always appropriate when working to determine particular worldviews, perspectives, and behaviors. Thus, I have chosen to identify the teachers in a group of six for the sake of space and overall perspective, not because I believe they are the same based on the fact that they are all White.

TROUBLING THE RELEVANCE OF DIVERSITY AND MAKING SOMETHING OUT OF NOTHING

Although teachers may read in textbooks or hear in lectures that teaching involves developing a conceptual repertoire related to understanding diversity, many of them still do not believe it will matter in their particular classroom. Many White teachers who attended largely racially and ethnically homogeneous (White) schools, for instance, aspire to and believe that they will return to their hometowns and teach in very similar schools. While they accept the reality that diversity matters for some teachers, they struggle to see how diversity matters for them. Consequently, teachers sometimes believe that emphasizing diversity is disadvantageous because it forces them to think

about issues that really do not or will not exist in their particular situations.
They fear that they are "making something out of nothing." Unfortunately,
these teachers sometimes do not realize that they may not be able to return to
their "dream" job or school. They may indeed teach in one of "those" highly
diverse or urban schools.

Fundamentally, many of the White teachers did not understand the relevance of diversity and teaching because they attended what they believed to be pretty homogeneous schools themselves (whether public or private).[7] In fact, my experience working to prepare these teachers revealed that many teachers did not see themselves as racial or cultural beings. They saw others as having a race or a culture, and they used themselves as the racial and cultural norm or standard by which others should be compared. That is, some saw (1) themselves, particularly White middle-class people, as the norm, (2) others as "diverse" or having a distinctive culture or race, and (3) a focus on diversity and teaching as irrelevant. Some teachers found it annoying, to a degree, that an emphasis would be placed on diversity because their worldview and frames of reference had not required such an emphasis, and they struggled to envision how diversity would play any real role or purpose in their professional lives as teachers.

It was difficult for some of the teachers to shift from mind-sets and ideas they had developed when they were students themselves—that is, to shift from thinking as a P–12 student to thinking as a teacher. Like Mr. Hall, teachers with whom I have worked over the years found it troubling that they would need to exert their energy thinking about diversity and teaching. As noted, one persistent problem regarding opportunity gaps is teachers' beliefs that it is not necessary or appropriate for them to see race, recognize how diversity matters, or understand the salience of diversity and teaching in the P–12 classroom. I have argued throughout this book that such avoidance in fact *contributes* to opportunity gaps. Many teachers had a "prove to me that diversity is worth my time" mentality. When teachers have such a mind-set, too much time can be spent in a teacher education course on trying to make a case for *why* diversity matters, rather than focusing on *what teachers can do* in their practices to address diversity and opportunity, and *how they can do it.*

The discourse of many courses I have taught over the years begins with *why* diversity really matters and *why* teachers should be concerned about it. This initial focus is logical. However, even after several weeks of my demonstrations on the importance of diversity, as shown through research articles and video clips, and despite their own observations of diverse classroom settings, some White teachers still hold on to persistent questions about the relevance of a diversity focus; they essentially want to "just teach math" or "just teach reading," and help their students "become good at it." It is true that when teachers observed or taught in diverse and/ or urban schools (through student teaching or practicum experiences, for instance), the emphasis on diversity in their teacher education program became more logical to them. However, there remained a recurrent wonder and frustration about how a focus on diversity would really matter in the grand scheme of teaching and learning. When asked during an interview how diversity mattered or would matter in her teaching, one teacher explained, "I don't think it did [matter] as much the first part of the semester because of the population I was with. I was teaching in [Oxford County] and the population was very much White. I had a class of twenty-two. I had two African American students and one from Vietnam. Everyone else was White. So I think I was thinking about it but again, that was part of my frustration at the beginning of the course where I felt like I had a lot more going on besides talking about diversity and cultures, and different cultures and how to consider that when you're teaching. But now my current . . . fifth-grade placement at [Jonesboro County is] about fifty-fifty [Black-White]. So it really is much more evident to me—the different cultures that are in my classroom. And I have thought about it."

Interestingly, the field experiences of the six teachers showcased in this chapter played a substantive role in terms of how they thought about the diversity focus in the teacher-education classroom. Similar to Dr. Johnson's experiences at Stevenson High School in a predominantly White social context, the six White teachers all seemed to feel that focusing on aspects of diversity and opportunity was irrelevant, inconsequential, and useless in their mostly White teaching and observation contexts. In many ways, the teachers in this chapter perceived the White students as "normal," and when they changed field sites to more "diverse" spaces, they began to see more clearly why we would be discussing anything beyond how to teach a particular subject matter in P–12. Teachers continued to point to firsthand experiences, whether through student teaching, practicum experiences, or personal experiences in contexts with an enormous range of diversity, as essential to their mind-sets and willingness to try different pedagogical and curriculum strategies in the P–12 classroom. One teacher reported, "[One of my teaching experiences] had English language learners from nine different countries. So, I've really had the opportunity to test out a lot of things we've been talking about in class and try and formulate my own opinions on them."

Not only was there a pervasive theme of "prove to me that diversity matters," there was also a concern that emphases on diversity may have been making them paranoid, or, as one teacher explained, "unnecessarily suspicious" and "obsessed" about it. Teachers worried that focusing "so much attention" on diversity would force them to see and think about issues that were not really there but were constructed through images that were painted in the teacher education classroom. One teacher maintained that she was concerned we were "making something out of nothing" by focusing on matters of race in particular. In her words, "I thought if you spend too much time on it—I think that maybe sometimes you can make things an issue that aren't an issue. And I don't know if that's just ignorance and my own lack of awareness and whatever." I discovered several of the teachers felt that attention to race and diversity meant that they would start "seeing things" and making up diversity-related matters that did not really exist or would not exist in the classroom when they began teaching.

For example, the same teacher stated: "Like I had a group of boys . . . they were all African American, and they all hung out together, but they were never hostile or mean or exclusive to anybody else. And nobody felt threatened by them. I wouldn't have thought anything of it. But now that we've talked about race and all that 'stuff' I was trying to figure out, why are they doing that [hanging out together]?"

This teacher's concern has been echoed by others I have taught over the years. Rather than perceiving her experience in a positive light, as one that allowed her to push herself to think about the underlying meaning of the "boys hanging out together," she was a bit suspicious and questioned why she was being guided to think about something that might not be a real issue. Frustrated, she explained further: "I don't know if it was anything that I even needed to think about because it didn't seem to cause any problems." The idea of racial and ethnic groups of students hanging out together to the exclusion of others is not a trivial social phenomenon. In her important book, *"Why Are All the Black Kids Sitting Together in the Cafeteria?" And Other Conversations About Race,* Spelman College president and psychologist Beverly Tatum poses this very question and then offers important insights into the kinds of support such groups provided for each other.[8] However, a group of Black students I approached with the same question at one school wondered why anyone would pose such a question to Black students. They then begged for an answer to another question they posed to me: "Why are all the White kids sitting together in the cafeteria?"

Another teacher remarked that it was important "not [to] specifically [make] problems where they didn't exist" and not "to make a big deal about it [race and diversity]." These six teachers often reflected back on their experiences as P–12 students and how similar they were to their classmates. While observing a "diverse" classroom, they were open to discussing race and diversity as they related to their mind-set, classroom practices, and the kinds of learning opportunities they would be able to offer their P–12 students, but they still were not convinced that diversity and opportunity were linked. As one student declared, "If a problem does come up, I don't want to automatically think it's something that I need to encourage and bring up . . . I've definitely learned how to relate to different people . . . to try to figure out what method works for each student . . . but I worry that I'm going to make a big deal . . . If there is a problem, if there is a conflict, then I'm just going to automatically attribute it to [issues of diversity]." Indeed, this teacher's point makes sense. Sometimes experiences well beyond those related to diversity are at the core of what is happening with students. Still, another student promised me in her interview that she certainly refused to "make problems where they didn't exist," and it seemed that the six White teachers showcased in this chapter were actually looking for reasons why a diversity- or race-centered rationale for what they experienced was inappropriate and incorrect.

FEARFUL TO JUST SAY IT

Some societal wisdom would suggest that the best way to address difficult issues is to ignore them—and certainly not to talk about them. Such a position—to avoid using particular words or to avoid certain topics—can actually result in unexamined mind-sets and practices that can leave teachers feeling hopeless. They may question the degree to which there is any hope of addressing particular topics because they feel disempowered to use particular words or phrases in a teacher education course or program, or even in a faculty meting once they have begun teaching. Teachers can be fearful that they will be ostracized or judged for their positions on difficult topics that are sometimes politically charged.

For many of the six teachers, it was difficult to even say the word *race* or to use terms like *Black*, *Latino/a*, *African American*, or *White*—especially early in a course. I have also observed that teachers can struggle to use words such as *immigration*, *President Obama*, *power*, *privilege*, and *oppression*. In class one day, I used the word *nigger*, explaining what I heard from a high school student as he was reciting the lyrics to a popular hip-hop song. Several teachers expressed how surprised they were that I felt comfortable using "that word," even in the context of quoting another. One teacher declared that he was never allowed to use such language growing up in his home and that he felt completely uncomfortable voicing the word, even when quoting. Ironically, the same teacher, adamant that he never used the word, admitted that his friends sometimes used the word *nigger* when sharing jokes. This teacher rationalized that it was acceptable for his friends because they were "just joking around."

Clearly, we socially construct words and phrases and give them power and meaning. I am not suggesting that teachers and teacher educators should not be mindful in selecting their words. However, when teachers are afraid to express certain words or phrases because they are concerned about being judged, they can miss out on promising opportunities to unpack mind-sets and belief systems that can be much more devastating to P–12 students than a teacher's use of an uncomfortable word or phrase. Other adults can serve as critical partners in helping them work through lingering issues. In short, I believe it is a disadvantage in teacher education when we hold White teachers' language hostage because of some power we have given to words. We should be focusing instead on the particular intention behind the words being used.

Teachers also are concerned that they will be considered politically incorrect if they use certain words. I have found that this fear has stifled important conversations that have the potential to expand teachers' mind-sets, particularly regarding diversity and opportunity gaps in P–12 classrooms. My observations suggest that teachers worry they will say something that will offend others, and they consciously avoid conversations about the very issues they should be grappling with in their teaching practices, such as what it means that their own parents called lesbians "dykes" when they were younger.

RACE AND RACISM—HISTORICAL AND FAMILIAL ROOTS

Much of what we learn about race and racism comes from family members (and our parents in particular). Attempting to gauge how educators have held on to deeply ingrained racist beliefs can help them work through them. While teachers may admit that their parents have held racist beliefs and views about others and have used racist language, they often fail to equate that language with actions. Inappropriately, teachers separate the racist language they have heard from their parents from racist acts. They fail to understand that language is indeed action.

While one teacher, as described in the previous section, expressed that he was never allowed to use what he called the "*n*-word" growing up, some teachers in this study confirmed what I have suspected and what the research literature has substantiated: teachers' views on race, racism, and other forms of prejudice are often rooted in their historical experiences, particularly within their families. Several of the six teachers showcased in this chapter reported that they had heard racist, sexist, and homophobic comments from their parents growing up. Rarely, though, did they report instances when they actually witnessed some actions of racism or sexism from their parents. Perhaps it is this disconnect—the fact that teachers did not equate words or mind-sets with action—that made it difficult for teachers to understand how their mind-sets, language, and beliefs could shape their practices. In terms of her familial roots, one teacher explained that her mother would express "racist" and "prejudiced" views about different groups of people, such as African Americans. The potency of parental views can have a lingering influence. Take, for instance, the number of people who continue to vote a parent's political party or who follow a parent's religious preferences long into adulthood. One teacher remarked how her mother would have "lost it" if she had decided to date a "Black guy" during high school. When asked if it would have mattered if the "Black guy" had been an honor student, she did not hesitate in her reply: "No."

Another teacher explained that she had come to believe that her mother was racist when she was growing up: "I [have been] worried by what I learned and understood about racial injustice and equality . . . [because of] my own mother's racial prejudice." Interestingly, it appeared that these two teachers' reflections about their mothers' "racial prejudice" seemed to have resulted in a desire to fight against it. In short, for a few teachers, reflection on some negative, insensitive, or inappropriate statement, action, experience, or mind-set, such as sexism, resulted in their wanting to be the opposite. This same teacher expressed: "I want my children to grow up in an integrated environment rather than the racial isolation I experienced growing up . . . I don't want my children to be racist, and they will not hear me talk in this [racist] way."

Promising experiences that seemed to disrupt deep-rooted familial issues related to race were those that placed teachers in real-life situations that required them to confront diversity personally, head-on. For instance, as explained previously, the teachers appeared to open up a bit when they observed a highly diverse teaching context. Experiences that placed White teachers in spaces they were unaccustomed to gave them opportunities to think about and question the roots of their experiences and how their lives had been shaped by particular norms and expectations not necessarily shared by all. One teacher explained that she had to be placed in a situation where she was the "minority" to recognize the kind of person and teacher she aspired to become: "I think very early on I was confronted with [racism], particularly from my mother . . . She was a very prejudiced lady, and I know that that influenced me early on." She went on to relate a real-life experience she had in the Peace Corps: "Right before I came to this program, I was with the Peace Corps for awhile, and that was my first opportunity of being a minority. And that probably was the main push to where I feel that I am today. Without that experience I would probably be a lot closer to the way I was raised, my background . . . So I think that that helped me to where I am today."

It is difficult to understand the struggles teachers have in making the diversity-opportunity connection without understanding their personal developmental trajectory and also how their familial experiences have molded their thinking and practices. Several teachers I worked with over the years have pointed explicitly to the negative "racist" and "prejudiced" experiences they had with their parents over the years, and examining these roots seems critical to understanding how to prepare White teachers (and all teachers) to address opportunity and diversity in the P–12 classroom.

I turn in the next several sections to the kinds of mind-sets and practices exhibited by some of the six White teachers that demonstrated the potential of addressing the diversity-opportunity connection. Like the exemplary teachers discussed in the previous chapters, many of the teachers with whom I worked over the years demonstrated the kinds of understanding, commitment, and development that I believe will prove essential in their becoming successful teachers of all students. Several teachers with whom I worked began their teacher education programs with some of the problematic issues described earlier in the chapter, but they progressed to achieve mind-sets and practices that can provide a solid foundation for their successful teaching practices.

CULTURAL CONNECTIONS AND ROLE MODELS

There is pedagogical promise when educators recognize the value in P–12 students having teachers with their racial and cultural background. When students interact with and are taught by someone from the same racial and cultural background, they are able to relate to the teacher through common experiences that boost students' confidence and sense of self-efficacy.

Although I recognize there is no such thing as a distinct African American culture, European American culture, or Asian American culture, the six teachers showcased in this chapter confounded race and ethnicity with culture when they discussed their positions. The teachers struggled to understand that there was no single African American culture. Similarly, Ms. Shaw, in the previous chapter, talked explicitly about her experiences in an "African American culture." However, the term *African American* denotes an ethnic group of people, not a singular, static cultural group; there is a wide range of diversity among African Americans although there are some consistencies inherent to the group. African Americans share a history of slavery, Jim Crow, and other forms of systemic discrimination, oppression, and racism that binds the group. They also possess a shared history of spiritual grounding, strength, intellect, and resilience through some of the most horrific situations that human beings have had to endure. However, while there are shared experiences, there are also many differences among people of the same race and ethnicity. Those differences can be vast; compare, for example, former secretary of state Condoleezza Rice and National Football League player Michael Vick (currently playing for the Philadelphia Eagles). The differences between these two African Americans are significantly greater than those of gender. It is critical that readers of this book do not essentialize or generalize the points discussed about any one racial or ethnic group. Readers should not consider the ideas discussed about any group to be static and pejorative.

When teachers understood the opportunity-diversity convergence, they started to understand micro- (classroom), meso- (institutional), and macro- (societal) level matters that had some influence over what happened to students. One teacher reported her concern about the low number of African American role models available for African American students in her school. She explained that she had developed a deeper understanding of what it meant to students to have role models of the same race or ethnicity in school. In her practicum site, she began to consider the enormous void of same-ethnicity mentors available to African American students in her school. She explained: "I worry that my African American students see so few positive role models that are their race in school. After our discussions in seminar, I have really begun to wonder what kind of message it is sending to our African American students . . . " The teacher went on to explain that many of the African American adults in her school were there in service roles: custodial and cafeteria workers in particular. The low numbers of African Americans in teaching positions in the school began to "worry" her because she was concerned about her Black students' ability to relate and connect to Black adults outside of service roles.

The teacher maintained how important role models had been in her own experiences as a "White girl" in school and how her teachers had even inspired her to become a teacher. In her words: "Growing up, I never had an African American teacher or principal. Actually, all of my principals and teachers were White. I never had an Asian or Hispanic teacher or principal either." However, she did have important connections with her White teachers and principals, and she believed that many of her Black students lacked this opportunity, which was problematic in her view. While her critique and concern appeared initially on the micro level as she reflected on the classroom environment, a more nuanced review of her concern suggested that she wondered about the school and district levels of effort to increase the numbers of African American teachers in her school. She questioned: "What are they [the district] going to do about this void for these kids?" Through empathy for her students, this teacher had developed the type of mind-set that I believe has potential for how she might approach her work in the future; she put herself in her African American students' shoes, a cognitive, conceptual, and affective shift that was not easy for many of the teachers with whom I worked.

POWER AND PROMISE OF TEACHING A BILINGUAL TEXT

There appears to be power and promise when teachers provide students opportunities to learn using bilingual texts. English language learners as well as native English speakers have opportunities to complement the learning available in a reading selection. In this way, bilingual texts can enhance learning opportunities in a classroom.

One teacher actually incorporated what she referred to as "Mexican culture" into her lessons in the classroom. She explained: "I just recently did this project with my kids. It was like Cinderella stories from different countries, and one of the stories was a Mexican Cinderella, and my girls from Mexico really wanted to have that story. So it was something that they could relate to." The teacher discovered firsthand that her Latina students could "relate to" the story; they got excited about reading it in their first language, Spanish. She explained that the Latina students "had a bunch of other people in their group as well . . . Part of the book was written in Spanish, and so they said they liked learning in Spanish along with the book, too. So that kind of opened my eyes as well. It was something that the girls from Mexico could relate to."

The teacher reported that the Mexican students felt very confident about the sections of the book written in Spanish, and they seemed to appreciate the opportunity to learn from a bilingual text. The teacher continued: "It made them [the Latina students] feel a little bit more comfortable, I think. It was also kind of an eye-opening experience for other people [students] . . . We talked a lot about how they're similar to the story that they know and how they're different. And we also talked about why those differences are there." Furthermore, the Latina students were able to be the authority on the text, and it provided them space to showcase some of their expertise with their classmates, such as knowing how to speak and read Spanish fluently. Thus, this experience suggests that the teacher started to see the promise in incorporating some bilingual texts in her classroom for the benefit of her students, especially her Latina students.

DANGERS OF STEREOTYPING AND EXPECTATIONS

Teachers can have good intentions about the instructional and curricular needs of students but actually do more harm than good if they begin to stereotype certain groups and lower their expectations such that these students are not meeting and exceeding the broader school, district, and state expectations.

Although I was always concerned that teachers could develop generalizations and stereotypes about students from any gender, racial, or ethnic background or group, I learned that at least four of the six teachers showcased in this chapter began to develop the heart to teach all students effectively. These teachers generally had good intentions, and although all of them seemed to struggle to understand how to meet the needs of all their students most effectively, their hearts seemed to be in the right place.

Unfortunately, good intentions gone wrong can dangerously affect students' academic, intellectual, and social success, in both the short and long term.[9] For instance, one teacher shared with me an experience related to assessment that I believe was potentially risky for her students: "I learned in my last teaching placement with a majority of African American students [that] they're very much more towards verbal learning. A couple of times I gave them a choice of assessments, written or verbal, and they almost always chose to tell me verbally."

The promising aspect of this teacher's words and conceptions about her African American students and assessment was that she attempted to recognize her students' strengths and be responsive to them. Many teachers would have continued with business as usual, failing to recognize that assessments by nature often measure only one dimension of what students know. While her realization was problematic in some ways, the teacher above learned from her students that they performed better on verbal assessments than on written ones. However, given the myopic ways those in power in education think about assessment, it is reasonable to ask whether this teacher was setting the African American students up for failure by not forcing them to follow the norm of written assessment. Unfortunately, P–12 schools shortchange students who fall outside the realm of what educators and others in power believe to be acceptable, normal, and appropriate forms of assessment: pencil and paper tests.

Moreover, was this teacher stereotyping the African American students she described as "very much more towards verbal learning"? Could it be that her African American students preferred to complete the verbal assessment because it required less effort and not because they were not capable of completing the written assessment? This teacher summed up the reality for many teachers when she stated, "If you're not paying attention to those things [how students learn and are assessed], then you're shortchanging that student if you're not looking at how they learn [and demonstrate that learning] the best." I would add to her position that if teachers are not paying attention to broader, more systemic, and structural realities that guide student performance and outcomes, such as the ways in which students are assessed, then they could potentially do more harm than good—even though the teachers have good intentions.

For teachers to understand the complexities just described, teacher educators themselves must know what issues to address with teachers and how. I address the role of teacher educators in teacher education in the next section.

TEACHER EDUCATORS IN TEACHER EDUCATION

While teacher educators have made important strides in preparing teachers for the diversity and opportunity gaps they may encounter in P–12 schools, we cannot assume that teacher educators, in general, are committed to such a focus. Like teachers, teacher educators are diverse themselves and have varying positions on what the focus of teacher education courses and programs should be.

Thus far, I have shared some of the challenges and the promise demonstrated by six White teachers. My work with them is representative of the kinds of experiences and insights I have had during my time working with teachers on developing mind-sets and practices related to the opportunity-diversity nexus connection. I turn now to discuss teacher educators. Preparing teachers to address the opportunity-diversity nexus is difficult work. While it may seem easy to critique teachers learning to teach, those of us preparing teachers also need to examine ourselves in our quest to educate teachers to teach all P–12 students well. Cochran-Smith stresses the importance of teacher educators investigating themselves and their own practices as they attempt to understand the teachers with whom they work.[10] For instance, she examined her own work and her teachers' constructions of race and was able to shed light on the complexities inherent in the teaching and examination of race in teacher education. Indeed, I have come to understand that "it is important for all teacher educators and others who work with pre/inservice teachers, especially those of us who take on issues of race and racism as part of our pedagogical project, to consider the ways in which we participate in and promote, albeit tacitly, White privilege."[11]

Preparing teachers to teach can indeed be vexingly complicated work in general, and preparing teachers to teach for diversity and increased opportunity for P–12 students can prove even more difficult. Because people enter teacher education programs with a range of needs, there is no one-size-fits-all program or practice. Cochran-Smith maintains that she had "become *certain only of uncertainty* [emphasis added] about how and what to say, whom and what to have student teachers read and write, and about who can teach whom, who can speak for or to whom, and who has the right to speak at all about the possibilities and pitfalls of promoting a discourse about race and teaching."[12]

Much of Cochran-Smith's concern focuses on how to develop a teacher education curriculum and related experiences that will successfully prepare teachers for life in the P–12 classroom. As discussed earlier, teachers' responses to racialized and diversity-centered curricula in teacher education vary. For instance, in my own work, which is consistent with Cochran-Smith's research, teachers' responses to diversity/race-central discussions, assignments, and activities on the classroom level ranged widely: some were receptive and reported new insights and consciousness relative to their P–12 students' needs; others were resentful and did not understand why such topics are necessary. When teachers' responses follow the latter—frustration by a focus on diversity or race—research suggests that resentment can overshadow the effort put forth by teacher educators. Brown wrote:

> Resentment is frequently reflected on teacher evaluations, whereas resistance is apparent in inadequate pre-class preparation, reluctance to engage in class discussions and activities, and a lack of commitment to required cross-cultural interactions and research.[13]

However, teachers alone cannot be blamed for their development and experience in a teacher education program or course. Teacher educators themselves must be prepared to structure teacher education programs in ways that allow teachers to develop and not to feel silenced or manipulated into situations that are inconsistent with how they have come to see and experience the world. For instance, teachers' resistance can result in their silence in the face of important information about racism, injustice, diversity, and inequity. This silence can manifest because teachers believe they are being forced to think in a certain way, which counters the idea that all in a teacher education classroom should feel empowered to voice their positions and to construct knowledge and ways of knowing.[14]

Still, the racial backgrounds, knowledge, experiences, and mind-sets of teacher educators themselves and how they understand and position themselves pedagogically and philosophically in the education of teachers should be considered in teacher education courses and programs. In other words, it is wrong to assume that teacher educators are automatically committed to preparing teachers to meet the complex and diverse needs of P–12 students, and it certainly cannot be assumed that they are committed philosophically, theoretically, practically, or empirically to such a focus. In chapter 1, embedded in my discussion of color blindness, I shared student and teacher racial demographics and suggested that we needed to be mindful of these data when discussing what researchers have called a demographic divide. In a similar way, I believe we need to pay more attention to the racial demographics of teacher educators. Figures 5.1 and 5.2 summarize these racial demographic trends.

These graphs display racial demographic information for both full-time and adjunct faculty in teacher education programs. (I included data for adjunct faculty because many teacher education programs across the country rely on adjunct instructors to teach and to supervise student teachers.) These demographic data suggest that we should be concerned about increasing the numbers of teachers of color not only in P–12 social contexts but in teacher education as well. My point is not to suggest that White teacher educators cannot provide optimal learning opportunities for students but that teacher educators of color can add an important layer of diversity that can help teachers develop the mind-sets necessary to teach effectively in P–12.

FIGURE 5.1

An emerging picture of the teacher preparation pipeline: Race and ethnicity of full-time faculty in professional education programs, fall 2007

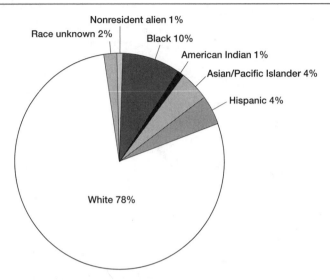

Adapted from M. Ludwig, R. Kirshstein, A. Sidana, A. Ardila-Rey, and Y. Bae, *An Emerging Picture of the Teacher Preparation Pipeline,* Report by the American Association of Colleges for Teacher Education and The American Institutes for Research for release at the briefing "Teacher Preparation: Who Needs It? What the Numbers Say" (Washington, DC: American Association of Colleges for Teacher Education and American Institutes for Research, 2010).

Teacher educators' own experiences with race-related matters are sometimes remote and vicarious.[15] Accordingly, as teacher education researcher Merry Merryfield writes:

> We know very little about the ability of college and university faculty and other teacher educators to prepare teachers in multicultural and global education. Do today's teacher educators have the knowledge, skills and commitment to teach for equity and diversity either locally or globally?[16]

Thus, the racial identity of teacher educators themselves and their commitment to diversity can have a huge bearing on teachers and on the kinds of learning opportunities available to them as they learn how to teach

FIGURE 5.2

An emerging picture of the teacher preparation pipeline: Race and ethnicity of adjunct faculty in professional education programs, fall 2007

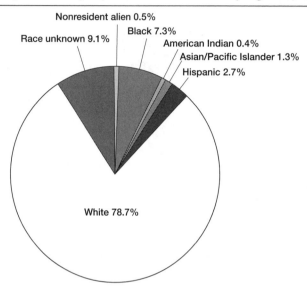

Adapted from M. Ludwig, R. Kirshstein, A. Sidana, A. Ardila-Rey, and Y. Bae, *An Emerging Picture of the Teacher Preparation Pipeline,* Report by the American Association of Colleges for Teacher Education and The American Institutes for Research for release at the briefing "Teacher Preparation: Who Needs It? What the Numbers Say" (Washington, DC: American Association of Colleges for Teacher Education and American Institutes for Research, 2010).

for diversity and close opportunity gaps that exist throughout U.S. school communities.

STRUCTURAL AND SYSTEMIC CONCERNS IN TEACHER EDUCATION

Because individuals create systems and structures, what teacher education programs emphasize will vary quite substantially depending on the views of those in the program. This variation can lead to uneven learning opportunities for teachers.

My analyses have revealed that there are no specified standard curriculum or instructional practices for teacher education programs, although the programs usually follow some specific standards and guidelines for accreditation through different associations, such as Teacher Education Accreditation Council (TEAC), National Council for Accreditation of Teacher Education (NCATE), and Southern Association of Colleges and Schools (SACS). From a broader curricular and instructional perspective, research suggests that it is not enough to have one stand-alone course on race, diversity, urban education, or equity in a teacher education program.[17] The goals of understanding *all* students and their experiences, developing racialized knowledge, and understanding trends and issues relative to diversity and opportunity should be at the core of teacher education programs. Ideally, issues of opportunity and diversity would be deeply integrated into the fabric and structure of a teacher education program. As a group of researchers observed:

> As instructors of one class in a large, complex program, we realize we can go only so far on our own. Our foundations course is marginalized from the curriculum and methods courses that students consider most important. If preservice teachers are to become more efficacious in teaching culturally diverse students and preparing all students to live in a democratic, multicultural society, we must work together as a program toward these ends.[18]

Curricular and instructional opportunities and experiences in teacher education, as well as the structure of teacher education programs, may need to change. Ladson-Billings found that "most [teacher education] programs were satisfied with adding 'multicultural content' rather than changing the philosophy and structure of the teacher education programs."[19] The core of teacher education programs—the nature and focus of the programs, the emphasis on certain issues over others—can be considered microlevel policy matters that need to be reexamined.

Where there is not a structural and systemic focus on opportunity and diversity in teacher education programs, the few isolated and marginalized courses that endeavor to prepare teachers can fail. At the core of those structural issues is (1) who teaches in these programs, (2) what they believe to be central to the curriculum, (3) who enrolls in the programs, (4) the kinds of historical experiences these people have had to contribute to the curriculum, and (5) the nature of their core commitments to opportunity and diversity.

Teacher education researcher Kenneth Zeichner explains that "it has come to the point that the term social justice teacher education is so commonly used now by college and university teacher educators that it is difficult to find a teacher education program in the United States that does not claim to have a program that prepares teachers for social justice."[20] The question is, are all these programs really *practicing* a social justice teacher education mission? If so, how can we build knowledge about what these programs are actually doing in order to build a broad curriculum base from which others can build and learn? Some faculty members in teacher education programs claim to have a social justice orientation. However, they may not practice their professed ideology in terms of decision making. With only one or two courses that offer a few sessions on race and racism, for example, it is no wonder that many teachers leave unprepared, or underprepared, to teach culturally diverse students. These P–12 students can then become the victims whom society, the media, politicians, parents, teachers, principals, board members, and other adults in and out of schools blame for all the problems in P–12 education.

In short, reshaping curricular and instructional emphasis related to diversity and opportunity gaps is especially important in teacher education (a) if there is not a range of courses focusing on race, opportunity, and diversity embedded in the program, and/or (b) if programs have difficulty recruiting teacher candidates who have a desire to teach in contexts with culturally diverse students, and/or (c) if students do not come into the program with some understanding of and affinity toward teaching for social justice. Even where such classes exist, students may not be open to such ideas. Again, they may resist a curriculum and instruction that diverge from what they believe to be important. Thus, I am suggesting that teacher education programs become more coherent in their focus and mission in preparing teachers to meet the complex needs of P–12 students. As teacher education programs are restructured, teacher educators should remember that their programs should be designed to address the needs of *all* teachers enrolled, not just White teachers.

PREPARING ALL, NOT JUST WHITE, TEACHERS FOR DIVERSITY

Teachers of color do not necessarily enter teacher education programs with a deep understanding of what it means to teach for diversity. Teacher education programs (including courses and related experiences) need to be structured to address the conceptual and practical developmental needs of all teachers, not just White teachers.

Teacher education policy makers (including professors involved in the process of accepting students into teacher education) sometimes embrace a more racially diverse population for one of several (selfish) interests. When admission policies and practices are adopted to increase racial diversity, they are sometimes justified as "benefiting" the interests and needs of White teachers.[21] In this line of reasoning, a diverse student/teacher population is important because White teachers can learn from non-White teachers.

This mind-set is rarely reciprocal; what about opportunities for non-mainstream teachers to learn from White teachers? Moreover, what about the developmental needs of the nonmainstream teachers? *All* teachers need and deserve preparation that can help them meet the challenges they will face in the P–12 classroom. Clearly, nonmainstream teachers learn from their White counterparts and vice versa, yet the intention and vision are sometimes one-sided. It is critical that teacher educators remember that nonmainstream teachers may come into a teacher education program unequipped to meet the needs of P–12 students. As I have come to understand, nonmainstream teachers may have been brainwashed into believing that they are inferior, and thus they may consciously or subconsciously tend to concentrate on the negative attributes and characteristics of their P–12 students and communities of color. As Tatum writes:

> In a race-conscious society, the development of a positive sense of racial/ethnic identity not based on assumed superiority or inferiority is an important task for *both* White people and people of color. The development of this positive identity is a lifelong process that often requires *unlearning the misinformation and stereotypes* [emphasis added] we have internalized not only about others, but also about ourselves.[22]

Course syllabi and related instructional and curriculum policies can imply that teacher educators are concerned about the needs of their White teachers and that culturally diverse teachers should simply learn "by default" or come into the learning environment with what they already need to succeed.

Ever more volumes are published to address the developmental, conceptual, pedagogical, philosophical, and curricular needs of White teachers, while the needs of culturally diverse teachers are considered far less often. In addition, a culturally diverse teacher is sometimes recruited to be a "spokesperson" for his or her race; for example, during class discussions, he or she is asked to address every issue facing his or her race in education. I have observed that such an expectation—for teachers of color to speak on behalf of their entire race—can cause these teachers to retreat from the teaching and learning exchange because they cannot—and, more importantly, *should not*—be asked to speak on behalf of their entire race or ethnicity.

Thus, in some instances, culturally diverse teachers have to learn from curricula and related experiences that are tailored to meet their White counterparts' needs.[23] Published curriculum materials such as textbooks used in teacher education programs often make recommendations "based on the assumption that preservice teachers are White."[24] This approach could alienate preservice teachers of color—for instance, what about the curricular and instructional needs of Asian or Latino/a teachers? As teacher education researcher Adrienne Dixson observes, the teacher education curriculum can look very much like the P–12 curriculum. It can privilege the positions, norms, needs, worldviews, and expectations of White people.[25]

BENEFITS TO DIVERSIFYING THE TEACHING FORCE

There appear to be benefits to the teacher education curriculum and contextual discourse when teachers and teacher educators are culturally and racially diverse. Of course, this diversity can and should include White teachers who have lived in different parts of the United States and world as well as those who possess other diverse characteristics, such as men in a female-dominated profession.

One of the six teachers showcased in this chapter explained to me in an interview, "She [the Asian teacher] shared how she felt . . . And I think that's what has helped me the most, just taking that stance [of the Asian teacher]." She found the Asian teacher's perspectives especially insightful, and she was able to link them to what she described as a "tangible reality."

Another teacher explained that the racialized experiences I shared as an African American teacher educator contributed to her new perspectives on "others." During a class discussion, this teacher kept questioning me about whether I always perceive myself as a Black male; that is, whether there are times when I forget that I am Black. She referenced this class discussion in an interview and explained that this exchange made a powerful difference in how she thought about others, particularly African Americans, and she linked it to her practice:

Teacher: Are there not times when you forget that you are Black? Are there not times when you forget that you are a Black male?

Milner: No, I always see myself as Black, and I always see myself as a Black male.

Teacher: Do you always feel the pressure of being Black?

Milner: I am always aware of the stereotypes and assumptions that surround my racial and gender identity.

Teacher: Do you ever wish that you could just be "Dr. Milner" the person and not Dr. Milner the Black person?

Milner: I see my professional identity as importantly intertwined with my racial and gender identity.

In our interview, the teacher explained: "I kept pushing you to speak whether . . . there were times when you could forget who you are in the sense that you didn't wonder, worry, it wasn't in the back of your mind that someone was seeing you as a Black man . . . to me the greatest impact was you being [sic] able to just state without any wavering on it at all that [you always] see yourself as Black." The gist of this argument is that having culturally diverse teachers as classmates and as teacher educators can potentially have a meaningful impact on the White teachers in a course or teacher education program. The question is, what about the culturally diverse teachers and their need for such influence?

CHALLENGES FACING CULTURALLY DIVERSE TEACHER EDUCATORS

Culturally diverse teacher educators sometimes face added pressure to represent their racial and ethnic group. While their representation may be seen as an asset, their voice and perspective can be marginalized or silenced because they are outnumbered in philosophical and conceptual discussions and debates. In addition, culturally diverse teacher educators are expected to serve on committees to represent "minority issues," and teachers and colleagues often look to them to solve complex problems related to diversity. Often, culturally diverse faculty are expected to teach diversity.

While I have argued for the need to increase diversity among both P–12 teachers and teacher educators, such diversity can bring challenges as well. During class discussions and related assignments, clashes sometimes ensue between teachers and teacher educators, especially when the teacher educator is African American and the teachers are White. As Ladson-Billings explains, teachers in the teacher education classroom may refuse to participate in discussions about race and culture when they disagree with what is being covered in the course. The result can be what she calls "silence as weapons." For an African American teacher educator, discussions about race and culture can be silently interpreted as the professor's "putting forth a particular political agenda."[26] Students may shut down when uncomfortable issues related to diversity and opportunities are discussed.

In my own teaching and research, despite my best efforts to provide spaces where race, diversity, and opportunity were at the top of the instructional agenda, I have observed teachers disengaging during class discussions, particularly when the topic was race and racism in the P–12 classroom. This counterproductive silence can leave teacher educators and their students perplexed about *what* should be covered related to race, *where* (in what contexts) race can be addressed, and, perhaps most important, *how* the issue might be explored.[27] What do teachers really think about discussions of diversity in teacher education? What is the nature of their silenced dialogue?[28] Why are they silenced? Why are they silent? And, most critically, how might their unstated concerns and positions show up in their P–12 practices?

Coupled with the concerns that can emerge when culturally diverse teacher educators work with mostly White teachers is the added pressure to assume what I have come to call a diversity-savior role. Culturally diverse teacher educators are sometimes expected to represent diversity in many situations and facets of a program. This means, for instance, that teachers from different racial and ethnic backgrounds consistently meet with culturally diverse teacher educators and expect them to help them solve diversity dilemmas from a range of perspectives. Furthermore, culturally diverse teacher educators are also often delegated to the one or two diversity courses in a program regardless of their subject-matter expertise or area of interest. They are often expected to serve on committees in order to have "diverse" representation. When these culturally diverse teacher educators serve on committees, they often are not listened to because they are outnumbered in terms of their cultural and racial background and belief system. Culturally diverse teacher educators are also expected to speak on behalf of their cultural and racial group for the benefit or interest of their colleagues—for example, to explain a behavioral pattern that they have observed from a culturally diverse teacher or student. White allies can be few and far between.[29]

SUMMARY

Unlike other disciplines where there is an accepted, standard, and under-stood body of knowledge, teacher education is much more dynamic, and perhaps it needs to be. There are, of course, positives and negatives to this reality that bring about bittersweet outcomes for both teacher educators and teachers. This chapter demonstrates some of the pervasive problems and promising possibilities that teacher education programs face in pre-paring teachers for the opportunity and diversity they will encounter in P–12 social contexts. While the field of teacher education has improved in providing teachers with curriculum and related experiences that address diversity, there are lingering broad issues to consider in the field:

- Increased external pressure to provide evidence of programs' effectiveness
- Structural incoherence between programs, where there is perhaps too much variation in terms of the level of curricular and instructional emphasis on opportunity and diversity
- Lack of consistency and commitment among teacher educators to ad-dress diversity
- Increasing the numbers of teachers and teacher educators of color and from diverse backgrounds (such as men) in the field
- Constructing and deconstructing curriculum and instructional expe-riences that meet the needs of all students, not just White students
- Addressing the uneven stress and burdens placed on teacher educators of color to be the diversity go-to person in teacher education programs

On a more local level, the six White teachers demonstrated some consistent themes that teacher educators should be aware of: (1) the White teachers had difficulty understanding the relevance of diversity for their own work, and they worried that they may have been making an issue out of diversity when it really did not matter; (2) the White teachers were fearful of offending those in the teacher education classroom, so they avoided using certain words, and even avoided particular politically charged topics for fear of saying the "wrong" thing; (3) the White teachers' positions (beliefs and mind-sets) were guided by and grounded in their familial history, especially their experiences with their parents; these histories helped shape the White teachers' views on diversity (especially race); and (4) the White teachers were sometimes in danger of stereotyping their students and lowering their expectations of them although this may not have been their intention.

Concurrent with problems and tensions that emerged among the White teachers showcased in this chapter were promising dimensions of their thinking and mind-sets. For instance, the White teachers in my study (1) started to make sense of the importance of cultural connections and role models for students; a teacher explained that the underrepresentation of teachers of color in her particular school was problematic, and they even started to look beyond their school to viewing the shortage of teachers of color as a "district" issue; (2) had good intentions and attempted to empathize with their students; their commitment to think about their work with students with both head and heart, I have found, can be the foundation for them to develop the mind-sets and practices that meet their P–12 students' needs; (3) began to incorporate aspects of diversity into their decision making, and they began to witness for themselves the benefits of, for instance, using bilingual texts in the classroom; and (4) in some cases wanted to disrupt and fight against the racist or homophobic language that they had heard growing up. These aspects of preparing teachers to address diversity and opportunities among their students bring about bittersweet challenges and possibilities that should be considered.

Conclusions and
Recommendations
for Practice

IN MANY WAYS, I regret having to end this book because there is so much more to say about bridging opportunity gaps and addressing diversity in education. Throughout this book, I have showcased teachers from two different P–12 learning environments, one high school and one middle school, who have worked to address diversity and opportunity gaps beyond those related to a perceived achievement gap. Also, I have showcased teachers who teach different subject matter: science, language arts, mathematics, and social studies. I have demonstrated that although these teachers attempted to maximize student potential, they had very different approaches and practices in doing so. I have stressed that all students bring layers of diversity—not just non-White students—so emphases related to opportunity and diversity should be incorporated in the educational experiences of all students, in a range of different educational contexts. In the preceding chapter, I wrote about some of the challenges and possibilities regarding diversity and opportunity gaps in P–12 classrooms that teacher educators must work through, drawing from my work in different teacher education programs. While I have outlined some of the challenges that the field of teacher education faces on micro-, macro-, individual, and collective levels, I have additionally provided snapshots of the kinds of practices and mind-sets that demonstrate promise for teaching in P–12 social contexts. I have made it clear that teaching and preparing teachers to teach can be concomitantly bitter and sweet, and that it is complex, difficult, and multifaceted work—especially when teachers are being prepared to address opportunity gaps.

Teaching inherently brings rewards and challenges. There were times when the teachers showcased in this book were at their best, and consequently students appeared to flourish. There were times, too, when teachers encountered difficulties as they worked to design and implement learning and related opportunities for students to build social and academic skills, knowledge, and ability. I have attempted to provide portraits of teachers and teaching that demonstrate the complex, yet promising, dimensions of what it means to teach in different contexts: urban and suburban schools as well as high and middle school. I have deliberately chosen varied portraits to avoid a propensity to look at any teacher, instructional practice, or teacher education program as a panacea, capable of "curing" deeply ingrained structural problems that educators may face in their classrooms and schools.

A FINAL LOOK AT THE DIVERSITY AND OPPORTUNITY GAPS EXPLANATORY FRAMEWORK

In concluding, I think it is useful to make explicit links between the mind-sets and practices of the teachers in this book and the five tenets of the framework introduced in chapter 1. Mr. Hall, Dr. Johnson, Mr. Jackson, and Ms. Shaw all understood how certain mind-sets could stifle opportunity as they designed their instructional practices for all their students. In particular, in their own relevant and responsive ways, each teacher rejected *color blindness* (and diversity blindness) and understood the salience, relevance, and permanence of race and racism in the fabric of society and therefore in schools. Mr. Hall did not initially believe race would be a critical component of his work as a science teacher, but the experience of being called racist by some students facilitated his reflection on race and racial influences in the science classroom. Ms. Shaw also grasped how important it was to understand race in her work because she reflected on her historical reality, having grown up predesegregation in the same school district where she now taught. Dr. Johnson had been called a racist in her early years at Stevenson High School, and some of her classes were taken away from her because of her emphasis on issues of race and racism as well as broader multicultural principles that she incorporated into her language arts curriculum.

Additionally, the teachers in this book understood that *cultural conflicts* were inevitable, and they developed practices through the building and sustaining of relationships to circumvent and work through them. However, the teachers did not always see cultural conflicts as a detriment to their success but as opportunities for them to learn, develop, and mature in the classroom. They used cultural conflicts as opportunity vehicles to learn from and with their students, and they recognized that cultural conflicts transcended race but were concerned with a range of inconsistencies that could exist between themselves and their students, such as generational (age) differences.

Dr. Johnson, in particular, was deliberate in her decision to help her wealthy, mostly White students understand and question a merit-based worldview in society. She focused her instructional curriculum on diversity, culture, and race in a predominantly White social context, where such issues were often completely ignored because people believed they were irrelevant. Through the construction of a safe, unintimidating, and non-threatening environment, Dr. Johnson helped her students think through the *myths of meritocracy* because she understood them as myths—a point that too many teachers fail to recognize, making it difficult for them to support student thinking around the construct. In particular, Dr. Johnson provided space for her students to think about how people earn and are positioned for success in life, and she used her own life experiences of marginalization, inside and outside the classroom, to provide learning opportunities for her students to grasp that success in society and education is not fully determined by the merits of hard work and ability.

Also, the teachers that I have showcased throughout this book refused to hold *low expectations and deficit mind-sets* for their students. Mr. Jackson astutely used student interests in hip-hop to "hook" his students and build relationships with them. He recognized the rich array of intellect, experience, and know-how that his students possessed and brought into the classroom, and he perceived their appreciation for and interest in hip-hop and popular culture as strengths from which he was able to draw and build. Mr. Jackson did not develop an oppositional stance against his students' interests but attempted to find value in what was of interest to them while simultaneously encouraging students to analyze and critique aspects of hip-hop and pop culture that were disadvantageous and dangerously harmful, such as some of the language used to describe women.

Also, Mr. Hall had high expectations of his students, and he refused to allow them to get away with mediocrity—even when they got upset with him for correcting them. He would confront his students when they were not reaching their potential or were acting out because he held his students in high esteem and maintained high expectations for them. However, Mr. Hall's high expectations far exceeded academic goals. He also held his students accountable for excellence in other areas of their learning and development, such as how they behaved with their friends and other teachers, not only in his classroom but in the broader school context.

In addition, the teachers highlighted in this book seemed to understand that they conducted their work in a particular social context and refused to adopt *context-neutral mind-sets* (and consequently practices). They recognized that their practices had to be tailored to be responsive to the needs of students (and other adults such as colleagues, administrators, and parents) in real, *particular,* school contexts. The teachers understood that knowing a particular subject matter such as mathematics, language arts, or science, while certainly necessary, was insufficient to successfully address the diversity-opportunity gaps that existed in their different spaces. All the teachers seemed to understand that people—a unique collection of adults and students—created the contexts in which they taught, and their challenge was to deepen their knowledge and skill about the idiosyncrasies inherent in their particular teaching situations in order to provide relevant and responsive learning opportunities for all their students. General strategies and principles that teachers develop to build their conceptual and practical repertoires are important; however, the skills and ability to translate, adapt, enact, and implement those strategies and principles at the appropriate times, with particular people, and with meaningful intent and rationale are more critical.

The six White teachers learning to teach in chapter 5 provided what I believe to be important insight into the kinds of challenges that we face in preparing teachers to address diversity and close opportunity gaps. While the White teachers grappled with understanding the role of diversity in their teaching, most of them developed into educators with strong potential to teach all students well. Collectively, the teachers in this book represented an important range of diversity: a White male teacher, two African American female teachers, one African American male teacher, and six White female teachers. I realize, though, that the perspectives of teachers from other racial and ethnic backgrounds (such as Latino and Asian) are not represented in this book. I am mindful of and sensitive to this void. Still, I am hopeful that readers can acquire a range of different insights and perspectives from the educators presented here.

I want to conclude with some practical implications and recommendations that teachers, teacher educators, administrators, and other educators might consider in their journey to address the opportunity-diversity connection and the opportunity gaps that too often exist in schools. I draw from mainly two areas: (1) research I have conducted over the years (including my work with the teachers in this book); and (2) the established research literature focusing on diversity, equity, and urban education.

Although this book is about opportunity gaps and diversity, a recurrent and purposeful theme has been the importance of teachers' ability to develop relationships with students. That is, I have come to understand that at the heart of effective, promising, and successful teaching in any social context is building and sustaining relationships with students.

BUILDING SOLID AND SUSTAINABLE RELATIONSHIPS

In theory and rhetoric, the notion that teachers must build relationships with students is logical and well accepted. For instance, I rarely, if ever, hear practitioners contest the idea that relationship building is a critical aspect to their success with students in any classroom or school. The question, however, is how do teachers and other educators build those relationships? Further, how do educators sustain relationships, when conflicts are looming, in order to maximize learning opportunities? Building relationships with students is about meeting students where they are, attempting to understand them, and developing connections with them. A forerunner to such an exchange requires that teachers are *willing to find the good* and the worth in students; all students possess positive characteristics and attributes, but these are sometimes overlooked and undervalued. Thus, teachers may have to refocus and sharpen their lenses for thinking about students, especially when they have known students only in a negative light. When teachers do not have a positive frame or an appropriate lens to view some students as capable of excellence or success, it can be difficult to recognize that all students, despite their differences, bring worthwhile talents with endless potential and capability into the classroom. Are teachers willing and prepared to recognize talent, potential talent, intellect, skill, excellence, and ability when they emerge in an unexpected social context or with an unlikely group of students?

It is essential to remember that students have sometimes internalized negative words, phrases, and perceptions about them, which can make it difficult for them to recognize their own potential or to trust and give teachers a chance to help them develop their talents and strengths. Teachers may find that they need to bridge gaps of self-doubt and worthlessness to help students recognize their own potential and promise. For instance, at home, students sometimes hear and internalize only what their parents and siblings say is "wrong" with them. Students may receive these kinds of messages from different adults or other family members:

- You will never amount to anything.
- You're ugly, and you are worthless.
- I regret the day you were born.
- You're too loud.
- You're not smart or athletic enough!
- You remind me of your "no good" mother [or father].

These statements can have lasting negative influence on students, which may consequently have significant impact on their success and interaction with other students and teachers. Moreover, negative words and perspectives that have been *spoken into students' lives* can make it difficult for them to become motivated to engage in the academic curriculum and/ or in social or athletic opportunities at school. To combat negative experiences students may have had and counter destructive language they may have heard, teachers must work to build the types of relationships that can outweigh the hurt. Teachers have to empower students to want to learn; to visualize themselves as different from the negative ideas they have been taught; and to believe they can develop the knowledge, skills, attitudes, and beliefs to build a successful future. But what specific practices can teachers develop and enact in their classrooms to build relationships?

Classroom Practices to Build Relationships

There are many micro- or classroom-level practices that can assist teachers in molding relationships with their students. Consider the following tasks and activities teachers can engage in to build relationships with students and learn from them.

- *Interview*—that is, talk to their students. Teachers sometimes spend infinite amounts of time talking *about* students to their colleagues or to students' parents, but minimal time actually talking *to* students themselves. This strategy suggests that teachers engage in conversations with students themselves to learn from and about them. Teachers can then incorporate this learning into the class curriculum and teaching. In my university classroom, I utilize this strategy. For instance, when I learn of a student's interest in a particular aspect of education, I remain mindful of that area of interest. When I am reading journals and books, or when I am engaged in research projects, I often make copies of writing or related information that may be of interest to that student and share the materials with him or her.
- *Develop assignments* that allow students to share experiences and interests with teachers. In language arts, assignments might include journal writing or essay writing. In social studies, assignments might include family history projects or local community-studies projects. In mathematics or science, assignments might include student-constructed word problems or community-based inquiry projects where students investigate the effects of environmental realities on health, crime, and/or poverty in their community.
- *Develop and implement classroom discussions* that allow students to be the center of attention. Teachers should not always be at the center of discussions but should allow students to share events and experiences in their community (home and school). Students should be allowed to share whatever information they feel comfortable discussing. For instance, when I taught high school English, I used to facilitate what I came to call "rap sessions" that allowed students to have conversations with each other and me about what was happening in their lives (inside and outside of school). The students developed categories/topics of interest that they wanted to discuss, and we selected topics out of a hat that allowed the students to debate issues or just to share their perspectives on a particular theme. The experience was inundated with learning opportunities: (1) it allowed students to think about and

construct a position; (2) it allowed students to develop counterpositions to debate classmates when they disagreed; (3) it helped students to learn to substantiate their positions, listen to others, and build coherent narratives; and (4) it provided students space for voice and authority in the classroom. The discussion sessions with students allowed them to develop voice and perspective, and they allowed me to gain knowledge about the students. When discussing her pedagogical approach and voice, hooks wrote:

> As a teacher, I recognize that students . . . enter classrooms within institutions where their voices have been neither heard nor welcomed, whether these students discuss facts—those that any of us might know—or personal experience. My pedagogy has been shaped to respond to this reality. If I do not wish to see these students use the "authority of experience" as a means of asserting voice, I can circumvent this possible misuse of power by bringing to the classroom pedagogical strategies that affirm their presence, their right to speak, in multiple ways on diverse topics.[1]

• *Attend an extracurricular activity* of a student (a football, lacrosse, or basketball game, a band concert, or a play/theatrical production, for instance), even when the teacher is *not* on duty. Such attendance is something that teachers on the elementary through high school level can do (even when elementary students participate in extracurricular activities through community recreation centers, for instance); it means something to students when teachers take time out of their schedules to visit an activity they are involved in. I shall never forget the time my third-grade teacher, Mrs. Sandra Zachery, attended my football game at a city park. Needless to say, I played at my highest capacity that game, and I remember feeling a great sense of pride that my teacher had supported me in this way. In the third grade classroom, I remember putting forth more effort after this experience and looking at my teacher with an intensified level of respect.

• *Visit a community site in students' communities* such as a grocery store, library, beauty salon or barbershop, community center, or church, synagogue, or other worship site (only if this is something that is consistent with the teacher's worldview or religious beliefs). In essence, when teachers immerse themselves in students' communities, they are able to learn about what is happening in students' neighborhoods and their worlds outside of the learning environment. I recall that my mother, who owned a beauty salon in my community, saw my second-grade teacher, Mrs. Louise Britt, every other Thursday, when she did her hair. Moreover, other teachers who taught my sister, me, and many of my friends also received services from my mother's beauty salon: Mrs. Cynthia Anderson, Mrs. Josephine Terry, Mrs. Essie Mcrae, and Mrs. Cheryl Gilbert, to name a few. Of course, I am completely confident that there were conversations about me and my academic performance during those appointments where my mother styled my teacher's hair. My second-grade teacher was building knowledge about me, the community, and other students in the community because my friends' parents also visited my mother's shop for services.

Activities like these have the potential to help teachers build important relationships with students and develop curriculum and instructional practices that are meaningful to students. There are also some broader school-related practices that have the potential to assist educators in building relationships—again, with the ultimate goal of addressing diversity and closing opportunity gaps.

Whole-School Practices to Build Relationships

In addition to supporting classroom-level practices that assist teachers in building and sustaining relationships, schools can also develop macro-level programs to cultivate relationships and simultaneously address aspects of diversity and opportunity gaps. Consider the following examples of practices schools can develop and enact:

- *Language-learning resource program for parents and families:* Such a program can provide families in the school community with opportunities to acquire a new or second language that can assist them in the school community and beyond. The chance to learn English, Spanish, Arabic, French, Chinese, and other languages, particularly languages represented in a school community, can help those in the community build relationships and engage in language acquisition at the same time. I learned from a parent in Ohio that a school was even looking to provide child care for parents interested in acquiring another language.

- *Parenting workshops:* Such workshops can help parents understand what Delpit describes as the "culture of power" and encourage them to partner with the school to maximize student learning opportunities.[2] Because parents sometimes do not understand all that is expected of them to help their students achieve social and academic success, the workshops could be structured to assist and empower parents to be active participants in their students' education. It is important that these workshops be designed to allow parents to have voice and perspective in the design and implementation of the workshop. Parents should not be told how to parent but should be provided information on strategies they can use to assist their children while simultaneously providing information about what educators (schools) need from parents in order for students to succeed. Indeed, I have rarely met parents who do not care for their children. However, I have often met parents who are not aware of how to support their children in a school culture. Some parents, for instance, may see their role primarily as an economic resource, not an educational one, and they need to be encouraged to become an educational resource for their children as well. Moreover, some parents vowed to themselves that they would never set foot inside another school after graduating because of the negative experiences they had as students themselves. Also, some parents may be intimidated by the discourse of a school, especially if they are not "well educated" themselves. All of these factors may be related to why parents are not actively involved in their children's education. The question is: what role might/should schools play in reversing parents' lack of involvement? Moreover, if parents did start showing up at school, would educators know what to ask them to do in order to support their children?

- *Diversity-related theme for the semester or year:* The development and implementation of a theme for the academic school year or semester can allow those in the community to build common knowledge about the theme and to incorporate aspects of the theme into curriculum and instructional practices throughout the year.[3] Students themselves could suggest a diversity theme, and the entire student body could vote on the top three themes, eventually selecting one. Possible themes might include opportunity, diversity, integrity, community service, poverty, or injustice. Such a schoolwide focus can allow for synergistic focus and aims, which allow students to learn and build knowledge about the importance and essence of the theme from multiple vantage points through multiple subject-matter areas. Parents, of course, should be involved and informed about the theme, and community members (such as professional athletes, community organizers, business executives, or entrepreneurs) might be invited to the school to provide narratives about their experience with a particular theme.

- *Schoolwide movie viewing:* Schools can consider holding periodic, annual, semiannual, or quarterly movie showings that invite the school community (parents, teachers, students, community members) into the school to address dimensions of diversity and opportunity. The movies can be used as "sites" for curriculum connections that empower students to grapple with complex matters, which can assist them in building knowledge, skills, and mind-sets transferable to other areas of their work and lives. Movies that can help students and others in the school community think about opportunity and diversity include *Boyz N the Hood, Crash, The Blind Side, Remember the Titans, Something New, Finding Forrester, Stand and Deliver, Lean on Me,* and *Good Will Hunting.* There is also a litany of teacher-centered movies that display White teachers as "saviors" of students living in poverty, students of color, and students whose first language is not English. It is critical for those in a learning context to remember that movies that paint a White educator as the savior to students "in need" send a particular message that can perpetuate unintended stereotypes. Moreover, movies such as *Lean on Me* can showcase an African American administrator in a light of rage and hostility, providing a picture that is one-sided and inconsistent with the experiences of many viewers.[4] Thus, by way of caution, I encourage movie selections that are balanced in perspective and that show marginalized people in a light of success, not only in roles of servitude, need, or hostility. In addition, I encourage those viewing the movies to use them as a site for discussion, and in particular as an opportunity to critique and analyze the major themes in the movies without taking the themes as uncomplicated or necessarily accurate.

- *Community-centered dinner:* Quarterly, semiannually, and/or annually, schools could host a dinner for parents (and other caregivers) and community members along with teachers, staff members, administrators, and students. I was mindful in my decision to include "other caregivers" in my list of those who should be invited. Educators must expand their notions of "parental" involvement to include the extended family. Older siblings might need to be involved if parents work late hours. Students' grandparents, aunts, uncles, and "othermothers and fathers," those who serve as surrogate parents, might also need to be considered. There might be a keynote address, or students might build the program's focus. I know of different schools in Tennessee that have adopted very different approaches to this idea. One suburban school actually has an annual formal dinner. An urban school in the same city holds a fish fry each year. Both events have standing room only. Food, perhaps, is the draw, but the goal is for parents to talk to each other and to educators about educational issues. All involved have a chance to make recommendations about the best approaches to support students.
- *Schoolwide book reading:* In their journey to build community, schools might also consider adopting a schoolwide yearly reading selection that showcases some aspect of diversity or opportunity. The

book should be read by all those in the community—students, teachers, parents, and staff—and teachers can use the reading as a site for discussion and curriculum construction across different age spans. Where possible, schools might select a reading that expands on the theme chosen for the year, or they might select a book that has a complementary movie. In both cases, students and others in the learning community can use the reading as an opportunity to share knowledge around a particular issue or theme and to voice their views of the major ideas in the book. Where possible, parents should be invited into the school to engage with their children in roundtable discussions about particular aspects and themes of the books.

Having established both classroom and school-level suggestions and strategies that teachers and schools can consider to build relationships with students (and their parents), I close this book with two, I hope, thought-provoking short stories about the necessity to continue focusing on diversity and opportunity in P–12 social contexts.

TROUBLING STORIES OF OPPORTUNITY AND DIVERSITY

I want to conclude with two personal stories that I believe capture some of what I hoped to convey in this book. The first story is about English language learners and opportunity, and the second is about societal perceptions that an emphasis on diversity and opportunity is not necessary.

Short Story 1: English Language Learners Can Benefit "Our Children"

Several years ago, I was invited to give a talk in a moderately large city in the northern region of the United States. During the visit, I was driven around and shown several local schools. My tour guide explained, quite proudly, that the district had begun busing immigrant "non-English-speaking" students to one of the "best" local schools in the district. Even more intriguing for my tour guide was the reality that the district had developed policies that would "pour dollar after dollar" into the school over the next five years so that the "non-English-speaking" students would "learn to speak English." What seemed to excite the tour guide more than anything was the reality that "our English-speaking students [mostly White, upper-class English speakers] in the school were also learning to speak different languages as well, mostly Spanish." It is also important to note that the tour guide did not stress how important it would be for the "non-English speakers" to maintain their native language and build or add to their first language. The emphasis was on the opportunity for the first language Spanish-speaking student to learn English.

What appeared obvious from the guide's description and responses to my questions about the policies and practices in the district and the school where the English language learners would be bused was his interest in the fact that the mostly White, upper-middle-class students were acquiring language and becoming bi- or trilingual. My tour guide and the policy- and decision-making body on the district board realized how important it will be for children from higher socioeconomic backgrounds to speak multiple languages in this increasingly diverse country (and abroad). The district and school were willing to negotiate and provide the resources necessary for the "non-English speakers" to "learn English" because they had figured out that the majority White and wealthy students would of course benefit from the various racial, ethnic, cultural, and linguistic backgrounds that would be represented in the school. There was a convergence of interests between those in power and the "non-English speakers."

I share this story because it is representative of the mind-set and commitments that some have regarding opportunity and diversity. My tour guide was resolute in his position that "our children get to learn Spanish." Sadly, opportunities for some groups of students are contingent upon the opportunities and benefits of those in power. It is when those in power determine that there is some benefit to them that people are willing to negotiate and do what is right. But we should do what is right because that is what we are supposed to do—not because we are expecting something in return. Opportunity for all our students should be designed so they can reach their full capacity, even when the benefits for those in power are not so obvious or compelling. What my tour guide seemed to forget in his description was that all students must be considered "our children," and that we should always be mindful of and committed to providing optimal opportunities for every student in our schools and districts, not just when we find compelling benefits for another, more powerful, group of students.

Short Story 2: Diversity Is What's Wrong with Our School Systems

The second story I share here is one that I experienced after providing professional development on "diversity and education" for a U.S. school district. After my presentation, I was interviewed by the news media, and below are some comments I received regarding my work with the district (note: the statements are taken directly from a public blogging Web site regarding my visit to the district):

> Paid for Propaganda, nothing less. In the beginning, Immigrants to America came here to learn our culture and to be assimilated into AMERICAN culture. The idea today is to forcefully insert your ideology upon Americans who do not agree with changing what has taken centuries to perfect. At least as near perfection as man is ever likely to achieve. The handwriting is on the wall, America, the writing began immediately after WW2 with the importation of masses of refugees totally different in culture. And values. What kind of idiots worked to bring in people who had just yesterday been conquered by America in War? Many bring a dagger to place in our backs. A nation must have a common language, familiar culture, and true LACK of the very thing you are hyping.

When I shared these comments with one of my colleagues, a White male, he was furious. I was not angry, however, because I was not surprised. The mind-set, belief system, and position of the writer indicates the range of ideology surrounding opportunity and diversity in the United States. I have worked for many years with teachers in professional development across the country who share this respondent's position and view, though their thoughts are not expressed in the language above. The real question is: how do teachers with such mind-sets and positions teach and provide opportunities for all students? Moreover, how do students, particularly culturally diverse students, fare when educators and others in society believe that they should just assimilate into a one-dimensional "American culture" that rejects other important cultural markers?

Similar comments came from another person who expressed his or her disdain with my presenting to teachers about "diversity and education" and also with the district for inviting me. Consider this statement, again copied directly from the blogging site:

> Diversity is what is wrong with our school system now. this is still america teach [h]ow to be american and think for themselves. the schools have become indoctrination centers. they can't read are right are think for themselves. miseducated is what you get out of Vanderbilt and miller they all live of tax dollars.

Again, some in society and consequently in education believe that matters of diversity are "what is wrong" in school systems all over the country. Based on what I hear from teachers and other educators (including principals and staff members), some educators do believe this to be true for their experiences. Such mind-sets and positions suggest that there is still much work to be done to transform mind-sets and belief systems related to the benefits and assets that all students bring to our learning contexts—even when we are not prepared to recognize those assets.

GET FIRED UP!

I have decided to convey words that I use to end so many of my class sessions and professional development workshops across the country: *get fired up!* The goal is to inspire, motivate, and empower readers to move ideas into action. Books, journal articles, newspaper articles, and a range of other social and professional media are inundated with reports of problems facing P–12 students and teachers across U.S. society. The reports often focus on problems of opportunity and diversity but too rarely focus on ways to address, counter, and disrupt the problems. I am hopeful that readers are now "fired up" about reenvisioning the possibilities of their curriculum development and instructional practices in various learning contexts.

I am also hopeful that educators will choose to build relationships with students and to treat them like *people* developing rather than people who are prisoners, focusing on rules to the detriment of learning the explicit curriculum (see the important work of Eisner and of McCutcheon regarding the nature and form of the curriculum).[5] I recall walking down a hallway in an urban elementary school in the Midwest when a teacher proclaimed: "We are not moving until I see a straight line." I was stunned as I noticed the third graders desperately trying to figure out how to construct the line straight enough so that they could "move." For six minutes, the teacher stood there with a look of disgust on her face because the students apparently could not make the line straight enough. I wondered what kinds of learning opportunities the students were missing during her six minutes of "teaching" the students that they would not move until she saw a straight line. This story is not unique. All over the country but especially in urban schools, teachers focus so much on rules that they sometimes forget they are working with human beings who are developing and grappling with a range of matters.

While I have spent a lot of time visiting urban schools (from elementary to high), I have also visited and observed suburban and independent schools. What I have learned is that despite these different social contexts, student behaviors are similar in many ways: students talk sometimes without raising their hands, they have conflicts with their classmates, they forget to complete their homework, they sometimes use profanity, and they even struggle to stand in a straight line. However, there is a stark difference between how teachers handle students' mistakes in suburban and independent schools. In many urban schools, students are treated like prisoners (see the important work of Noguera for more on this), while in suburban and independent schools, students are treated as individuals who are learning and developing.[6] In many urban and highly diverse schools, students are learning how to follow rules but are rarely learning how to develop their own academic, social, and political awareness and positions on issues. In this way, urban and highly diverse schools are preparing their students for jobs that require this skill: to take orders. Suburban and independent schools are preparing their students to develop and *give* orders. It is important to note that I am not suggesting that teachers should not help students understand rules and the consequences for not following them. We must have rules and laws in society and schools in order to live and function. However, focusing on rules more than on helping students develop knowledge and skills is problematic—yet pervasive in schools across the United States. I hope educators will "get fired up" and do something about inequity and unjust situations wherever they find them.

IN CONCLUSION

If viewed separately, the individual portraits of these teachers and their practices provide some powerful narratives of teachers working to address the diverse needs of all their students. However, collectively, the narratives in this book provide important broader implications beyond local, individual classroom situations. Educators are invited to assess their current situations, draw meaning from these narratives, and transfer the lessons learned that are relevant and appropriate for their practices. I have chosen to share in this book the kinds of practices, mind-sets, strategies, and ideas that I have seen in my own empirical work over the years as well as insights garnered from an established body of educational research, theory, and practice. Thus, it is critical that readers consider the broader implications and recommendations offered both tacitly and overtly.

In a similar vein, I encourage educators and teachers in particular to change (that is, transform and improve) their individual practices with students in their classrooms in order to address opportunity gaps that may exist. When teachers transform their individual practices, their students inevitably have an opportunity to benefit. But I want to pose another set of questions for individual teachers to ponder as they transfer lessons in this book to their particular classrooms: What would happen if a group of teachers transformed their practices to address opportunity gaps? What if an entire school decided to refocus its efforts to build on some of the principles, recommendations, and suggestions discussed here? In what ways might students benefit when teachers in the collective transform the very fabric of an entire school? The answers to these questions are dynamic. Fundamentally, I believe that individual teachers can make a difference; but I believe that groups of teachers, schools, districts, regions, and entire states can make a *huge* difference in addressing opportunity gaps that exist in P–12 social contexts. Thus, while I certainly am hopeful that individual teachers will change their practices, I am even more hopeful that groups of teachers and administrators will come together to change and improve broader institutional, systemic, and structural factors for the benefit of students.

I am not only optimistic about the possibilities for teachers and students, I am also *hopeful* about what could be for them as well. As Cornel West wrote in the preface of the important book *Restoring Hope: Conversations on the Future of Black America*:

> Hope is not the same as optimism. Optimism adopts the role of the spectator who surveys the evidence in order to infer that things are going to get better . . . Hope enacts the stance of the participant who actively struggles against the evidence in order to change the deadly tides of wealth inequality, group xenophobia, and personal despair. Only a new wave of vision, courage, and hope can keep us sane—and preserve the decency and dignity requisite to revitalize our organizational energy for the work to be done. To live is to wrestle with despair yet never to allow despair to have the last word.[7]

Thus, I conclude this book with optimism and hope (and perhaps hope more than optimism) that educators will be courageous enough to do what is right on behalf of students, all students, every day, even when no one else is looking and even when no one else will. The teachers in this book remain, as do I, critical of current social, historic, economic, and political ills and concurrently optimistic and *hopeful* about the change that can emerge when we refuse to be defeated in education.

Epilogue

IN THIS EPILOGUE, I describe how I came to learn about and share the practices of Mr. Hall, Dr. Johnson, Mr. Jackson, Ms. Shaw, and the six White teachers presented in this book. I also briefly reveal important information to help readers understand *what* I did in collecting these stories about the teachers and the social contexts in which they worked or learned, *why* I made certain decisions in collecting and reporting the narratives, and *how* I was able to conduct the research. I begin with a brief discussion of my research journey to explain who I am as a social scientist and how I have come to engage in what I believe to be my life's work and my professional calling.

A BRIEF GLANCE AT MY RESEARCH JOURNEY

Since 2001, I have been interested in the roles teachers play in students' opportunities to learn and in how teachers can enable and support student development in different sociocultural contexts. While in graduate school, I participated on a research team with educational anthropologist Peter Demerath, who helped me develop my research knowledge and skills as I learned to study real people in real places. Indeed, he taught me to make the familiar strange and the strange familiar as I attempted to understand people, places, and practices. I was able to build and sharpen my research skills on that team because we pushed each other to think more deeply about what we were observing, how we were developing conjectures, and how we would represent what we learned to others. I was propelled to respond to important epistemological questions like how I came to know what I believed I knew and what evidence I was drawing from to make claims.

My earliest research as a participant on that team was conducted in a suburban school, what I have called Stevenson High School in this book. With colleagues and a mentor, I studied student culture and student identity development. For a thorough synopsis of the work we engaged in at that school, see "The Secrets of Their Success: A Middle-Class Logic of Individual Advancement in a U.S. Suburb and High School," by Demerath et al.[1] Though my research skills and abilities deepened and my understanding of student culture and identity at Stevenson High intensified, I still found myself wondering about the influence of teachers on the construction of students' culture and on identity development. Thus, my individual research began to take on a different shape and focus. I increasingly became interested in matters of diversity (especially race), and I wanted to know about social interactions between students and between teachers and students. Moreover, I was interested in the curriculum and the role race played in the classroom. Thus, as I attempted to understand some of these interests more clearly and precisely, I began to study the practices of several teachers at Stevenson High, including Dr. Johnson. I became intrigued by the ways in which she talked about her role in the mostly White context and, perhaps more than anything, I was motivated to learn more about her and her practices and interactions because her students seemed so captivated by her, her curriculum development, and her teaching methods.

My interests in race and student learning opportunities did not shift much after I completed my graduate studies. When I moved to Vanderbilt University, I immediately began collecting stories about the teaching, learning, curriculum, and diversity (mostly race) nexus. I first studied this interplay at a local urban high school. Later, I moved my research project to a local urban middle school, what I refer to in this book as Bridge

Middle School. There, I studied the practices of six teachers. I showcase three of them in this book: Mr. Hall, Ms. Jackson, and Ms. Shaw.

It is also important to note that I am a teacher volunteer at another local urban middle school in the city. In this capacity, I serve as a language arts teacher for eighth-grade male students. In that space, I intentionally do not collect any systematic data or attempt to write in any systematic way about my experiences with the students. I have chosen not to publish research articles and books about that volunteer work because I believe it is important for researchers and professors to provide service while receiving from the many teachers and students who teach them about their work. My volunteer work at the local middle school has taught me much. The principal invited me to work with a group of eighteen male students who had not passed the state-mandated test in language arts. Many of them were considered difficult to teach. My experience there has been important for many reasons. For instance, it has allowed me to test some of the principles and ideas I have come to believe and that I share with teachers in professional development as well as in my teacher education courses. In addition, it allows me to stay grounded in real classroom problems and never forget about the many teachers and students who are unable to enjoy and reap the benefits of opportunities that have potential to make a difference in their lives. All of these experiences have shaped me, helped me analyze and write about the evidence presented through these narratives, and propelled me to write this book.

BRIDGE MIDDLE SCHOOL

First, the names of all the people and places showcased in this book are pseudonyms to maintain their anonymity. Constructed in 1954, Bridge Middle School is an urban school in a relatively large city in the southeastern region of the United States. According to a Bridge County real estate agent in 2006, houses in the community then sold for between $120,000 and $175,000. There are also a considerable number of rental houses zoned to the school. Many of the neighborhood students from higher socioeconomic backgrounds who are zoned to Bridge Middle School attend private and independent schools in the city rather than Bridge. The practice of sending students to private and independent schools rather than their zoned school is very common in the district. A larger number of students from lower socioeconomic backgrounds attend Bridge.

Bridge Middle School is considered a Title I school, which means that the school receives additional federal funds to assist with instructional and related resources. It accommodates approximately 350 students. While the demographics are constantly evolving, the most current information available revealed that 59.8 percent of the students at Bridge were African American, 5.6 percent Hispanic American, 31.6 percent White, 0.3 percent American Indian, and 2.8 percent Asian American, a truly diverse learning environment in terms of racial and ethnic diversity. The free and reduced lunch rate increased between the 2002 and 2006 academic years, from 64 percent to 79 percent, respectively. In 2006, there were twenty-seven teachers at the school, 45 percent of them African American and 55 percent White. Seven of the teachers were male and twenty were female. Tables 1, 2, and 3 summarize this data.

TABLE 1

Ethnic background of students at Bridge Middle School, 2006–2007

African American	European American	Hispanic American	Asian American	American Indian	Total students
59.8%	31.6%	5.6%	2.8%	0.3%	354

TABLE 2

Racial background of teachers at Bridge Middle School, 2006–2007

Race	Percentage
Black	45
White	55

TABLE 3
Students receiving free or reduced lunch, 2002 and 2006

2002	Increase	2006
64%	15%	79%

Bridge Middle School is known for competitive basketball, wrestling, track, and football teams. The school building is brick, and windows are usually open during the spring and summer. There is a buzzer at the main entrance of the school. Visitors ring the bell, are identified by a camera, and are allowed to enter by one of the administrative assistants in the main office. When I visited the school, I signed a logbook in the main office before proceeding to the teachers' classrooms, the cafeteria, or the library. During my first month of conducting this research (September 2005), one of the hall monitors insisted that I go back to the main office to get a red name badge, so I could be identified as a visitor/researcher. They were serious about safety at the school. The floors in the hallways were spotless. There was no writing or graffiti on the walls. Especially during the month of February (2006 and 2007), Black history/heritage/celebration posters and bulletin boards occupied nearly all the wall space in the hallways and classrooms.

Why Bridge Middle School

I selected Bridge Middle School because it was known in the district and community as one of the "better" middle schools in the urban area. For instance, when I asked practicing teachers enrolled in my classes at the university to "community nominate" some of the "strong" and "better" urban schools in the city, Bridge Middle School was consistently nominated.[2] In addition, people in the supermarket would also mention Bridge as one of the "better" schools in the district upon my queries. When I met with a school official at the district office to gain entry into a school, he also suggested Bridge as a place to work. I wanted to learn in a school with teachers and students who were considered urban and highly diverse and also successful at working through difficult situations.

STEVENSON HIGH SCHOOL

Stevenson High School is an economically affluent midwestern suburban high school. It accommodates approximately 1,650 students, with a mostly homogeneous population. Specifically, during the time of the study, 86 percent of Stevenson High students were White or European American, 4 percent were Black or African American, and 10 percent were Asian American; 2 percent spoke limited English, 2 percent came from low-income homes, 7 percent received special education, and the turnover rate was 3 percent. In 2010, prices for houses on the real estate market in the district ranged from around $150,000 to $930,000. It is one of two high schools in the Stevenson County District.

Stevenson High School is known for competitive soccer and lacrosse teams. Constructed in 1992, the school building is brick, and the architecture is modern and sophisticated. A large portion of the common area is carpeted, and parts of it resemble a coffee shop more than a school cafeteria. Students often congregate here before school, during lunch, and after classes. The hallways are light and airy, and artwork is displayed throughout most of the hallways, including original pieces by Stevenson High seniors.

Why Stevenson High School

As mentioned, during my doctoral studies, I was invited onto a research project that was taking place at Stevenson High School. Later, I decided to continue working at Stevenson to collect narratives for my independent research. I chose to work at Stevenson because the space allowed me to understand the interplay between teachers' identities (especially their racial and ethnic identities) and their skills, abilities, and choices in developing and implementing student learning opportunities. Also, the context allowed me to study how, whether, and to what extent issues of diversity and multicultural education were incorporated into student learning, by whom, and why in the mostly White and wealthy social context. Finally, the social context allowed me to understand social relationships and interactions between students and teachers, especially in the mostly

White context. In particular, my research with Dr. Johnson allowed me to consider what issues of diversity really meant in a predominantly White teaching context when a teacher deliberately developed, implemented, and transformed her curriculum and lessons with racial and cultural meaning as central features of the work.

TEACHER EDUCATION PROGRAMS

I have worked with preservice teachers in different teacher education sites over the years. While I have worked with teachers from diverse backgrounds, the majority have been White and female. These teacher education programs have varied in terms of size, research emphasis, and commitment to issues of diversity and social justice. I included what I consider representative stories of six White teachers in this book to provide a picture into some of the tensions, challenges, and possibilities that can emerge when teacher educators and teacher education programs attempt to foster and support teachers' learning, thinking, and practices related to diversity and opportunity.

HOW I COLLECTED THE NARRATIVES

This book reports on a collection of qualitative studies. In qualitative research, researchers systematically design studies to learn, in depth, about real people in real places and situations. Readers are then able to transfer what they read into their own practices, based on aspects of the research that they find applicable and relevant to their particular situations. Qualitative research allows researchers to construct stories of participants that are grounded in the participants' reality; in my study of these teachers, I was able to uncover not only important dimensions of their practices but also their conceptions, beliefs, and thinking about those practices. I learned with, from, and about the teachers through three primary data sources and techniques: (1) interviews, (2) observations, and (3) document analyses.

Interviews

Interviews played an important role in my ability to develop and convey the narratives of each teacher.[3] In particular, I conducted interviews with each of the teachers to gain their perspectives about what I was learning and observing regarding their curriculum and instructional practices related to diversity and opportunities. I conducted these interviews over time to gauge how their thoughts and positions shifted at different time periods. The interviews typically took place during the teachers' lunch hour, planning block, or after school. Interviews with the participants were taped. I (rather than a transcriptionist) transcribed the tapes for Dr. Johnson to gain a deeper level of intimacy with the data; I hired a transcriptionist to transcribe the interviews with the other teachers.

Social Context Observations

In addition to conducting interviews, I observed the teachers in their teaching practices. My ability to observe the teachers in their classroom and in the broader school community allowed me to deepen my understanding of the contextual nuances and the contextual nature of their work and the social context. I also attended other school-related activities such as a band concert, a school play, and an honor roll assembly, and I visited and observed in other locations in the school, such as the library and the cafeteria. I wanted to gain as much knowledge and perspective about life at the two schools as I possibly could as I attempted to construct the narratives shared here.

I was typically in the schools for the entire day, one day a week. Most mornings, I was in the school before the bell rang, talking to students and teachers as well as reviewing my field notes or documents, which were recorded or collected, respectively, throughout the study. Although I participated in some of the classroom tasks, I was more observer than participant. In some cases, I participated in group discussions or commented on themes as they emerged in a particular reading, especially in the language arts courses. Most of the time, however, I simply observed the classroom contexts and wrote notes in my notebook.

Document Analyses

In addition to participating in interviews and allowing me to observe their classroom practices, the teachers also shared their plan books and/or other documents that shaped their thinking about what they would teach, how, and why. Teachers and students allowed me to review their assignments as well, such as worksheets, novels they would read, lab assignments, videotapes, and other materials, to help me gain a deeper understanding and knowledge base relative to the thought processes and goals that guided their decisions. Moreover, my ability to analyze documents enabled me to draw connections between what I learned in interviews and what I observed.

ANALYZING THE DATA

Data from interviews, observations, and documents I analyzed were hand coded. Essentially, my analysis followed a recursive, thematic process; as interviews and observations progressed, I used analytic induction and reasoning to develop thematic categories. Because findings were based on observations, interviews, and document analyses, the patterns of thematic findings emerged from multiple data sources, resulting in triangulation. For instance, when a teacher repeated a point several times throughout the study, I called this a "pattern." When what the teacher articulated during interviews also became evident in his or her actions, in documents, or in the students' actions, I called this a "triangulational pattern." In my analyses, I attempted to uncover what urban educational researcher Marvin Lynn expresses as the teachers' "thoughts, ideas, and histories" to understand and construct their stories.[4]

SITUATING MYSELF WITHIN THE STUDY
AND THE STORIES

Throughout the representation of the stories and discussion, I deliberately use first person because, in a sense, I am telling my own narrative as much as I am telling the stories of the participants. As an African American male researcher and a former English teacher in a predominantly Black U.S. secondary school, I have attempted to understand the stories of these teachers. In addition, I use first person to distinguish my own experiences from those of the participants.

WHY NARRATIVES

I have chosen to share what I learned about these teachers and their relationship to opportunity and diversity through stories or narratives. As the researcher, I constructed the stories based on what I observed, the documents I analyzed, and the interviews I conducted. The idea is that teachers' (and others') stories provide an entry into the real human condition. Researchers study narratives that research participants tell and then shape broader narratives to convey results to consumers of research. In qualitative research, we have come to understand that "lived experiences can be translated into rich narrative stories useful for both teaching and research" (emphasis added).[5] Many narrative researchers believe that people come to see themselves situated within various story lines of events, situations, and experiences. Narratives provide people an opportunity to enter into the experiences of people they may not have access to otherwise. Thus, the narrative can be described as the study of the stories that people come to experience, live, represent, and tell in the world and in education.[6]

Notes

Foreword

1. A. Lareau, *Unequal Childhoods: Class, Race, and Family Life*. (Berkeley and Los Angeles, CA: University of California Press, 2003).

2. G. Michie, *See You When We Get There: Teaching for Change in Urban Schools*. (New York: Teachers College Press, 2005).

Introduction

1. T. C. Howard, *Why Race and Culture Matter in Schools: Closing the Achievement Gap in America's Classrooms* (New York: Teachers College Press, 2010).

2. M. W. Apple, "Understanding and Interrupting Neoliberalism and Neoconservatism in Education," *Pedagogies: An International Journal* 1, no. 1 (2006): 21–26.

3. Beginning in the late 1980s, alternative teacher education programs, such as Teach for America and Teach Tennessee, began increasing their visibility and concurrently their relevance in U.S. society. Debates that focus on whether there should be alternative teacher certification programs are obsolete. Alternative teacher education programs are likely permanent programs in the United States, and politicians, researchers, parents, and others have shifted the discourse from whether these programs should exist to discourses that consider their comparable effectiveness—that is, alternative versus traditional programs.

4. G. A. Duncan, "Critical Race Ethnography in Education: Narrative, Inequality and the Problem of Epistemology," *Race, Ethnicity and Education* 8, no. 1 (2005): 93–114; M. A. Gooden and T. Y. Nowlin, "The Achievement Gap and No Child Left Behind: Is There a Connection?" in *No Child Left Behind and Other Federal*

Programs for Urban School Districts, 2006, Advances in Educational Administration, vol. 9, ed. F. Brown and R. Hunter (Oxford: Elsevier, 2006), 231–248; C. Lewis, "African American Male Teachers in Public Schools: An Examination of Three Urban School Districts," *Teachers College Record* 108, no. 2 (2006): 224–245; D. B. Martin, "Researching Race in Mathematics Education," *Teachers College Record* 111, no. 2 (2009): 295–338; H. R. Milner, "Critical Race Theory and Interest Convergence as Analytic Tools in Teacher Education Policies and Practices," *Journal of Teacher Education* 59, no. 4 (2008): 332–346.

5. K. Gutierrez and B. Rogoff, "Cultural Ways of Learning: Individual Traits or Repertoires of Practice," *Educational Researcher* 32, no. 5 (2002): 19–25; J. J. Irvine, *Educating Teachers for Diversity: Seeing with a Cultural Eye* (New York: Teachers College Press, 2003); C. D. Lee, *Culture, Literacy, and Learning: Blooming in the Midst of the Whirlwind* (New York: Teachers College Press, 2007); S. Nieto, *The Light in Their Eyes: Creating Multicultural Learning Communities* (New York: Teachers College Press, 1999); R. H. Sheets, "From Remedial to Gifted: Effects of Culturally Centered Pedagogy," *Theory into Practice* 34, no. 3 (1995): 186–193.

6. J. A. Banks, *Cultural Diversity and Education: Foundations, Curriculum, and Teaching* (Boston: Pearson, 2006); C. A. Grant and C. E. Sleeter, *Doing Multicultural Education for Achievement and Equity* (New York: Routledge, 2007).

7. G. Gay, *Culturally Responsive Teaching: Theory, Research, and Practice* (New York: Teachers College Press, 2000), 116.

8. P. L. Carter, *Keepin' It Real: School Success Beyond Black and White* (New York: Oxford University Press, 2005).

9. Sport management researchers John Singer and Kwame Agyemang, building on the important work of African American studies scholar and educational researcher Mwalimu Shuja, stress the important distinction between "schooling" and education. Singer and Shuja encourage those of us in education to shift our emphasis from schooling practices to educational practices. Understanding the distinct differences between the two (schooling and education) has compelling implications. See J. N. Singer and K. Agyemang, "Understanding the (Mis)education of African American Male College Athletes: Toward a Multilevel Framework" (presentation, College Sport Research Institute annual conference, University of NC, Chapel Hill, North Carolina., April 22, 2010); and M. J. Shuja, ed., *Too Much Schooling, Too Little Education: A Paradox of Black Life in White Societies* (Trenton, NJ: Africa World Press, 1994).

10. G. Ladson-Billings, "From the Achievement Gap to the Education Debt: Understanding Achievement in U.S. Schools," *Educational Researcher* 35, no. 7 (2006): 3–12.

11. J. J. Irvine, foreword to *Culture, Curriculum, and Identity in Education*, ed. H. R. Milner (New York: Palgrave Macmillan, 2010).

12. Ibid., xii.

13. J. Sheurich and M. Young, "Coloring Epistemologies: Are Our Research Epistemologies Racially Biased?" *Educational Researcher* 26, no. 4 (1997): 4–16; M. Foster, "Race, Class, and Gender in Education Research: Surveying the Political Terrain," *Educational Policy* 13, no. 1 (1999): 77–85; G. Ladson-Billings, "Preparing Teachers for Diverse Student Populations: A Critical Race Theory Perspective," *Review of Research in Education* 24 (1999): 211–247; H. R. Milner, "Race, Culture, and Researcher Positionality: Working Through Dangers Seen, Unseen, and Unforeseen," *Educational Researcher* 36, no. 7 (2007): 388–400.

14. D. Y. Ford, *Reversing Underachievement Among Gifted Black Students: Promising Practices and Programs* (New York: Teachers College Press, 1996); H. R. Milner, "What Does Teacher Education Have to Do with Teaching? Implications for Diversity Studies," *Journal of Teacher Education* 61, nos. 1/2 (2010): 118–131; J. E. Morris, "Can Anything Good Come from Nazareth? Race, Class, and African American Schooling and Community in the Urban South and Midwest," *American Educational Research Journal* 41, no. 1 (2004): 69–112.

15. C. B. Dillard, "The Substance of Things Hoped for, the Evidence of Things Not Seen: Examining an Endarkened Feminist Epistemology in Educational Research and Leadership," *International Journal of Qualitative Studies in Education* 13, no. 6 (2000): 661–681.

Chapter 1

1. L. Johnson, "'My Eyes Have Been Opened': White Teachers and Racial Awareness," *Journal of Teacher Education* 53, no. 2 (2002): 153–167; A. E. Lewis, "There is No 'Race' in the Schoolyard: Colorblind Ideology in an (Almost) All White School," *American Educational Research Journal* 38, no. 4 (2001): 781–811.

2. A. Lorde, *Zami: A New Spelling of My Name* (Trumansburg, NY: Crossing Press, 1981), 81.

3. J. A. Banks, "Citizenship Education and Diversity: Implications for Teacher Education," *Journal of Teacher Education* 52, no. 1 (2001): 12.

4. The curriculum can be defined as what students have the opportunity to learn in schools (see E. W. Eisner, *The Educational Imagination: On the Design and Evaluation of School Programs* [New York: MacMillan College Publishing, 1994]; G. McCutcheon, *Developing the Curriculum: Solo and Group Deliberation* [Troy, NY: Educators' Press International, 2002]). In *The Educational Imagination,* curriculum theorist Elliott Eisner postulates several important forms of the curriculum: (a) *the explicit curriculum* concerns student-learning opportunities that are overtly taught and stated or printed in documents, policies, and guidelines, such as in course syllabi or on school Web sites; (b) *the implicit curriculum* is intended or unintended but is not stated or written down and is actually inherent to what students have the opportunity to learn; the implicit curriculum is also referred to as the hidden curriculum; (c) a third form of curriculum, *the null curriculum,* deals with what students do not have the opportunity to learn. Thus, information and knowledge that are not available for student learning are also a form of the curriculum because *students are actually learning something based on what is not emphasized, covered, or taught.* What students do not experience in the curriculum become messages for them. For example, if educators are not taught to question, critique, or critically examine power structures, the students are learning something—possibly that it may not be essential for them to critique the world in order to improve it. From Eisner's perspective, what is *absent* is essentially *present* in student learning opportunities.

5. G. Gay and T. Howard, "Multicultural Teacher Education for the 21st Century," *Teacher Educator* 36, no. 1 (2000): 1–16; K. Zumwalt and E. Craig, "Teachers' Characteristics: Research on the Demographic Profile," in *Studying Teacher Education: The Report of the AERA Panel on Research and Teacher Education,* ed. M. C. Smith and K. M. Zeichner (Mahwah, NJ: Lawrence Erlbaum Associates, 2005), 111–156.

6. J. J. Irvine, *Educating Teachers for Diversity: Seeing with a Cultural Eye* (New York: Teachers College Press, 2003).

7. G. Gay, *Culturally Responsive Teaching: Theory, Research, and Practice* (New York: Teachers College Press, 2000), 205.

8. G. Ladson-Billings, "Toward a Theory of Culturally Relevant Pedagogy," *American Education Research Journal* 35 (1995): 465–491.

9. Irvine, *Educating Teachers for Diversity*; S. Nieto, "Lessons from Students on Creating a Chance to Dream," *Harvard Educational Review* 64, no. 4 (1994): 392–426; V. Siddle-Walker, "Valued Segregated Schools for African American Children in the South, 1935–1969: A Review of Common Themes and Characteristics," *Review of Educational Research* 70, no. 3 (2000): 253–285.

10. C. E. Sleeter and H. R. Milner, "Researching Successful Efforts in Teacher Education to Diversify Teachers," in *Studying Diversity in Teacher Education*, ed. A. F. Ball and C. Tyson (Washington, DC: American Educational Research Association).

11. M. Foster, *Black Teachers on Teaching* (New York: New Press, 1997); Irvine, *Educating Teachers for Diversity*; H. R. Milner, "Developing a Multicultural Curriculum in a Predominantly White Teaching Context: Lessons from an African American Teacher in a Suburban English Classroom," *Curriculum Inquiry* 35, no. 4 (2005): 391–428.

12. Lewis, "There is No 'Race' in the Schoolyard."

13. D. Y. Ford, "Identification of Young, Culturally Diverse Students for Gifted Education Programs," *Gifted Education Press Quarterly* 20, no. 1 (2006): 2–4.

14. Culture can be defined as a group of people who possess and share deep-rooted connections such as values, beliefs, languages, customs, and norms. Yet culture is not a static concept, "a category for conveniently sorting people according to expected values, beliefs, and behaviors" (A. H. Dyson and C. Genishi, *The Need for Story: Cultural Diversity in Classroom and Community.* [Boston: Harvard University Press, 1994], 3). Rather, culture is dynamic and encompasses other concepts that relate to its central meaning. The supplemental categories that make up culture include, but are not limited to, identity (race and ethnicity), socioeconomic status, class, economic status, sexual orientation, geography, and gender.

15. M. Foster, *Black Teachers on Teaching* (New York: New Press, 1997); T. C. Howard, "Telling Their Side of the Story: African American Students' Perceptions of Culturally Relevant Pedagogy," *Urban Review* 33, no. 2 (2001): 131–149; Irvine, *Educating Teachers for Diversity*.

16. J. A. Banks, *An Introduction to Multicultural Education*, 2nd ed. (Boston, MA: Allyn and Bacon, 1998), 22–23.

17. L. Delpit, *Other People's Children: Cultural Conflict in the Classroom* (New York: New Press, 1995).

18. Ibid., 24.

19. Classroom management continues to be a serious concern for most educators, especially new educators (see S. A. Melnick and D. G. Meister, "A Comparison of Beginning and Experienced Teachers' Concerns," *Educational Research Quarterly* 31, no. 3 [2008]: 39–56). Educators' concerns are sometimes exacerbated when considering classroom management in urban and highly diverse

settings. In the thirty-ninth Annual Gallup Poll, Rose and Gallup found that the public consistently ranked "discipline" as one of the top five problems that schools face (L. C. Rose and A. M. Gallup, "The 39th Annual Phi Delta Kappa/ Gallup Poll of the Public's Attitude Toward the Public Schools," *Phi Delta Kappan* 89, no. 1 [2007]: 33–45), and White educators, in particular, consistently point to classroom management with culturally diverse students as one of their weakest areas of preparation (H. R. Milner, "Disrupting Deficit Notions of Difference: Counter-narratives of Teachers and Community in Urban Education," *Teaching and Teacher Education* 24, no. 6 [2008]: 1573–1598).

20. Delpit, *Other People's Children*.

21. P. A. Noguera, "Schools, Prisons, and Social Implications of Punishment: Rethinking Disciplinary Practices," *Theory into Practice* 42, no. 4 (2003): 341–350.

22. M. Haberman, "Pedagogy of Poverty Versus Good Teaching," *Phi Delta Kappan* 73, no. 4 (1991): 290–293.

23. J. Anyon, "Social Class and the Hidden Curriculum of Work," *Journal of Education* 162, no. 1 (1980): 366–391; Haberman, "Pedagogy of Poverty Versus Good Teaching"; J. Kozol, *The Shame on a Nation* (New York: Crown Books, 2005).

24. R. J. Skiba, R. S. Michael, A. D. Nardo, and R. L. Peterson, "The Color of Discipline: Sources of Racial and Gender Disproportionality in School Punishment," *Urban Review* 34, no. 4 (2002): 317.

25. Ibid.

26. P. McIntosh, "White Privilege: Unpacking the Invisible Knapsack," *Independent School* 90, no. 49 (1990): 31–36.

27. J. M. Henslin, *Essentials of Sociology: A Down-to-Earth Approach*, 5th ed. (Boston: Pearson, 2004), 174.

28. I. Randolph-McCree and E. Pristoop, "The Funding Gap 2005: Low-Income and Minority Students Shortchanged by Most States," Special Report by the Education Trust (Washington, DC: Education Trust, 2005), 2.

29. M. Cochran-Smith, "Uncertain Allies: Understanding the Boundaries of Race and Teaching," *Harvard Educational Review* 65, no. 4 (1995): 547.

30. G. Ladson-Billings and B. Tate, "Toward a Critical Race Theory of Education," *Teachers College Record* 97, no. 1 (1995): 47–67.

31. M. W. Apple, "Understanding and Interrupting Neoliberalism and Neoconservatism in Education," *Pedagogies: An International Journal* 1, no. 1 (2006): 22.

32. I am grateful to Lee Druce and Matthew Davis for representing this data in graph form for me.

33. J. MacLeod, *Ain't No Makin' It: Aspirations and Attainment in a Low-Income Neighborhood* (San Francisco: Westview Press, 1995), 11.

34. B. M. Gordon, "The Necessity of African-American Epistemology for Educational Theory and Practice," *Journal of Education* 172, no. 3 (1990): 88–106.

35. D. Y. Ford, *Reversing Underachievement Among Gifted Black Students: Promising Practices and Programs* (New York: Teachers College Press, 1996), 84.

36. D. Y. Ford and T. C. Grantham, "Providing Access for Culturally Diverse Gifted Students: From Deficit to Dynamic Thinking," *Theory into Practice* 42, no. 3 (2003): 217.

37. Milner, "Disrupting Deficit Notions of Difference."

38. C. M. Steele, "A Threat in the Air: How Stereotypes Shape Intellectual Identity and Performance," *American Psychologist* 52 (1997): 613–629.

39. F. Rios, ed., *Teacher Thinking in Cultural Contexts* (Albany: State University of New York Press, 1996).

40. P. E. Barton, *Parsing the Achievement Gap: Baseline for Tracking Progress* (Princeton, NJ: Educational Testing Services, 2003).

41. W. F. Tate, "'Geography of Opportunity': Poverty, Place, and Educational Outcomes," *Educational Researcher* 37, no. 7 (2008): 397–411.

42. M. Roza, *How Districts Shortchange Low-Income and Minority Students* (Washington, DC: Education Trust, 2006), 11.

43. J. A. Banks, *Cultural Diversity and Education: Foundations, Curriculum, and Teaching* (Boston: Pearson, 2006); T. C. Howard, *Why Race and Culture Matter in Schools: Closing the Achievement Gap in America's Classrooms* (New York: Teachers College Press, 2010); Milner, "Developing a Multicultural Curriculum."

44. Banks, *An Introduction to Multicultural Education*, 23.

45. Banks, *Cultural Diversity and Education.*

46. C. Jenks, J. O. Lee, and B. Kanpol, "Approaches to Multicultural Education in Preservice Teacher Education: Philosophical Frameworks and Models for Teaching," *Urban Review* 33, no. 2 (2001): 87.

47. P. Freire, *Pedagogy of the Oppressed* (New York: Continuum, 1998).

48. McCutcheon, *Developing the Curriculum.*

Chapter 2

1. I am grateful to Vincent Windrow for helping me understand the importance of a learner assuming the proper posture to learn. Teachers can teach when students are ready to learn.

2. P. Freire, *Pedagogy of the Oppressed* (New York: Continuum, 1998).

3. C. R. Monroe and J. E. Obidah, "The Influence of Cultural Synchronization on a Teacher's Perceptions of Disruption: A Case Study of an African-American Middle-School Classroom," *Journal of Teacher Education* 55, no. 3 (2004): 256–268.

4. L. Delpit, *Other People's Children: Cultural Conflict in the Classroom* (New York: New Press, 1995).

5. G. Ladson-Billings, "Fighting for Our Lives: Preparing Teachers to Teach African American Students," *Journal of Teacher Education* 51, no. 3 (2000): 206–214.

Chapter 3

1. J. A. Banks, "Multicultural Education and Curriculum Transformation," *Journal of Negro Education* 64, no. 4 (1995): 392.

2. J. A. Banks, "Teaching Literacy for Social Justice and Global Citizenship," *Language Arts* 81, no. 1 (2003): 18.

3. b. hooks, *Teaching to Transgress: Education as the Practice of Freedom* (New York: Routledge, 1994).

4. C. West, *Race Matters* (Boston: Beacon Press, 1993).

5. W. E. B. DuBois, *The Souls of Black Folk* (New York: Fawcett, 1903).

6. P. McIntosh, "White Privilege: Unpacking the Invisible Knapsack," *Independent School* 90, no. 49 (1990): 31–36.

7. A. E. Lewis, "There is No 'Race' in the Schoolyard: Colorblind Ideology in an (Almost) All White School," *American Educational Research Journal* 38, no. 4 (2001): 781–811.

8. E. Buendia, A. Gitlin, and F. Doumbia, "Working the Pedagogical Borderlands: An African Critical Pedagogue Teaching Within an ESL Context," *Curriculum Inquiry* 3, no. 3 (2003): 291–320.

9. Ibid.

10. C. A. Banks and J. A. Banks, "Equity Pedagogy: An Essential Component of Multicultural Education," *Theory into Practice* 34 (1995): 153.

11. P. Freire, *Pedagogy of the Oppressed* (New York: Continuum, 1998).

12. Banks, "Teaching Literacy," 18.

Chapter 4

1. To substantiate this point, see the important work of Ladson-Billings, which showcases successful teachers from different racial backgrounds of African American students: G. Ladson-Billings, "Toward a Theory of Culturally Relevant Pedagogy," *American Education Research Journal* 35 (1995): 465–491.

2. For a thorough overview of this line of thinking, see S. Fordham and J. A. Ogbu, "Black Students' School Success: Coping with the Burden of 'Acting White,'" *Urban Review* 18, no. 3 (1986): 176–206.

3. For good examples of counternarratives, see J. E. Morris, "Can Anything Good Come from Nazareth? Race, Class, and African American Schooling and Community in the Urban South and Midwest," *American Educational Research Journal* 41, no. 1 (2004): 69–112; and H. R. Milner, "Disrupting Deficit Notions of Difference: Counter-narratives of Teachers and Community in Urban Education," *Teaching and Teacher Education* 24, no. 6 (2008): 1573–1598.

4. R. Suskind, *A Hope in the Unseen: An American Odyssey from the Inner City to the Ivy League* (New York: Broadway, 1998).

5. V. Siddle-Walker, "Valued Segregated Schools for African American Children in the South, 1935–1969: A Review of Common Themes and Characteristics," *Review of Educational Research* 70, no. 3 (2000): 253–285.

6. Hip-hop, some would argue, is a culture that allows youth to engage in customs and experiences that allow them to express themselves through music, film, art, and other forms of expression that can run counter to more mainstream and dominant forms of living and being in society. Hill explains that educators have successfully incorporated features of hip-hop culture in the P–12 classroom to make teaching and learning more relevant, responsive, and accessible to youth (M. L. Hill, *Beats, Rhymes, and Classroom Life: Hip-Hop Pedagogy and the Politics of Identity* [New York: Teachers College Press, 2009]). From his empirical perspective, hip-hop can be used to "improve student motivation, teach critical media literacy, foster critical consciousness, and transmit disciplinary knowledge" (p. 2).

7. J. G. Irizarry, "Representin': Drawing from Hip-Hop and Urban Youth Culture to Inform Teacher Education," *Education and Urban Society* 41, no. 4 (2009): 490.

8. M. Haberman, "Pedagogy of Poverty Versus Good Teaching," *Phi Delta Kappan* 73, no. 4 (1991): 290–293.

9. J. P. Gee, "The Classroom of Popular Culture: What Video Games Can Teach Us About Making Students Want to Learn," *Harvard Education Letter* 21, no. 6 (2005).

10. J. Duncan-Andrade and E. Morrell, "Turn Up That Radio, Teacher: Popular Cultural Pedagogy in New Century Urban Schools," *Journal of School Leadership* 15 (2005): 284–304.

11. P. Freire, *Pedagogy of the Oppressed* (New York: Continuum, 1998).

12. Ibid., 53.

13. G. McCutcheon, *Developing the Curriculum: Solo and Group Deliberation* (Troy, NY: Educators' Press International, 2002).

14. Duncan-Andrade and Morrell, "Turn Up That Radio, Teacher," 284.

15. Ibid.

16. M. Foster, *Black Teachers on Teaching* (New York: New Press, 1997); J. J. Irvine, *Educating Teachers for Diversity: Seeing with a Cultural Eye* (New York: Teachers College Press, 2003).

17. Foster, *Black Teachers on Teaching*; M. Foster, "The Politics of Race: Through the Eyes of African-American Teachers," *Journal of Education* 172 (1990): 123–141; R. W. Irvine and J. J. Irvine, "The Impact of the Desegregation Process on the Education of Black Students: Key Variables," *Journal of Negro Education* 52 (1983): 410–422; S. King, "The Limited Presence of African-American Teachers," *Review of Educational Research* 63, no. 2 (1993): 115–149.

18. Siddle-Walker, "Valued Segregated Schools," 265–266.

19. V. Siddle-Walker, *Their Highest Potential: An African American School Community in the Segregated South* (Chapel Hill: University of North Carolina Press, 1996).

20. L. C. Tillman, "(Un)Intended Consequences? The Impact of *Brown v. Board of Education* Decision on the Employment Status of Black Educators," *Education and Urban Society* 36, no. 3 (2004): 282.

21. V. O. Pang and R. Gibson, "Concepts of Democracy and Citizenship: Views of African American Teachers," *The Social Studies* 92, no. 6 (2001): 260–261.

22. Freire, *Pedagogy of the Oppressed*.

23. Siddle-Walker, *Their Highest Potential*.

24. G. McAllister and J. J. Irvine, "The Role of Empathy in Teaching Culturally Diverse Students: A Qualitative Study of Teachers' Beliefs," *Journal of Teacher Education* 53, no. 5 (2002): 433–443.

25. P. H. Collins, *Black Feminist Thought: Knowledge, Consciousness, and the Politics of Empowerment: Perspectives on Gender*, vol. 2 (New York: Routledge, 1991); Irvine, *Educating Teachers for Diversity*.

Chapter 5

1. C. E. Sleeter, "Epistemological Diversity in Research on Preservice Teacher Preparation for Historically Underserved Children," *Review of Research in Education* 25 (2001): 209–250.

2. H. R. Milner, "Reflection, Racial Competence, and Critical Pedagogy: How Do We Prepare Preservice Teachers to Pose Tough Questions?" *Race, Ethnicity, and Education* 6, no. 2 (2003): 193–208.

F. B. Tenore, "An Analysis of the Subject Positions Offered and Denied in Three Conceptions of Teacher Development" (major area paper, Department of Teaching and Learning, Vanderbilt University, 2009).

3. P. Grossman et al., "Teaching Practice: A Cross-Professional Perspective," *Teachers College Record* 111, no. 9 (2009): 2055–2100.

4. L. Darling-Hammond, R. Chung, and F. Frelow, "Variation in Teacher Preparation: How Well Do Different Pathways Prepare Teachers to Teach?" *Journal of Teacher Education* 53, no. 4 (2002): 286–302.

5. H. R. Milner and M. Smithey, "How Teacher Educators Created a Course Curriculum to Challenge and Enhance Preservice Teachers' Thinking and Experience with Diversity," *Teaching Education* 14, no. 3 (2003): 293–305.

6. J. C. Laughter, "Change Agents: Empowering White Female Preservice Teachers Through Dialogue and Counter-narrative" (PhD diss., Vanderbilt University, 2009). Available at http://etd.library.vanderbilt.edu/available/etd-06302009-150423/.

7. I realize that there is no such thing as a homogeneous school.

8. B. D. Tatum, *"Why Are All the Black Kids Sitting Together in the Cafeteria?" and Other Conversations About Race* (New York: Basic Books, 1997).

9. H. R. Milner, "But Good Intentions Are Not Enough: Theoretical and Philosophical Relevance in Teaching Students of Color," in *White Teachers/Diverse Classrooms: A Guide to Building Inclusive Schools, Promoting High Expectations and Eliminating Racism*, ed. J. Landsman and C.W. Lewis (Sterling, VA: Stylus Publishers, 2006), 79–90.

10. M. Cochran-Smith, "Learning and Unlearning: The Education of Teacher Educators," *Teaching and Teacher Education* 19 (2003): 5–28.

11. C. L. Ryan and A. D. Dixson, "Rethinking Pedagogy to Re-center Race: Some Reflections," *Language Arts* 84, no. 2 (2006): 181.

12. M. Cochran-Smith, "Uncertain Allies: Understanding the Boundaries of Race and Teaching," *Harvard Educational Review* 65, no. 4 (1995): 546.

13. E. L. Brown, "What Precipitates Change in Cultural Diversity Awareness During a Multicultural Course: The Message or the Method?" *Journal of Teacher Education* 55, no. 4 (2004): 326. Also see B. D. Tatum, "Talking About Race, Learning About Racism: The Application of Racial Identity Development Theory in the Classroom," *Harvard Educational Review* 62, no. 1 (1992): 1–24.

14. E. Ellsworth, "'Why Doesn't This Feel Empowering?' Working Through the Repressive Myths of Critical Pedagogy," *Harvard Educational Review* 59, no. 3 (1989): 297–324.

15. G. Ladson-Billings, "Preparing Teachers for Diverse Student Populations: A Critical Race Theory Perspective," *Review of Research in Education* 24 (1999): 211–247.

16. M. M. Merryfield, "Why Aren't Teachers Being Prepared to Teach for Diversity, Equity, and Global Interconnectedness? A Study of Lived Experiences in the Making of Multicultural and Global Educators," *Teaching and Teacher Education* 16 (2000): 430.

17. H. R. Milner, "Preservice Teachers' Learning About Cultural and Racial Diversity: Implications for Urban Education," *Urban Education* 41, no. 4 (2006): 343–375; H. R. Milner, "Race, Narrative Inquiry, and Self-Study in Curriculum and Teacher Education," *Education and Urban Society* 39, no. 4 (2007): 584–609; H. R. Milner, "Critical Race Theory and Interest Convergence as Analytic Tools in

Teacher Education Policies and Practices," *Journal of Teacher Education* 59, no. 4 (2008): 332–346.

18. K. S. Cockrell et al., "Coming to Terms with 'Diversity' and 'Multiculturalism' in Teacher Education: Learning About Our Students, Changing Our Practice," *Teaching and Teacher Education* 5 (1999): 363.

19. Ladson-Billings, "Preparing Teachers for Diverse Student Populations," 221.

20. K. Zeichner, "Reflections of a University-Based Teacher Educator on the Future of College- and University-Based Teacher Education," *Journal of Teacher Education* 57, no. 3 (2006): 328.

21. Here, I am referring to the course syllabus, and the goals and objectives outlined on it as policy. See J. Agee, "Negotiating a Teaching Identity: An African American Teacher's Struggle to Teach in Test-Driven Contexts," *Teachers College Record* 106, no. 4 (2004): 747–774; A. D. Dixson, "What's Race Got to Do with It? Race, Racial Identity Development, and Teacher Preparation," in *Race, Ethnicity, and Education: The Influences of Racial and Ethnic Identity in Education*, ed. H. R. Milner and E. W. Ross (Westport, CT: Greenwood/Praeger, 2006), 19–36; G. Gay, *Culturally Responsive Teaching: Theory, Research, and Practice* (New York: Teachers College Press, 2000).

22. B. D. Tatum, "Professional Development: An Important Partner in Antiracist Teacher Education," in *Racism and Racial Inequality: Implications for Teacher Education*, ed. S. H. King and L. A. Castenell (Washington, DC: AACTE Publications, 2001), 53.

23. Dixson, "What's Race Got to Do with It?"

24. Agee, "Negotiating a Teaching Identity," 749.

25. Dixson, "What's Race Got to Do with It?"

26. G. Ladson-Billings, "Silences as Weapons: Challenges of a Black Professor Teaching White Students," *Theory into Practice* 35 (1996): 79.

27. Cochran-Smith, "Uncertain Allies."

28. Delpit, *Other People's Children.*

29. B. D. Tatum, "Teaching White Students About Racism: The Search for White Allies and the Restoration of Hope," *Teachers College Record* 95, no. 4 (1994): 462–476.

Conclusion

1. b. hooks, *Teaching to Transgress: Education as the Practice of Freedom* (New York: Routledge, 1994), 84.

2. L. Delpit, *Other People's Children: Cultural Conflict in the Classroom* (New York: New Press, 1995).

3. I am grateful to William Moseley, headmaster at the Ensworth School in Nashville, Tennessee, for sharing this idea with me.

4. For an excellent discussion of this issue, see M. A. Gooden, "What Does Racism Have to Do with Leadership? Countering the Idea of Color-Blind Leadership: A Reflection on Race and Growing Pressures of Principalship," *Educational Foundations*, in press.

5. E. W. Eisner, *The Educational Imagination: On the Design and Evaluation of School Programs* (New York: Macmillan College Publishing, 1994); G. McCutcheon, *Developing the Curriculum: Solo and Group Deliberation* (Troy, NY: Educators' Press International, 2002).

6. P. A. Noguera, "Schools, Prisons, and Social Implications of Punishment: Rethinking Disciplinary Practices," *Theory into Practice* 42, no. 4 (2003): 341–350.

7. C. West, *Restoring Hope: Conversations on the Future of Black America*, ed. K. S. Sealey (Boston: Beacon Press, 1997), xii.

Epilogue

1. P. Demerath et al., "Decoding Success: A Middle-Class Logic of Individual Advancement in a U.S. Suburb and High School," *Teachers College Record* 112, no. 12 (2010).

2. G. Ladson-Billings, *The Dreamkeepers: Successful Teachers of Black Children* (San Francisco: Jossey-Bass, 1994), 147.

3. I. Seidman, *Interviewing as Qualitative Research: A Guide for Researchers in Education and the Social Sciences* (New York: Teachers College Press, 1998).

4. M. Lynn, "Education for the Community: Exploring the Culturally Relevant Practices of Black Male Teachers," *Teachers College Record* 108, no. 12 (2006): 2501.

5. S. P. Rushton, "Using Narrative Inquiry to Understand a Student-Teacher's Practical Knowledge While Teaching in an Inner-City School," *The Urban Review* 3, no. 1 (2004): 61–79.

6. M. He, "A Narrative Inquiry of Cross-Cultural Lives: Lives in the North American Academy," *Journal of Curriculum Studies* 34, no. 5 (2002): 513–533; J. Phillion, "Becoming a Narrative Inquirer in a Multicultural Landscape," *Journal of Curriculum Studies* 34, no. 5 (2002): 535–556.

About the Author

H. Richard Milner IV is associate professor of education and a founding director of the graduate program Learning, Diversity, and Urban Studies in the Department of Teaching and Learning at Peabody College of Vanderbilt University. Professor Milner is also a faculty affiliate in education at Fisk University in Nashville, Tennessee. A former high school teacher, Milner has served as a visiting professor in urban education at the University of Texas-Austin and was named a visiting lecturer in the graduate program of education at York University in Toronto, Canada, where he taught in the Language, Culture and Teaching program. His teaching, research, and policy interests concern urban education, teacher education, English education, and the sociology of education. Professor Milner's research and scholarly contributions have been recognized with an Early Career Award from the American Educational Research Association and the Carl A. Grant Multicultural Award from the National Association for Multicultural Education. He is the incoming senior editor of the journal *Urban Education*. Professor Milner has also edited several books, including *Race, Ethnicity, and Education* (coedited with E. Wayne Ross, 2006), *Diversity and Education: Teachers, Teaching, and Teacher Education* (2009), and *Culture, Curriculum, and Identity in Education* (2010). Professor Milner consults with schools and districts concerning diversity and opportunity both domestically and internationally.

Index